IN PILLNESS AND IN HEALTH

A MEMOIR

HENRIETTE IVANANS

To L. who told me I could do it.

To K. who never has to read it.

And to my father, because now I understand.

CONTENTS

PROLOGUE

Before Daddy died, I was raised Catholic. I knew about Adam and Eve, and David and Goliath. I had memorized The Lord's Prayer, reciting it in church and morning services at private school. Yet, I'd never felt anything other than pride as I nailed each syllable. I had it down, but was never uplifted. I had never experienced prayer.

At age 7, the stench of alcoholism was choking our family of four. At night, my chest caved in as death swirled around my bedposts. The party line remained *Daddy just needs to go on vacation,* but I smelled the lies, pungent as skunk. I knew the truth. Daddy was dying. Anguished and alone, I craved a peace no one could provide. Not my mother, or church, or school. So one night I made up my own prayer.

"Dear God. Please keep Daddy alive until I am 20."

With these words, I was able to fall asleep as my father drank in the next room. My prayer was a curious divine request I'm not sure I understand even today. Did I think I would no longer need a father at age twenty? That I would be married and happy and on my way? What I do know is it was not the words that brought me comfort, but rather a connection I found every night with something greater than myself. Something I believed was out there.

Three years later, Daddy died at age 38. I was 10. I never prayed again.

Well, for another 32 years.

1. XANAX 2011

My husband, Kevin had never denied me anything. Sunday October 9th, 2011 was no different. Six months earlier, he had given me his kidney. That morning, all I needed were my pills.

I could hear him walking in and out of the house, packing up our one car with his tripod, lights, and zipping up the pockets of his camera bag. He had to be in Orange County by noon to work a wedding. Plenty of time to first pick up my Xanax. Dragging my shaking hands through my hair, I glanced at the alarm clock. 10:07 am. Why was he dawdling? Why hadn't he arrived at Rite Aid at 9:59 am as the pharmacy's steel door rolled up, offering its medicinal charms to the world? He was such an ass.

All 97 pounds of me quivered in bed. I was not sick, but dopesick. A bag of bones wracked no longer with the nausea associated with renal failure, but straight up addiction. My legs twitched under the sheets, knowing my prescription was ready. I rubbed at my eyes with agitated fingers, aimless fingers that had no purpose unless they were plucking pills from the bottom of their plastic home.

The day before, we had been told it was "too soon" to pick up my prescription—the dreaded phrase sinks the hungry heart of every pharmaceutical whore. Throwing myself across the counter, I'd angled my scrawny frame towards the pharmacist, trying to explain why she needed to release my pills.

"Now that I look at your file," she said, scrutinizing the computer screen, "you've picked up 135 tablets this month, well over the regulated 90. I can't release this until tomorrow."

"How did you get so many extra pills?" Kevin whispered, his skin a lighter shade of pale.

"I don't know. It's fine. Don't worry."

My husband did not wait in one of the plastic chairs where I had slumped many a day, willing my body to sit up on the faintest wisp of adrenaline, knowing my drugs were but minutes away. He moved ever closer toward me, hands tucked into his armpits. Always there. My parent. My protector. My prison guard.

I twisted my body past the cash register. The pharmacist raised her eyebrows.

"But my doctor said it was fine. You can call..."

I have often wondered how pharmacists are trained to deal with an addict's aggressiveness. Is there a course in Pharmacy College? Special lectures? A supplemental pamphlet? *How to Beat a Drug Addict Off Your Counter.* Could she smell the panicked manipulation wafting off my skin? I know I could.

With a withering stare, she scythed away my ramblings. I had slipped under her professional radar once to score an additional 45 pills. I wasn't about to con her again.

"Sorry, I can't do anything. Next."

I did not look at Kevin as we walked away. His silence radiated hot. My pills would be released at 10:00 am the next day. 18 hours from now. 1080 minutes. 64,800 seconds. How would I survive until then?

Pills have been a part of my life since I was 14 years old and diagnosed with Chronic Kidney Disease. At the age of 42, after two kidney transplants, pills had become my life. The life-saving immunosuppressives: Cell-Cept, Cyclosporine and Prednisone so my body would not reject Kevin's kidney. The mind-altering ones: Xanax, Ambien and Klonopin. The soul-altering ones: Codeine, Morphine, Dilaudid,

Roxicodone, Vicodin, Norco, Percocet and Tramadol. And Her. The love of my life: Fiorinal. I had no awareness of anything other than pills. I lived and breathed inside the vacuum of their container, powerless to climb my way out. Not because the side effects of my immunosuppressives had stunted the growth of my fingernails, but because I couldn't. Pills gave me my identity. They were my raison d'être. They were my parents, lovers and friends. I was married to pills.

As I heard Kevin drive away, I collapsed onto the mound of stale sheets. Long gone were the days when I would assist him at a wedding. No longer did I stand at the end of the aisle, undistracted by the bride and groom's first kiss, but attentive to my own husband's every move. Anticipating what lens he might need, wiping his brow with a cloth, or passing him a handful of fresh batteries for his flash pack.

When the reception kicked into high gear, I would lean against a wall with a well-deserved glass of wine in my hand as Kevin ran around taking pictures. Tears would spring to my eyes as I mused, *We are such a great team.*

The floorboard creaked. I peeked out from beneath a damp wash-cloth. Kevin stood in the doorway with that familiar crumpled white paper bag in his hands. Finally! He tossed it on top of me and left. *What the hell is he so mad about?*

I reached for the bag. My heart flipped. Xanax tablets are tiny, but this bag felt alarmingly light. I ripped it open, masterfully avoiding the overenthusiastic spattering of staples. I scanned the label. My breath caught. Quantity: 12. 12! I scanned again, willing the number to change from 12 to 120. Motherfucker. I had forgotten I had two Xanax scripts going: My standing refill of 90 and an additional 12 I had manipulated my nephrologist into prescribing. Kevin had picked up the wrong script.

My stomach clamped in fear. I couldn't get through the day with 12 tablets. Once upon a time, that would have lasted me a week. But over the year I had been taking Xanax, I tossed back 3, sometimes 4 at a time, pulverizing them with my molars. Their magic powder melted my tight bones into gelatinous flesh, and unlaced knots of tension into free-floating strands of calm. They were so close. So tempting. It was like asking a body to get up and walk away once it has lurched into the throes of orgasm.

If I took even one of these controlled tablets the pharmacy would not release the other prescription. Kevin had to go back. Now. My head began to sweat. The warm beams of October light that this Canadian transplant worshipped became an irritation. My sublime California King mattress, the bed where I had been loved, cherished and obeyed, became an irritation. The husband who had so believed in my ability to become a movie star, and became heart-broken when I did not, my Prince who had given me his kidney was now my biggest irritation.

My temples began to throb. *God. Help me.* If Kevin didn't exchange this bottle, I would not survive. I could not make it through the day without that bottle of 90 tablets.

Deep inside this tunnel vision, I was trapped. All I had been able to see for the last six months since our kidney transplant was pills. Along this myopic journey, there was no point in looking out the windows. There was nothing to see. There existed only the same stations I needed to arrive at—doctors' offices, pharmacies, and other people's medicine cabinets. The people, places, and things revealed along the way held no interest for me. They merely dotted the land-scape, distractions that might derail me from my destination. I sat defiantly, belted into the front seat of this bullet train focused only on getting what I wanted, and where I thought I needed to be.

2. XANAX 2006

The first time I tried Xanax, I stole it from my mother-in-law. I was trapped in Winnipeg, Canada for Christmas 2006. Not literally trapped, but with the kind of winters that sweep through this small prairie city, this scenario is never ruled out. For long, long months, winter dominates. Brutal arctic temperatures pound the city with a gavel of unrelenting cold. I could never warm up, outside or in.

Most December afternoons found the eight of us—Kevin, his sister, Kim, her husband and two kids, and Kevin's parents—huddled around my mother-in-law's tiny kitchen table. We would drink bottomless cups of weak, black tea and pick at the plethora of empty calories (Christmas cookies, fudge, shortbread) they call "Dainties." And they would chat.

Listening to them was about as interesting as watching paint dry. Scratch that. At least when you watch paint dry, something is happening. The unwanted color or mistreated wall painted a disrespectful beige, or neglected with no paint at all is undergoing a transformation. A brilliant metamorphosis affects as the new color seeps into the drywall. Here at the kitchen table, nothing happened. The conversations felt like Groundhog Day—sports, church and musical theatre—each day a repeat of the last, and all things of zero interest to me. The only thing anchoring me from flying off the handle was the grip I had on my lukewarm cup of tea.

"More tea, Kim?" my MIL asked, neglecting me.

Inwardly, I rolled my eyes. I sat coiled, tense like a serpent, daring someone to piss me off so I could justify a poisoned strike. Aching to shed my skin, but there was nowhere to go.

Outside, the heavens revealed endless hues of gray. If the color were a paint chit it would have been called "Suicidal Sludge." If you were not coated in dandruff-like snowflakes, you were dodging dirty mountains of rock-hard ice and snow. It was filthy weather that matched my mood.

"You OK, sweetheart?"

I nodded at my husband, even as I stewed in wifely obligation. No one else seemed to notice me. What I could not see was that if I didn't care about their conversations, why should they care about me? I leaned back from the table. There was no solution but to swallow the wave of anger consuming me with my tea. Or have another Dainty.

~

I HAD A HABIT, a daily habit as reflexive as a morning cup of coffee. I took Tylenol 1 with Codeine every morning, swallowing up to 18 tablets at a time.

I did not take them because I was in pain. Tylenol 1 is for headaches, backaches etc., but I took them because they got me high. Every day began inside a cloud of empowering protection: limp, but strong, drifting, yet anchored. My daily fix-it.

Upon awakening, I would turn over, and reach for the fat, plastic container of 200 caplets I had purchased over the counter (Oh, Canada!) at the neighborhood drug store. Then I would crack the lid, being careful not to stir my sleeping husband, and pour a mound of pills into my palm. I would separate the pile into three piles of 5 or three piles of 6—or some variation there of—and swallow, gulp, gag, until they were gone. Then I would lie back and wait, chasing that soft Codeine cloud of escape.

I had been taking Codeine daily for over nineteen years. At first, I took 2-3 tablets, then 5-6, then 8-12. By 2006, I gobbled over 15-18 tablets for my lusting flesh to feel any relief. This resulted in a back wave of nausea, constipation and depression. It was an insidious cycle I was determined to break. Every morning I prayed *Maybe this time it'll work. What if I take one more pill? Or maybe one less?* But Codeine's magic carpet ride no longer unfurled for me. It remained rolled up in a corner of the bedroom while I lay next to my husband, craving relief that no longer came.

Caught inside this torturous cycle I persisted, swallowing every morning, and then going on with my day. My health was a main dish I served with pride. I exercised, ate well, and took my transplant medications as prescribed. Addiction remained a gluttonous side dish I picked at. I had not yet discovered the magical elixir that was alcohol, the euphoric camaraderie of the opiate family, the catatonic escape of benzodiazepines, or the utter obliteration of barbiturates. The tentacles of addiction were winding through my brain like a wily weed. Yet I was unable to feel what was growing inside of me.

∼

ON ONE OF the last days of this Christmas trip, I was alone. Defiant, I had backed out of some outdoor sports activity that Winnipeggers love so much. (How can skating in -20 degree weather be anything but punishing?) I often played my well-worn Sick card without hesitation. No one argues with a kidney transplant patient.

Standing in my mother-in-law's unofficial corner of the kitchen was not planned. It was predestined. The germination of a seed that had been planted in my brain months ago. I knew Kevin's mother took the benzodiazepine, Xanax for anxiety. I was becoming an unconscious student of addiction, my ears opening wider to these nuggets of information, spurring me with a fluttery restlessness to try things I had never before dared.

Along this tiny stretch of counter, she hoarded a canister of thirty or more pens, uneven stacks of papers, and newspaper clippings. The tiled backsplash was littered with post-its. It was an impossible-to-decode system of notes, anecdotes and reminders that made sense to no one but her. This, I could relate to. I made lists myself, ever since I was 6 years old. Constantly, compulsively. Jotting down everything from: What I need to do. What I want to do. What I have done. What I want to buy. Where I have been. Where I would like to go. This pointless scribbling felt as vital to me as breathing. If I trapped every thought, idea and objective and then recorded it all, I could breathe. Apparently, my mother-in-law subscribed to the same nonsensical idea that peace and serenity was born in an office supply store aisle, and then reared on wallpaper of chaos. At least we had that in common.

I knew where they were. I cracked open one of the cupboard doors perpendicular to the sink. On the inside she had taped even more lists. They fluttered up from below. I eyeballed the shelves, cataloguing a standard inventory of ketchup, jams, and sweeteners for those endless cups of tea. There on the bottom shelf were three prescription bottles. I inhaled slowly. I had stolen a single pill two times before, but never from someone I knew. My pulse skip-skip-skipped along to the beat of a little girl playing hopscotch. This game was fantastic fun. I was the only player. I knew I would win.

I had left the light off. It was late afternoon and the day's weak winter sun had wisped away. The kitchen's only glow came from a single streetlamp. Its white beam angled in through the slightly cracked window. Crisp air brushed my skin. I could barely breathe. Anticipation lodged in my throat like my medication sometimes did. Anticipation that someone might come home and catch me. Anticipation for what these pills might do.

Selecting from my version of the Christmas Dainties, I turned the first bottle towards me. It was for heartburn. Meh. I turned the second one around. For depression. No thanks. Swiveling the final bottle around, I smiled. Alprazolam. Generic for Xanax. Bingo! Like any good student of addiction, I had Googled.

My hand formed like a steel claw in one of those mechanical stuffed animal games you find by the exit at Denny's. Impulse purchase. Impulse steal. I lowered my hand, steady, my fingers taut with energy I did not understand. Clamping my fingers around the bottle, I pulled up my prize. The label read *Alprazolam. 0.5 mg. 4 times daily as needed.* At the time, I did not know this was a moderate prescription. Four times a day just seemed like an awful lot to me. Surely she could spare a few.

Once the bottle was in my hand, walking away felt impossible. There was no stopping my thoughts. *I want this. I deserve this. Why can't I have this?* I ignored the proverbial white angel offering up an uninspired protest. *But it's stealing! You aren't prescribed these pills!* A new voice commanded. With cunning, dominatrix-like power it straddled my soul. *She has refills. She won't even notice.* I popped the cap and poured 8 tablets into my trembling palm, shaking not with fear, but electrified by adrenaline.

I palmed the 8 pills, swaddling 7 of them inside a cloth inside my eyeglasses case and slipped the 8th into the front pocket of my jeans. A tiny pouch above the regular pocket, the perfect size for quarters, Chapstick or stolen medication. I fingered the pill, my flesh cool as ice. I was born to do this. Mistress of the Swipe. I did not think about how Xanax might interact with my immunosuppressives. Tonight, I would slither away from a wintry world that froze me out, both inside and out.

When Kevin and his family returned home, we gathered around the table to recap the outing I had successfully dodged. Out came the Dainties.

"More tea, Kim?"

No longer seething, I waited, perched on the edge of my chair. I had just swallowed the pill, and was terrified I would miss my inauguration into the calming world of benzodiazepines. Then it hit me. Hard. Like a bucket of hot water flung with a single toss onto my icy discontent. My eyelids fluttered shut, my limbs melted, and I disappeared into a sea of plush stuffed animals, released from the steel claw grip inside.

Leaning back against my chair in quiet victory, I tuned out the conversation at hand. I gave my mother-in-law a congratulatory glance. *Jesus. No wonder you take these.* Xanax melted everything away. All my fears and discontent disappeared with just one pill. If Codeine was a side dish I picked at, Xanax had just introduced me to the buffet.

"Looks like Mrs. Smith isn't doing well. Bob and Susan are really worried about her."

Who the hell are Bob and Susan? And why are they worried about Mrs. Smith?

I released the grip on my mug. With Xanax swimming through me, I just didn't care. No one was talking to me. They were talking over me and under me, and around me, but it didn't matter. Nothing mattered. Xanax was talking to me, and I was just fine.

3. PREDNISONE

"Where are we?"

Disoriented, I lifted my 13-year old head. In the rear-view mirror my hair stuck to my face in damp clumps. My cheeks were stained a feverish red.

"Lie down, Henriette," Mum said softly. We were arriving at the Hospital for Sick Children. My mother had been called up to Parry Sound, a tiny bay town three hours north of Toronto where I had been vacationing on my girlfriend's parents' boat. Moaning, I curled into the back seat as our Pacer jolted across the streetcar tracks of downtown.

Things had not been easy for our small family after my father died three years earlier. To save money, Mum bought enormous blocks of generic cheese. We drank powdered milk. Our living room was decorated with wicker garden furniture. Through a combination of scholarships, sweat and tears, she had been able to keep me enrolled at BSS (Bishop Strachan School), the private girls' school I had attended for eleven years. But in September, I would begin at an advanced placement, co-ed public high school.

Just 24 hours earlier, everything had been perfect. From the reflective blue of the water to the forever-blue sky that startled after the endless, gray Canadian winter. My girlfriend and I squealed with joy as the yacht chopped along Georgian Bay. My eyes closed against the spray, as my long, strawberry-blond hair whipped across my face. A natural kink was emerging. Whether it was from the invigorating mist or puberty, I didn't know, but sure didn't like it. Exhausted after playing in the water all day, we gnawed on corn on the cob, the buttery niblets dropping down the tops of our bathing suits.

After we docked that evening I remained outside, staring at the velvet sky. A handful of stars blinked steadily like a visual Morse code, celestial bodies sending me a message. I squinted, dragging my finger across the sky, trying to cluster the glimmering letters into words. Into the story they wanted to tell. I brought my knees up to my chin. Nothing this beautiful could exist without meaning. The stars sparkled mystically, communicating a secret language I could not learn fast enough.

I shivered, drawing my arms around me. Something was in the air that still summer night. It feathered across my tanned skin. Was it just that the air was too clean, and unfamiliar to my urban lungs? A loaded sigh escaped my lips and floated into the blackness of the bay. Is that when it slinked inside me? Infecting my bean-shaped babies as I slept? Or was it already done?

Our race to the Hospital for Sick Children was my second bout with fever (The Yacht Fevers). My first bout (The First Fevers) occurred in December 1981 as I was studying for my 8th Grade Science Exam. After ten days as an inpatient, the doctors' best guess was an acute kidney infection. One they believed could be washed away on a chalky pink stream of antibiotics. Eight months later, on the waters of Georgian Bay, the fevers returned. Three days of a high temperature with no other symptoms. Henriette, we have a problem.

When Mum and I arrived at the hospital, my medical mystery was upgraded to include a nephrologist (kidney specialist), Dr. B. Seven months later, in March of 1983, the fevers would return one last time (The Final Fevers). Cold washcloths, fizzy pop, and Mum's elegant fingers stroking my forehead, tried and true panaceas were rendered useless inside another 72-hour inferno. I could do nothing but lay there, helpless against the Unknown Virus.

When The Final Fevers retreated, Dr. B. ordered a kidney biopsy (a diagnostic test where tissue samples are collected for analysis). The Unknown Virus remained unidentified. It wasn't Mononucleosis or Streptococcal Throat. Not lupus or another autoimmune disorder. At age 13, with no genetic predisposition, I was diagnosed with Chronic Kidney Disease (CKD), or more specifically: Glomerulonephritis (inflammation of the kidneys' filters). There are three outcomes to this chronic condition: Kidney transplantation, dialysis, or eventually, death.

~

THERE ARE certain moments in your life you never forget. Milestone moments. Backpacking around Europe. Your graduation from college. The birth of your first child. It should be noted that I never achieved any of these particular milestones. I cancelled my backpacking trip around Europe because my kidneys went into End Stage Renal Failure. I went to theater school after I dropped out of college. And it was too challenging to have children with a kidney transplant.

May 19th, 1983 was my milestone moment. From that day forward, Pills ran the show. At age 14, I began taking a regimen of toxic medications designed to prolong the life of my kidneys: 1) Imuran (immunosuppressant), 2) Baby Aspirin (blood thinner) and 3) Prednisone (steroid). Dr. B. warned me about Prednisone.

"I've never taken it myself," he admitted, "but I hear it tastes pretty bad."

Aw, sweet, but really, how bad could Prednisone taste?

Pretty fucking bad. You wouldn't think it to look at It. It is a small, round pill. White. Odorless. Benign. By all appearances, the one you least expect to do damage. So the only way Prednisone can stand out from Its pharmaceutical brethren is to slay from within.

To say It tastes revolting would be insulting to Its insidious brilliance. It doesn't just coat your tongue—It marinates it. Its discharge is bitter, intensely so, as if It has been fermenting for years. If It was alcohol it would be 80% proof. After swallowing, your tongue is instantly smashed on Prednisone.

That first morning, It slayed. I choked. It smeared. I gasped. I wanted to spit It out like a dog, but then I would have to start over. This drug was no joke. I had to get some skills, and fast.

I hid It inside cheese, or cold hotdogs, but that just made swallowing more problematic. I gagged as it busted out of my ingenious food-ball traps, flooding my mouth with its skunky ejaculate. God forbid I accidentally chew it. I think I would have imploded on the spot.

The entire experience felt shocking and mean, like a driver who gives you the finger just because you're going the speed limit. Thank God I didn't have to take It at night.

Aside from this morning ritual, and monthly blood work, I never thought about CKD. I didn't feel sick, or look sick. My primary focus was on getting my boobs and period. Trying to explain to a 13 year-old girl what will happen when her kidneys fail would have been like giving a military recruit a pamphlet entitled *WAR WILL SUCK* and expecting them to understand the horrors that await them.

I would suffer with Prednisone-weight-gain-induced Anorexia Nervosa. It would weaken my gums, stain my teeth, and puff up my cheeks. Moonface. There was the morning nausea, irritability and constant headache. I understood Prednisone was a steroid I needed to take to prolong the life of my kidneys, but the side effects were punishing. No question about it. Prednisone and I were the original frenemies.

~

TWELVE YEARS LATER, when Kevin asked me to marry him, there was no way for him to know I was already taken.

Getting married had not necessarily been on my list. Becoming a big, fat movie star, yes. After dating for two years, Kevin proposed on New Years' Eve 1994. That night we cocooned in a claw foot bathtub as a trendy bath bomb exploded in the water around us, languidly melting into swirls of hot pink. Our young relationship often worked like this—explosive arguments dissolving into loving periods of calm. We rode the Dickensian line: The Best of Times. The Worst of Times. That night was most definitely The Best. Marriage just made sense.

By 1995, Kevin was a lead in *Miss Saigon* and I was on a series called *Liberty Street.* My seven-year old kidney transplant from my mother was thriving. We lived in a two-story rental on the same street where I had grown up. We had money and friends and were in love— truly, madly, deeply. Just like in the movies.

A friend asked me how I knew Kevin was The One. He was talented, funny, adventurous, sexy and sensitive, but *He's just Kevin* was the best I could ever come up with. I don't know that my answer would be any different today.

Kevin had me pegged from the start. *You come into a room with your fists up.* I never saw this as a flaw I needed to deconstruct. *You'd fight, too, if you'd had my life.* To my fiery inner tween—slammed by death, and branded with disease—everything was suspect. So I kept my fists in front of my face, and often, in front of his.

If my fiancée was studying me, I had learned Kevin was guided by an internal moral compass so finely tuned he walked a righteous path that often left him paralyzed. He worried. A lot. For my young groom-to-be, too much had happened too fast—our booming careers, the adorable house, and our love.

"I feel like something's going to happen."

"What? You're crazy! Nothing's going to happen." I scoffed. I had already been through enough heartache for a lifetime. As far as I was concerned, I deserved this bliss. The Worst of Times had passed me by.

MAY 27TH, 1995. Our Wedding Day.

ON ONLY SIX hours of fitful sleep, I awoke in a room with a view at

Toronto's Royal York Hotel. Swallowing my regular morning pills, Cyclosporine (immunosuppressant), Inderal (blood pressure), Prednisone, and 6 tablets of Tylenol 1 with Codeine, I walked over to the window.

I had been told not to worry if it was raining. Rain was a good sign. A desired omen on someone's wedding day. I had been praying for sun. I yanked open the curtains. Blue as far as the eye could see, from the cotton-flecked sky to the polluted waters of Lake Ontario. Unconditional blue.

I feel like something is going to happen.

By my wedding day, I had been taking Prednisone for 12 years, and it still ran the show. It even informed what dress I chose. The sweetheart neckline plunged away from my face, distracting from my moonface. I hired the hair and makeup people from my TV series to blend away the mounds. As the gown zipped behind me with a delicate whoosh, I moved to the mirror. I saw the puffy hills of my cheeks. Noted the tiny gobble under my chin. My heart sank. I did not see a beautiful bride.

Down by the altar, Kevin stood with his hands clasped behind his back, waiting for married life to begin. Gliding towards him my skin tingled. In his crisp tuxedo and short blond hair, he rivaled any depicted prince. The organ swelled and the congregation rose. Over the melodic kerfuffle, we locked eyes. I burst into a nervous giggle.

Bathed in my groom's merciful gaze of love, everything disappeared: our family, friends, the minister, and Prednisone. I still had moonface. I still had a kidney transplant. But reflected in his unconditional blue eyes, I was no longer sick. I was whole. Dropping my fists upon the swishing folds of my princess gown, I took his hands in mine.

"I, Kevin, take thee Henriette, to be my lawfully wedded wife. To have and to hold, from this day forward, for better for worse, for richer for poorer, in sickness and in health..."

He paused, and then squeezed my hand.

Three hours later, I would betray my new husband in the bathroom of our marital suite by swallowing 6 more Tylenol 1 with

Codeine before the reception. On our first night as husband and wife, I would sleep with the controlled substance, Fiorinal, racing through my veins, and awake to swallow Cyclosporine, Inderal, Prednisone, and 6 more Codeine.

Kevin might have proposed to me, but he had married Us all.

4. FIORINAL 2008

I was going to be a star. I knew it. I had always known it.

The problem was no one else seemed to.

I had been auditioning in Los Angeles for over 10 years, and as much as I hated to admit it, I had become a cliché. The unemployed actress with a pile of headshots in her car, her agent's number on speed dial, and a compulsion to check her voice mail for auditions fifty times a day. And a drowning feeling that never went away.

By 2008, Kevin and I had been married for 13 years. He supported my flat lining career with his headshot photography business. Kevin began playing the bagpipes again with a local band, while I volunteered at an animal shelter. My transplant was 20 years young and kicking renal ass. We had just bought a half-acre property in Shadow Hills, a beautiful ranch-filled pocket north of LA, and had disposable income for wine-tasting train rides to Portland. Corny nicknames. Godsons. Friends, family and a big, fat basset hound named Daisy. For the most part, we were happy.

I often took this list for granted, focusing on the spaces in between the lines, the tantalizing lights of Hollywood blinding me to everything but my unrealized stardom.

∾

ADJUSTING my sunglasses in the rear-view mirror, I reveled in my rock star self. My satin dress clung to my hips like a lover's sweaty skin. Smacking my lips together, I flipped my butter-colored locks over my shoulder as if on cue. I was Movie Star ready.

I had just screen-tested for Ron Howard for the role of a "Young Diane Sawyer" in his upcoming film, *FROST/NIXON*. I had killed it. I was looking at The Next Big Thing.

My Hollywood dream had been simple: To nurture my Canadian career—a steady stream of small roles—into a flash flood of lead parts and artistic challenges. That had been The Plan, but with every year my name was not up in lights, my agonizing case of career-blue balls incited me to try almost anything.

Instead of studying Pinter, I now studied the sundry shades of white-blond hair on reality TV. Then I drank the sugar-free Kool-Aid and went blond. I bleached my teeth. Had my fanged incisors rounded. Ran five miles a day. And was always, always on some version of a diet, never managing to achieve that "lollipop-body" look. (Big head. Stick body.) With reverent determination, I studied actresses made scrawny from coffee and cigarettes. I puzzled over stars who would wax, nip and tuck themselves into plucked chickens, then tan to a rotisserie gleam inside halogen beds. Then I studied myself and wondered why, although I followed the Hollywood Recipe down to the very last ingredient, I never felt full.

As I merged onto the 405 N for home, I replayed the audition, designing an illusory blueprint of how my life would unfold from here on out. *After I shoot the film, I'll be able to get a great agent. Then I'll get a publicist. Then...* I could feel it fluttering in my stomach. Anticipation like the agonizing seconds as a man works his way down your torso to your wriggling pelvis. I was ready for the stunning payoff to a tantric career that had left me painfully unsatisfied.

Gone was my love of the craft. The girl who would spring out of bed at 6 AM for a role in an unpaid short film had disappeared. I now resented every fruitless audition, every flip of the coin when a producer chose another's head over my tail.

What if I don't get it? I bit down on my lip tasting gloss, then blood.

It would be several days, possibly weeks before the role was cast. Out the passenger window I noted the miniaturized moments whizzing by—tiny homes, tiny people and tiny lives. I was going home to the same: Dinner, laundry and television.

You never get the part. That voice. *You are a loser. You are a waste of space.* More and more, it was the one I heard. Lowering the window, I let the wind whip my cheeks. My finger jammed at the radio until Nirvana's ruthless sound filled my ears. I cranked the volume, egging the grunge explosion to drown the voice in my head. *Fuck. Off.*

I darted into the neighboring lane without warning, smirking as I accelerated past the pack. The engine's roar. Cobain's suicidal screams. More. I wanted more. I squirmed against the vibrating bass, the nostalgic riffs blasting me away. Now the car was my Time Machine where I could will a world of my own design. In here, I reigned as law-breaker, superstar, god.

I swelled beneath my dress, suddenly wet. Glancing out the window, I surveyed the glut of cars. My heart pounded. *Can I do this while driving?* I loved masturbating in public places. Inside a restroom stall at a wedding or in a random Starbucks toilet, but this scenario was unexplored territory.

I spotted Kevin's kilt in the back seat—weighted layers of wool ideal for concealing movement. Placing my left hand on the wheel, I twisted my body back and to the right. Grabbing the kilt, I yanked it over and onto my lap. Then I eased out of the fast lane, adjusting to the flow of traffic. I would have to coast along between cars my size, realizing the height of a trucker's cab might serve as a voyeuristic platform. It never occurred to me this might be distracted driving, maybe even a misdemeanor, and even if it had, it wouldn't have stopped me.

I reached underneath the kilt, sighing with the relief of flesh-on-flesh contact. *Concentrate. Just stay around sixty-two MPH.* Driving While Masturbating was so thrilling I was almost ready to come. My fingers quickly picked up the pace, from eager to hard to fierce. A moan echoed inside the car startling me. *I am actually doing this.* I could feel myself building to climax, tension as pain. My fingers dipped in, out and around, my cunt desperate for release. My foot began to descend heavy on the right.

Then I felt the twitch, that telling drop between your legs when you have reached the point of no return. Proud abandon filled my ears. My fingers dug into the soft leather of the steering wheel. I bucked upward, straining against complete surrender beneath this curious chastity blanket. I cried out. My eyes fluttered shut, then widened, uncaring if anyone was watching, as my orgasm crashed against the steel constriction of my thighs.

Shaking, I smiled, certain I had gotten away with something. But what? I reached under the wooly skirt one more time to finger myself in wonder. Bringing my musky fingers up to my nose, I inhaled. Adult. Real. My body's twitches were fading. Even the thump from the dashboard seemed diluted. The thrill so quick to come had already vanished.

More. I always wanted more than what I had. I did not want to go home and didn't know why. I switched back over to the fast lane, trying to outrun my ballooning anxiety. I needed something. Now. *I wonder if I have any Fiorinal?*

My heart skipped a beat. It was that simple. Suddenly, I was full. The mere thought of Her like a match sparking my obsession. Ordering Her was like preparing to go on a date you know will end in a great fuck. The ritual of Her trumped any ritual to come before it: Getting ready for my first date. Any hospital discharge. The morning of my wedding.

I pressed the icon on my steering wheel. "Bluetooth Audio." it sputtered.

"Call CVS." I said. The call clicked through to an automated system. I tapped through a couple of prompts, then pressed "3" for the pharmacy.

~

I GOT my first migraine when I was 17.

I was studying in my bedroom, nestled beside a stack of books.

The only sound in the room was the concentrated scratching of my pen. A bookish, yet results-oriented teen, my focus wasn't so much on what I learned, but on the grade I received.

Foreboding plopped into my gut as a single raindrop. Then another. And another. Then sheeting pain. Howling tore through my brain. I dropped my book and dug my fingers into my temples. My stomach roiled with nausea. Flung out to sea, so far, so fast, it was unlike any headache I had ever experienced.

Grabbing the Extra Strength Tylenol, I ignored the instructions: *Take 1 to 2 capsules once every 4 hours.* They couldn't have meant for this kind of pain! I tossed 4 back with a swig of water from the bathroom tap. Delirious, I paced my bedroom desperate for relief that never came. Defeated, I went fetal until dawn.

That morning, I awoke to scattered homework and a dull ache across my neck. My fingers shook as I gathered the incomplete assignment.

Later that morning, I whispered to a friend in class. "God, I had such a crazy headache last night. I took 4 Tylenol."

"Wow," she said, alarmed. "That's a lot."

Was it? It had not occurred to me to try 1 or 2 capsules first. Four capsules had made total sense. Fists up. Fight. Fight. Fight. I didn't know that I had just experienced a migraine, and that no one conquers a migraine. You just try to survive it.

∿

FOUR YEARS LATER, I was complaining of these headaches to my second Canadian nephrologist, Dr. C. who had seen me through my first kidney transplant. My symptoms were: nausea, vomiting, ocular disturbance, a physical allergy to light and sound, and pain, ferocious, unrelenting pain.

Migraines are the tornadoes of the neurological world. Your typical tension headache— that nine times out of ten can be eradicated with a bottle of water and a jog around the block— might rate as an F0 (light winds, fast moving clouds.) My teenage neurological blitzkrieg rated an F5 (homes ripped from their foundations and flung into the air like confetti). By age 21, I was getting these headaches two or three times a month, each one lasting several days at a time.

Although a nephrologist and not a neurologist, Dr. C. explained that these were not just brutal headaches, but migraines. The foreboding feeling was a like a warning system (a.k.a the aura). A brief window of time before a migraine touches down. Mine would strike the back of my head or neck, or sometimes in-between my eyes.

In 1991, Dr. C. prescribed me Fiorinal (Butalbital/Aspirin/Caffeine) with a warning.

"You must take it the moment you feel the aura, or it will not be effective. And be careful. They are strong."

It is with a wistful irony that I remember Our first time together. That night, I stood washing dishes in a condo I shared in my final year of theater school. A feeling of unease hummed in my neck. My stomach dropped. The aura had landed. Dripping, I peeled off the rubber gloves and went into my bedroom.

Fiorinal was waiting for me in a basket with all of my other medications. I read and reread Her label. *Take 1 or 2 capsules at the onset of migraine.* My heart pounded as I stared fascinated, at the lone, glamorous, double-blue capsule I had just rolled into my palm. I fingered Her gently. *What is it going to do to me?* Despite my escalating Codeine abuse, I hesitated. My stomach cramped, churning with bile. The thought of another migraine tearing through my body and soul was enough motivation. *Fuck it.*

I threw Her into the back of my throat and swallowed. Then I lay down on my bed and waited. After about twenty minutes, my migraine was flattened, unable to funnel into those hysterical winds of pain. And from that moment on, I was infatuated.

Codeine had helped my headaches, but never saved me from physical pain. My soul sang with almost divine relief. I was so grateful to Her, in the same way you are grateful to the first man who can bring you to orgasm. You never knew this feeling was possible, but after you've had it, you never want to live without it.

Infatuation is like a wily weed. It does not need respectful and tenacious maintenance the way love does. It can develop one of two ways. Wither away when a new infatuation is introduced, or patiently subsist, freakishly sustaining itself without sunlight or water. With nothing but time as fertilizer.

Over seventeen years, Her directions had become open to my interpretation. I would take a few extra pills here and there for myriad reasons: 1) to enhance the buzz of a beer 2) because 4 seemed to work so much better than 1, or 3) when there was no migraine at all. I never sought more than my monthly script of 30, especially when it was upped to 60. After pick up, I would consume all of Her in a few short days. This was followed by two and a half weeks of white knuckling it as I counted down to Refill Day. I never asked for more. I never exceeded the monthly amount. It wasn't abuse. I just took Her a little more quickly than prescribed.

By 2008, I was obsessed. I did not realize how deep my infatuation went, until I found myself craving Her acrid smell, and longing to finger her plastic shell. Aching to disappear with Her for days on end. When obsession takes root, there is only one way for it to grow. Wild.

~

STEP 1: The Ordering of the Medication.

"PHARMACY."

"Oh, hello. Good afternoon." Light. Polite. I needed this call to go smoothly. "I was wondering if you could check on a refill?"

"Patient's name?"

"Henriette Ivanans-McIntyre."

"For what medication?" I could hear him typing in the background.

"Um, Fiorital?" I feigned. This was key. To never look too eager.

"Fiorinal," he corrected. "Yes, you do. Would you like me to fill it for you?"

"Yes. Thank you."

"Give me half an hour."

In porn, this moment would be known as the money shot. Now that She was ordered, I was free to explode in ecstasy all over the car. Yet, I continued to pretend I was so not into this transaction. Although I wasn't doing anything illegal by ordering Fiorinal, I had no intention of taking Her according to directions. So whom was I manipulating the phone call for? Not the pharmacist. He didn't appreciate my professionally trained voice inflections, or my genius pretense that I was so noncommittal about this drug I had forgotten its name. He wouldn't care if I took my pills as prescribed or not. He wouldn't think about me after I left the pharmacy any more than I would think about him.

"And how late are you open?"

I knew it was open 24/7. That's why I had picked this CVS. I placed the question there with a quiet flourish, not to convince the pharmacist I wasn't doing anything wrong, but myself.

"24 hours."

"Thank you." I replied, hanging up. My chest erupted with joy, hard and loud. As if a team of cheerleaders had stormed the field, screaming Her name. *Gimme an F! F! Gimme an I! I! Gimme an O! O!* Operation Refill complete, I maneuvered the car off the freeway, and onto the San Fernando Valley side streets, detouring south towards my Burbank CVS.

Timing is everything when you are having an affair. I didn't want to call Kevin and let him know where I was just yet. It would be too hard to pretend I wasn't on the freeway. If I got home much later than I told him, I would have to pick a reason why other than that perennially golden LA excuse: traffic. Maybe get a receipt to prove I had been running errands. Or straight up lie and say I had been to the chiropractor or even the gym, even as my workout gear lay untouched in the back seat.

Kevin ran his photography business from home, and we shared one car, so we were together a lot. Which is not a bad thing when you love your husband, but it is a tricky thing when you are in love with something else.

It was hard to determine what Kevin knew about my increasing binging. He was starting to speak up, noting *I can tell when you're on them* or *Your personality changes.* I chose not to pay attention to what he said. As long as he didn't stand in Our way, I really didn't care what Kevin thought, and as I pulled into the pharmacy's parking lot, I was no longer thinking about my husband at all.

Flipping down the visor mirror, I slid on a generous layer of lip-gloss. I always made an effort to look nice before I saw Her. My pupils were black, glinting with Her magnetic force, goading me towards a dark dance choreographed just for Us.

Clip, clip, clip. My heels echoed across the parking lot. Fiorinal empowered me. Around Her I soared, in spirit and stature, insecurities like my stunted growth from kidney disease dissolved. I had always felt awkward about my height, but in this moment, invincible —all legs and no regrets.

I entered my church. The antiseptic smells of witch hazel, hemorrhoid cream and Epsom salts comforted me like Roman Catholic incense swirling around the sanctified on their knees. Here I would drink the holy water. Here I would be saved.

Fiorinal and I had discovered something that made our relationship even stronger. *In Vino Veritas.* This was how we would really bond. We did not care for the subtleties of pear notes or a blackcurrant after taste. We were fans of what was cheap and cold. My customized cocktail was simple: the coldest possible chardonnay and a fistful of blue plastic pills. No mixologist could ever trump this winning combination. Hold the fruit, straws and tiny umbrellas. I took my absolution straight up.

I grabbed a sale-priced Mondavi and pretended to peruse the label. Really I was just fondling the nape to see if it was cold enough. Almost perfect. Nothing that a few ice cubes couldn't cure. Then I marched towards the pharmacy.

. . .

Step 2: The Purchasing of the Medication.

A BOTTLENECK of customers jammed the analgesic aisle. I joined the crooked, toe-tapping line, slumping my shoulders along with the others: the plaid-clad, blue-collared workers, the disheveled, scrunchied housewives and the hopped-up hipsters. My greatest fear was to approach the counter and have the pharmacist report they were out of stock.

An elderly man was rambling on about his medication regimen, then his insurance, then, could they check that his generic medication was the same as the brand name? *Oh, my God. How can an old man talk so much?* Shifting my weight from one foot to the next, I rested the bottle along the back of my neck. Nice and cool. I wanted to yank him by his shirt collar and hurl him into a display of *One Direction* singing toothbrushes. I tried to make eye contact with one of my fellow prisoners-of-wait, to commiserate in mutual irritation. Everyone was either dialed-out, heads up, scanning the water-stained ceiling tiles or dialed in, heads down, scrolling on their phones. We were nothing if not a motley crew of disconnected pill poppers.

"Next!"

I approached the counter. The backs of my knees quivered as the cashier retrieved Her from a hanging hook on the back wall. *Thank you, God.* Folding over the top of the bag, he stapled it shut. My mouth watered. She was so close now. I calmly placed the wine on the counter and offered my debit card. I smiled brightly. He ignored me.

"Have you ever taken this medication before?" I wanted to laugh in his face.

"Yes. Thank you." I replied. He lifted the bag. Our eyes met. I watched as it dangled from his arm over the DMZ of the pharmacy counter. No longer his, but not quite mine. His eyes narrowed as my fingers curled around empty air. I grabbed the bag and pirouetted away, tucking the wine under my shoulder and charging through the front doors.

This was the feeling I wanted every moment of every day. Like fucking Christmas morning. Like fucking *on* Christmas morning. In this dance of anticipation, I was about to fall into my partner's arms and succumb to every inch of Her charms; crossing over from *Hen* to *Her,* losing myself one delicious misstep at a time.

I slid into the car, tucking a damp tendril of hair around my ear. Organizing my bags on the passenger seat, I glanced up to make sure no one was around. Sometimes I wondered if anyone else was doing what I was doing. Taking their controlled medication before heading home, despite a prescription label that warned: *Do not drive on this medication.*

Mostly, I chose not to think moments like this through, never connecting the dots between my secretive adventures and how, a few days later, I would be dope sick and full of remorse. Just like alcoholics were men in trench coats who sat on park benches and drank from bottles concealed in paper bags, drug addicts were ne'er-do-wells who lived under bridges, jamming needles into their arms slamming heroin eight times a day. I did not know, that addicts, like pills, came in all shapes and sizes.

The label also read, *Avoid alcohol while on this medication.* I chose to focus on the part that said *Alcohol may intensify effect.* Wasn't that a good thing? I was prescribed this medication. It was medicine I needed.

My heart slowed as I lifted Her from the bag. *Ker-thunk. Ker-thunk.* Oh, there She was! Her sweet white mushroom cap topped Her peach-plastic shell. Palming the lid, it popped open with a satisfying crack. The acrid smell caressed the fine hairs of my nostrils, promising what I could not deliver for myself—freedom.

STEP 3: The Swallowing of the Medication.

IGNORING THE DIRECTIONS, *Take 1-2 capsules every 4-6 hours for migraine*, I tossed 3 into the back of my mouth, swallowing them with a swig of warm water from a bottle off the floor of the car.

The dashboard read 3:26 pm. It took 15-20 minutes before I felt anything. I would almost be home by then. I remembered a scene in an HBO movie-of-the-week called *Norma Jean and Marilyn* starring Ashley Judd and Mira Sorvino. Sorvino, convincing as the lustrously loaded Marilyn, sits on the floor, a satin gown spread beneath her as blanket for her narcotic picnic of delights. She titters about her tricks of the intoxication trade to that evening's partner in crime.

"I like to open them up and sprinkle them into the bubbles," she breathes into his ear. Marilyn cracks her Seconal tablet in half, languidly sprinkling it into her champagne. "It hits you faster..."

Faster, faster. It's never fast enough...

Cruising north on Hollywood Way my every hair bristled, vigilant, ready to receive the first signal that She had landed. It was a subtle nudge, a metal taste at the back of my throat. My brain surged on. Everything became sharper, brighter—the cars, the road, the lights of the dashboard—even as a layer of chiffon floated over me. Blissfully swaddled, my life ahead no longer seemed overwhelming, but manageable. Worth the drive home.

～

I PULLED to the top of our steep driveway and turned off the ignition. I hated the abrasive silence. The mechanical crackle and pop of the engine shutting down. My heart sank as I removed the keys, ejected from my Time Machine. Present day stood just a few feet away. I hated having to share Her with him.

Reaching into my purse I grabbed Her, glancing up to see if Kevin had emerged from the house. Palming two more capsules, I crumpled the bag and receipt into a teeny ball. I jammed the paper muffler inside the bottle, silencing my 55 remaining friends. Then I hid Her in an inside pocket of my purse. If necessity is the mother of invention, perhaps creativity is its daughter.

I knew this ritual was pointless. I was fooling no one. When I walked through the front door, I would not make a beeline for our darkened bedroom after a quick pit stop for a cool washcloth. I had no migraine. Eventually, Kevin would see I was intoxicated. But I loved my husband very much, and was resolute in hiding my betrayal for as long as possible.

Tossing back the two pills, I swigged again from the bottle of warm water. A dribble escaped down my chin as I gagged, then smirked. She had not failed me. She had brought me home.

"Where have you been?" Kevin exclaimed as I slinked through the front door.

Oh, my god, he's such a fucking pain in the ass. I marched over to the freezer and slid the wine onto the top shelf next to the edamame. Slamming the door shut with my hip, I wobbled on my heels. *Boy. That was just the first 3! I have to pace myself. 10. Tonight, I will take 10. Max. I can do it. If I take 20, I'll be sick in the morning, and... Is he still talking?*

"Traffic." I threw over my shoulder.

The pills were rolling over me now. Barbiturate bugs gnawing on the wires of my brain. I looked at Kevin, his arms crossed, hands tucked up into his armpits. His face looked like it hurt. He had really been worried. Waltzing across the kitchen, I threw my arms around him, my irritation melting along with the two other pills.

"Oh, sweetheart! It was amazing!"

Out it came, a thick stream of enthusiasm detailing the screen test from beginning to end. OMG! Ron Howard totally looked like Ron Howard! Auditioning was like a date with *Richie Cunningham* where we debated whether or not to split a cherry cola at *Arnold's*.

My tongue tripped on the "r" in "Ron." Soon I would be slurring. I would have to avoid certain letters and substitute specific words altogether, choosing to say, for example, "SNL" instead of "Saturday Night Live." It was time to crack open the wine and get drinking. When I was loaded, he got upset. Tipsy, he could handle.

Kicking off my heels, I wobbled again. I grabbed at the kitchen counter, catching myself. Kevin stared. After thirteen years of marriage, I still couldn't figure him out. Was his neutral expression love or suspicion?

His tone was often flat. Never did Kevin proclaim his love for me in anything but straightforward declarations. When he listened, I wanted him to say something. When he said something, he almost never said the right thing.

Nor was my husband a writer of love letters. He had never been able to stroke my soul with an exquisite string of words perfectly arranged and presented like a pearl necklace I could wear close to my heart, grazing my breastbone for private pleasure, then occasionally pull out to show girlfriends that they might draw an envious gasp, that I might draw comfort from their envy, that I might make myself feel bigger by making them feel smaller.

Fiorinal nudged me. *Who cares what Kevin thinks! You're going to be a STAR!*

It was 4:49 pm. Drinking after 5 pm: Sophisticate. Drinking before 5 pm: Alcoholic. *Close enough! It's 5 clock somewhere!*

STEP 4: Mixing Alcohol with the Medication.

I HATED DOING this in front of Kevin. His eyes followed me everywhere —from the fridge to the drawer to the bottle. Placing our state-of-the-art corkscrew over the bottle, I pressed a side lever that locked onto the nape and then up. The air sucked out with a sensual slurp. My stomach flipped. Could my husband see how much I wanted this drink?

"You want some?" I asked, my hand hovering inside the cabinet, secretly hoping he would say no. Yet recognizing the more fucked up Kevin became, the less likely he was to notice how fucked up I was. I did not think this thinking was fucked at all.

"Sure."

I pulled out two glasses and filled each halfway. Kevin was not a big drinker, so I knew he wouldn't complain about the stingy pour.

The plummeting *glug, glug, glug* delighted my ears. In a lovely and surprising move, Kevin raised his glass. Proudly. I thought.

"It sounds like you are going to get it."

That was definitely the right thing to say. We clinked glasses. He looked me straight in the eye, whereas I dared but for a second. I turned away, craving private reverence as I went in for that first sip. My lips pillowed over the crystal edge, parting sensually. The pungent fumes blasted away my lingering anxiety. I tilted the glass back and swallowed. Then swallowed again. My throat burned with pleasure.

"Thank you, sweetheart." Then I turned away from my husband to finish the wine.

~

A FEW HOURS LATER, I was packing away the remains of dinner to an 80's pop groove. I had avoided eating by serving Kevin food in his office. (She went down so much better on an empty stomach.) Floating over to the fridge, I tossed the Tupperware box into the freezer. Catching my mistake, I snorted, laughing to myself in that sinister drunken way.

STEP 5: The Hiding of the Medication.

I SWILLED the last drops of wine, holding my empty glass against the eerie glow of the stove light. Lipstick smears and greasy fingerprints marked its once pristine edge. *I need more pills.* I racked my brain, parting through the veils of paranoia woven thick over the passing hours.

I would hide my pills all over the house: in my shoes, inside sweater pockets, or in between towels. Once Kevin knew She was in the house, his back went up and he questioned everything. *When did you pick it up? How many did you take?* I had learned how to keep Her safe from his interrogations.

Was She in the corner cabinet below and to the right of the kitchen sink? One shelf inside this cupboard ran parallel with the sink's length, running long and deep to the back of the wall. We kept almost nothing on this shelf, as it was too difficult to angle your arm back and retrieve anything. This was my Secret Cupboard.

I peered around the corner of our kitchen, straight across the dining room, and into Kevin's office where I could make out his shoulder and a portion of the back of his head. He was sitting at his desk, bathed in a florescent halo from his computer screen. Over the music, I could hear the tappity-tap-tap of his keyboard. He was nestled. I had to get to Her and find out how much was left. She was getting in the habit of disappearing on me way too fast.

I had to be quick. Our cabin is very small. Kevin could stride over to the kitchen in ten silent steps. I squatted beside the Secret Cupboard's door, snaking my arm towards the back. My fingers clawed at the wood shelf, grasping nothing but air. My neck flushed with sweat. I was certain I had left Her in here. With another frantic thrust backwards my fingers grazed plastic—the thin of the container, and then, the thick of the cap. I seized hold, knocking Her over in my panicked lust. Feeling my grip, She rattled with relief. Shoving Her into a tea towel, I cradled Her against my chest.

I couldn't count them here. If Kevin left his office, I wouldn't be able to hear him with the music playing. If I shut off the music, he would be able to hear the spilling of the pills on the counter. It was Bedroom or Bust. I tiptoed across the main section of our living room and around another corner into our bedroom, holding Her close. I felt a flicker of discomfort, not enough to trip me up, and certainly not a Charley horse to take me down, but there was something treasonous about a wife sneaking away from her husband on feet that did not even touch the ground.

STEP 6: The Counting of the Medication.

. . .

I SLIPPED INTO OUR BEDROOM, and coughed as I locked the door. The tapping of his keyboard rose up through the thin drywall that separated Kevin's office from our bedroom. Hmmm. If I could hear him typing, he'd be able to hear the plunking of the pills. I selected a new-age radio station on the TV. Then I poured the pills onto the bedspread.

The bright blue plastic popped incongruous against the soft green bedspread chosen for its calming potential—green like grass, grass like nature, nature like calm. Fuck that. I had seconds to get these counted and hidden again. Quickly, I separated them into groups of 2—2, 4, 6, 8, reaching 48. 48! That meant I had already taken 12 pills! My stomach dropped. How had that happened?

Fuck it! I had tons left. I plucked another 3 off the bed before scooping up the 45 remaining pills with the bottle's edge. Okay. 15. I wouldn't go past 15. That meant I could take these 3, with more wine. I was sure I had another bottle hidden somewhere.

At this point in Our relationship, any plan I came up with began to unravel before I had finished designing it. I would rather drink on a deliberately empty stomach than eat dinner with my husband. I would rather tiptoe behind a locked door and count pills than meet his eyes over a loving toast. She was now the architect, but I still thought I was drawing up the plans.

The 3 pills lolled melancholy in my palm as if they knew they would be the final hit of the night. I could barely keep my eyes uncrossed, stand without leaning, or talk without slurring, but this thought truly saddened me. I knew if I just kept taking more—1 more, 2 more, 5 more—something better would reveal itself to me. I just didn't know what.

Glancing at the bottle, something different caught my eye: 1 refill. One refill! I had completely missed that! That was all I needed to see. I wobbled in relief, smiling from behind closed eyes. Assured of more, I spilled 5 capsules onto the bed. 8 more pills. 20 total. But no more.

≈

IN THE BATHTUB, I lay motionless behind another locked door. The hot water rose in steamy wisps, lulling me close to catatonia. My eyes fluttered in the back of my head as I dragged my arm across the top of the water. I allowed myself to sink down, hovering below a watery line gone frighteningly still. This was no cause for alarm, for I had reason to surface: To swallow more pills.

I had now taken 18 pills. I thought about the remaining 2 in my bedside table drawer, hidden in between the pages of Mary Karr's *Lit* —the beloved memoir about an atheist alcoholic who found Catholicism. Kevin would never look there. He did not read much, and he certainly wouldn't open a novel about...or would he? Would he find the pills? Would he like the book? My head was thick with nonsense. Forming a thought was tedious work, like chewing through tough meat with very little payoff.

STEP 7: The Betrayal of the Medication.

DESPITE MY WELL-DESIGNED BLUEPRINT, I had arrived once again at the place I had sworn I would not, and I barely remembered leaving. I had not yet taken the last 2 pills, but I knew I would. No matter where I hid them, or how many times I counted them, they had already been swallowed. I was already dopesick, wondering when Fiorinal and I could be together again. There was a knock at the door.

"Are you OK, sweetheart?"

"Yeah," I slurred.

"You've been in there for an hour." Kevin's voice was tight.

An hour? Already? Our time together was never long enough.

I did not think about what he might say in bed, inconvenient questions I struggled to answer with a flaccid tongue. Maybe if I stayed in here long enough, he would fall asleep. I loved my husband. I really did. I thought I loved him more than anything. But in that moment—it feels impossible to write it—I loved Her more. I loved Her more.

I chose not to think about morning, knowing She would be gone. That I would beg for Her through the tremors, nausea and hallucinations. Her ear-scraping withdrawal would scream the truth. The knowledge that every time We stole away together, I knew was turning away from my career, and Kevin.

Sinking beneath the lukewarm water, I thought about my refill and smiled. The only way to survive Her, was more of Her. I did not know this yet, but I was losing the power of choice. But that was Her power. Convincing me I still had one.

It's only once-in-a-while. I can still become a star. For the most part, we are happy.

5. MORPHINE

Kidneys are fist-sized organs located in your mid-lower back. They are surrounded by millions of filters called glomeruli. These filters regulate urine output and remove waste from your bloodstream. Kidneys also regulate your blood pressure by balancing your body's salt and water. They balance vitamins, minerals, and the protein EPO necessary to produce hemoglobin, which feeds red blood cells, which provides oxygen, which provides energy. Everyone can live with approximately 1/3rd of one kidney. That is all you need. Which means almost everyone has a spare. (This is not a PSA for organ donation, but it wouldn't kill you to check your donor card.)

For a kidney transplant to survive, the recipient's immune system must be suppressed. This allows the body to accept the kidney as its own, and not reject it as a foreign object like a flu bug. For optimal absorption, you take your medication twice a day, 12 hours apart. But immunosuppressives are toxic, and the minute you swallow these drugs, they begin to destroy the thing suppression of your immune system is meant to protect, i.e. your transplant. It's a little like chemotherapy destroying healthy cells as it kills the malignant ones.

The second the donor's kidney is placed into the recipient's body it is flushed of the donor's bodily fluids (not unlike an oil change) and then pumped full of IV immunosuppressives (like the ignition turning over). That is the moment the transplant actually begins to die (like a car once driven off the lot, depreciates with every mile). With a suppressed immune system, I catch viruses and infections more easily, and they last weeks longer than you, The Healthy. It's like I'm always a little bit sick.

In 1998, on one of my bi-annual visits to Toronto, Dr. C. ordered an investigative, outpatient biopsy at the then Toronto General Hospital. After 10 years with my transplant, this procedure would determine how far my transplant had deteriorated.

"We will likely see about 30% of the kidney destroyed."

I do not know what bubble I was living in at the time—a World Wide Web-less world where I couldn't instantly research the life expectancy of my transplant. It feels ridiculous to write, but I was ignorant and just didn't know. Gone was the 14-year old girl who researched the side effects of Prednisone at the Metro Toronto Reference Library. Once I had my transplant at 19, I swallowed my pills every morning, and then barreled through the day, not ungrateful, but willing to take my transplant for granted, like running water or the sunrise.

Monitors and IV poles with cords draped over their sides cluttered the procedural area. The walls were lined with cupboards, labeled shelving, and a sink. Lying on the gurney, I scrutinized the drab walls. Were these colors chosen to further depress patients in case their sedatives did not work? It is noteworthy, that on this particular day, I was not sedated with anything.

As I wove conspiracy theories on a mental loom, Kevin poked his head through the curtain. His eyes darted all around, taking in the institutional blahness as he moved to stand behind me. After seven years together, this was the first time my husband had seen me lying in a hospital bed. The front of his thighs grazed the top of my head. His fingers danced lightly on my shoulders, unsure of where to land.

"Where are they going to put the needle?" he asked.

A transplanted kidney is placed into your abdomen where the surgeon connects it to the ureter, which connects to the bladder, and to blood vessels that supply blood to and from the leg. My original kidneys were left in place. Removing them would have required an additional and traumatic surgery called a nephrectomy (which is what my Mum endured in donating one of her kidneys to me). This surgery is only necessary if the kidneys have become enlarged from Polycystic Kidney Disease, or are a source of infection. With Glomerulonephritis, this surgery was unnecessary because over time, my kidneys would simply shrivel away.

My transplant was on the left side of my abdomen. This was where they were going to extract, via needle, a few samples of tissue. The ultrasound technician covered the area with sterile cloths, leaving a 2" x 5" patch of exposed flesh over the kidney. The area had already been sterilized, and then frozen with local anesthetic, which burns as it enters your bloodstream. About as bad as a bee sting.

My gurney stood next to an ultrasound machine. The probe—the mushroom-like head of the ultrasound's cord—lay on my belly, ready to monitor the kidney's location. Then the doctor brought the needle out, and let me just say, I was impressed.

The kidney biopsy is not for the faint of needle. Your standard-sized needle for routine blood work is small (1/2" to 1"), a prick you barely feel if you get the veteran tech, the one who can tie you off, swab your arm and poke you with one hand while juggling a Starbucks with the other. The IV needle is a little more complicated. There are specialized IV nurses for this, called in when it's difficult to find a vein, but that needle is still of average size.

The renal transplant biopsy needle however is a honey: Eight inches long, thick, and swabbed to gleaming perfection. It flickered under the cool light, a lean mean medical spear ready to pierce through my abdomen and go deep-me diving. This needle is so badass it is literally called, "The single packing semi-automatic biopsy" needle, because it retracts once it has collected a sample. Damn.

The technician placed the probe on the Sharpie-d "X" on my kidney. He checked the monitor, and then double-checked the marked area. The doctor came forward and inserted the biopsy needle into a slot in the center of the probe and prepared to plunge.

"You doing all right?" the doctor asked.

I nodded, one arm resting behind my head. I was proud to walk my husband through an example of my medical narrative in the way someone else might show their spouse the neighborhood they grew up in. *See, sweetheart? The Toronto Western Hospital? That's where Mum and I had the transplant* or *That's Sick Kids, where they gave me an experimental blood pressure medication that made me lose my sense of taste for three months.* These buildings and procedures were, for better or worse, where I had grown up.

Kevin touched the exposed skin between my gown's straps. His fingers were cold.

"I have to go to the bathroom," he whispered, tremulous, and then wisped away in a ghostly move.

The doctor looked up. "Is he alright?" I smiled.

"He just hasn't been through anything like this before."

When he came back, his hands were wet. Had he thrown up and washed his hands or just splashed cold water on his face? Did he stare into the mirror and wonder what he had gotten himself into? He had married a chronically sick woman, but until that day they hadn't met.

"Are you ok?" I asked, as he slipped back into the room, resuming his place at the gurney.

"I'm fine." Kevin slipped his hand beneath my folded arm and took my hand in his. Together, we watched the needle plunge.

Eight hours later, I returned to the hospital bleeding clots the size of dates. For two days, my kidney refused to stop gushing a blood-red stream of resentment from between my legs. It was pissed. Clutching the bedpan in agony, the hours dragged. Tears blinded me to all sight. But through it all, was Kevin.

It was my husband's medical baptism by fire, or flesh, as it were. After shedding the role of Fainting Man, he returned as the Hero. No matter how he was feeling, Kevin would stand beside me. No matter how deep the plunge, he always came back for more.

The results of the biopsy were just as Dr. C. predicted. Eight out of the twenty-five collected glomeruli were destroyed—about 31% of my kidney. At age twenty-nine, I felt the way I had at thirteen. I did not look sick or feel sick. I was never very good at math, but I could see how this was all going to add up. So I just kept going. When you have known illness for seventeen years, you don't look a medical gift horse in the mouth, you ride it into your future.

∼

TEN YEARS LATER, in February 2008, we were driving to Cedars-Sinai Medical Center: Kevin, my sister-in-law, Kim and her two children. There were five of us in the car, but I was the only one I cared about.

I had just returned from Toronto, couch surfing with friends for a couple of weeks. It was my biannual trip due north to purchase immunosuppressives et al., taking advantage of prices (under a purchased Canadian health care plan) that were a fraction of the cost in California (under my current American health care plan). Dr. C. prescribed my medications and after purchasing several 200 caplet over-the-counter bottles of Tylenol 1 with Codeine, I was on my way back to L.A.

The night before I flew home, I'd checked my private voice mailbox that The Toronto Hospital Transplant Clinic sets up for every patient. Here the staff leaves your latest blood results, updates about West Nile Virus outbreaks (potentially fatal for the immuno-suppressed) or just a general reminder to get your flu shot before flu season starts.

The outgoing message irritated me as both of my names had been pronounced incorrectly. *Henriett- Eee-Van-Is.* She'd clipped my first name and butchered my last. Every time I pressed pound to confirm I was indeed who they thought I was, I wanted to sneer *You suck* at the automated clown.

"Hi Henriette, it's Theresa. Your creatinine has jumped from 1.6 to 2.6. Get blood work immediately upon returning to Los Angeles. Let me know you got this."

Bile rose in my throat. Suddenly, I didn't care about the affronting outgoing message. This was not good. This was catastrophically bad. The normal range for creatinine (the most accurate blood test used to assess kidney function) is 0.4-1.2 for The Healthy. My range had been nothing out of the ordinary for a transplant patient of over 20 years. It had been fluctuating between 1.4-2.3. A spike like this—10 points— was not likely to be lab error (one point on either side).

When I landed, Kevin and I drove straight from LAX to Cedars- Sinai's West Tower where I had my blood drawn. Two days later, 2.6 became 2.8. A second round of blood work was ordered. Two days after that, the phone rang. It was Dr. D., my beloved nephrologist with whom I had been working for eleven years.

"Your creatinine is 3.1. We need to do a biopsy."

"What, like now?"

"Now. You might be rejecting."

You are not asked politely to step into the place you suddenly find yourself. You are shoved through some kind of portal into a place where nothing touches you, some metaphysical dimension where you touch things, but cannot feel. I pondered this as I packed up my hospital bag with my unfortunate wisdom of experience: earplugs, electric fan (as white noise against the silence) laptop, phone, charg- ers, pen and paper, book, and reading glasses. The items felt weight- less, yet my arms labored to pack any of it at all.

The constant chatter in the back seat made my skin crawl. I cracked my window to let in some air. I wasn't even sure why they had to tag along. This wasn't a trip to Disneyland.

"Do you have everything you need?" Kim called from the backseat.

Anger spread hot through my chest. This was no staycation! The nicer my sister-in-law was, the harder I wanted to punch her in the face.

"Yes," I mumbled, staring out the window.

"You OK?" Kevin whispered.

I shook my head. My husband knew I was on the verge of erupting.

"I think we're a little stunned," he offered in a thin voice. Kevin could always offer something kind to a room, even if he didn't feel like it. I could not. He gave me a second look that warned *Keep it together* which only made me want to throw it all away.

As we merged onto the freeway, my skin surged with adrenaline. I felt, maybe not a thrill, but curiosity of the unknown. I couldn't deny it. Hospital admissions were always a little bit exciting. As a transplant patient, I got extra attention in the medical midst of it all.

Being a transplant patient also allowed me to judge your overreaction when you were hospitalized. It is always more complicated for me. I am forever anchored to my chronic condition. You are not. You don't have one. Whatever you have is acute and will eventually float away like medical waste bobbing on the ocean foam. It is always worse for me.

Yet, as we approached Cedars, my stomach twisted. Less adrenaline, more fear. A 3.1 creatinine was bad. There would be nothing exciting about a rejection episode. I turned away from the window and watched Kevin drive. I wanted to grab the wheel from him and yell, *We have to turn around!* Somehow I knew if we pulled into the ER and a piece of my kidney was taken away, nothing would ever be the same again.

"I'm scared." I whispered.

"I know." He placed his hand on my thigh, and then stroked it forward to the kneecap, tickling it with fingers spread wide. He had a way of kneading my kneecap that gave me shivers when we were dating, a sensual claiming of this body part. Today, it was the clutch of a parent, his five-fingered assertion that I was not alone.

~

Post-biopsy, I lay holding a saline bag upon the needle's point of entry. My instructions were to keep pressure on the kidney for four hours. I had no pain. None of the staff seemed worried that I would bleed again. Indeed, I was preoccupied less with what the next few hours would bring and more over results that might hemorrhage my kidney's future. My fingers curled tighter around the salt-water weight. My head throbbed.

"Can you turn off the lights?" I inhaled his scent as Kevin reached over me to shut off the light: Vanilla and pine. My heart fluttered as he left for the cafeteria. Kim and the kids had gone home.

Carefully, I turned my head to look out the floor-to-ceiling window. My view was of the North hospital tower, the courtyard and surrounding buildings—the entire healing hamlet that is the world famous Cedars-Sinai Medical Center. Scrubs whizzed by in a blaze of color. Lab coats flared out behind doctors like white capes. Visitors bore flowers and shiny balloons bobbing behind them in the wind. I shifted slightly, my heart squeezing with envy. People taking their life for granted: Jobs. Legs. The ability to buy an overpriced coffee. No one telling them, *Nope! You can't do that today! Today, the single packing semi-automatic biopsy needle will steal a piece of your kidney, and a little bit of your soul.*

I shouldn't have been envious. Up until yesterday, I had been doing exactly the same thing. Striding through life with unconscious delight. You just don't realize how much you want to hold a balloon bobbing in the wind until you can't.

Three days later, it was official. My transplant was in acute rejection. In 2008, kidney transplants from 1988 almost never lasted twenty years. They rejected. Sometimes at five months. Sometimes five years. Sometimes ten. It was no surprise the kidney had gone into rejection after twenty years.

Acute rejection is treated with massive doses of steroids to prevent the episode from progressing into chronic rejection. The plan was to use IV steroids to pull my creatinine spike back from the 3's and into the low 2's, if not lower. My catalytic creatinine of 3.1 translated into a kidney function of 19% GFR (Glomeruli Filtration Rate) or Stage 4 Renal Failure.

In 2008, it was challenging to stop a rejection episode twenty years into a transplant's life. In 2019, transplantation science understands my immune system had built up undetected antibodies that attacked my (Mum's) kidney. Today, cutting-edge tests exist that monitor the development of antibodies. When they are detected, antibiotics are prescribed and immunosuppressives increased to quell antibody development.

I never thought to ask *Why is this happening?* That would have been like asking Earth why it chose that particular day to pull off an 8.2 earthquake. Earth's response: *Why are you so surprised I cracked open and you fell inside? You've been living along a fault line all along.*

It never occurred to me to fess up to years of Codeine abuse. My morning, over-the-counter buzz felt so innocuous. I never shared this ritual with anyone, especially Kevin. I never put Codeine on my list of medications at hospital check-in. It was stored in my inpatient locker in case of emergencies like Health Envy, or acute kidney transplant rejection.

First up, was a three-day round of IV steroids or Pulse Steroids: Methylprednisolone and Dexamethasone. Steroid therapy is the administration of greater than normal doses of glucocorticoids (steroid hormones produced by the adrenal cortex that have anti-inflammatory properties), when rapid immunosuppression is the goal. IV steroids are like steroids on steroids. Like mainlining caffeine while you chug your morning Joe. Or if you freebased crack while smoking meth. You get the idea.

The goal was to trick my body into thinking the kidney belonged to me by temporarily killing my immune system. For 72 hours, my life revolved around a swollen bag hanging from a metal hook. Every few hours, a deflated sack would be replaced with another bag bursting with fresh poison. Every afternoon the nurse scrolled down the computer screen to view the morning's blood draw. My creatinine remained essentially unchanged: 3.0, 2.9, 3.1.

Will I lose my kidney?

Giant tears dripped off my chin, as I clutched the receiver with both hands. "Tomorrow your creatinine will go down," Kevin promised. And in that moment, I believed him.

The first course of steroid therapy was pronounced unsuccessful. The kidney was still in rejection. It is curious that transplant doctors say the kidney is rejecting, when in reality it is my immune system that is rejecting the kidney. Maybe theirs is the better turn of phrase, because I chose to believe my body wanted the kidney to stay.

By early evening, Kevin would appear in the doorframe. He was my oasis, shimmering from the top of his baseball cap to the tips of his cowboy boots. At the sight of him a delicious smile would stain my face, impossible to remove, like grape Popsicle or red wine. As he approached the bed I'd spread my arms wide, burying my face into his neck, inhaling skin still tingling from wind and weather beyond the hospital walls. He would take my hand, being careful not to squeeze where the IV needle jutted out, and for a moment, everything was all right.

Most nights he was so tired, he would crawl into bed beside me. We'd giggle as he tried to fit his body around mine in the narrow bed, tangling, then untangling himself from my IV tubes. We would watch the overhead television, gorging on some reality TV as comfort food for the soul, and forget about our day. Photo shoots, laundry, the dog, an hour-long commute, and the next round of poison about to be injected into our lives.

After a two-day break, a longer and stronger round of Pulse Steroid therapy began.

For the nuclear version of Methylprednisolone, the nurse wore thick latex gloves. I remember the shade: A stunning and incongruous Tiffany-blue. Her fingers whirled through the routine, popping the bottom of the bag with a needle, and then threading it through a metal curlicue at the tip of the pole. Mesmerized by the blur of blue, I wondered, *How toxic is this drug that she needs gloves to hang it?*

There was a rush of cold as the drug entered my veins. *Please.* I whispered to some nebulous transplant god. *Please. Please. Please.*

The pain was almost instant. Nausea gripped my gut. I began to see double. "I'm getting a massive migraine," I croaked. The nurse nodded.

"Where is it on the pain scale?"

The pain scale? The nurse motioned to the chart on the wall. It is possible I was asked this back in Canada, post-transplant, but in that moment I had no recollection of a sliding scale for pain. With colored circles as animated faces (pale greens through bright red) the chart depicted escalating levels of pain: "0-1" is no pain (alert and smiling), "2" is mild pain (can be ignored), "3-4" is moderate pain (interferes with tasks), "5-6" is moderate pain (interferes with concentration), "7-8" is severe pain (interferes with basic needs), and "9-10" is worst pain possible (bed rest required).

Very quickly I put together the idea that she was offering me drugs. The higher the number, the greater amount of pain meds. Canadian hospitals are notoriously tight with pain medication. I was sent home with Tylenol 3 after my kidney transplant, which is barely a step up from the Tylenol 1 with Codeine I would purchase over the counter. In 2019, America prescribed 75% of the world's painkillers. Suddenly, I felt very patriotic. I loved the idea of a pain scale!

I wanted to say 10. The pain was harrowing. I was certain my face resembled the scrunched up 10 — a bright red circle with tears dripping onto a thick, black frown. Yet my instinct was to rein it in. I needed pain relief, so why was I afraid to be honest? I didn't want to seem eager for drugs, even though I legitimately needed them.

This paradox felt like the times I walk weak-kneed through Customs though I've done nothing wrong. I stare unblinkingly at the Customs' officer, every twitch of my eye calculated, voice inflections scanned for what I think he wants to hear. What action will get me the desired result: Letting me enter the country instead of pulling me aside to be searched. This hyper-insistence of my innocence feels like an untruth because it is. I am not really manipulating the officer, but myself into believing I have control over whether or not I am searched.

My theater-school-trained instinct was to grab my head in agony, but would that be too over-the-top? If I lay corpse-still, would it seem too slick? How should I play this? Did I have to play this? A searing heat shot through my head. I could barely open my eyes. This pain was the real deal, yet I was scared if I said 10 she wouldn't believe me, and if I said 7, the amount wouldn't be enough.

"Eight and a half?" I lied.

"We can help you with that. Have you ever had Morphine?"

It had been on the tip of my tongue to say I had a prescription for Fiorinal at home, and could they please give me some of that, but then she said Morphine. I'd never had Morphine before. Morphine is intense pain relief they gave to cancer patients at the end of their life. Morphine sounded great. Now I didn't want Fiorinal. I wanted Morphine.

Morphine was nice. It helped. My head cleared. The nausea lifted. It did its job—kill pain—yet I felt underwhelmed. I did not understand what I had expected until a friend called that afternoon.

"Morphine. That must have been nice." she tittered. I paused before answering.

"It helped, but it didn't take all the pain away."

This was half-true. It had taken away all my physical pain, but it had not been enough. Morphine felt like the tip of what could have been a fantastic, mind-blowing fuck. I wanted a longer, and more satisfying drug experience. The kind people tittered about.

Later that afternoon, my steroid-induced migraine returned. I could barely stand the tappity-tap-tap of my nurse entering a new order for pain management: Dilaudid. Inserting the syringe into my IV line, she pulled the plunger top back, and then slowly pushed this new narcotic through the barrel.

Almost instantly my bones melted like a pad of butter into a warming pan. I sank into the suddenly soft mattress. Kevin appeared awash in golden halo of light. Nothing had ever looked as beautiful as the sight of my husband's face swimming before mine.

"Who could give you a kidney?" he asked, rubbing my forehead.

Siblings, ideally twins, are the best possible living donors. Kevin's brow tightened as we discussed my slim prospects. My family lives in Denmark and Israel, and my Mum and brother live in Canada. In 1999, my brother had randomly declared he would not be comfortable giving me a kidney. Then, before I could catch my breath, demanded, *Are you mad?* Lost inside a stunned silence, I never ventured to ask why, and he never explained himself. This knowledge shadowed my husband's face with a darkness that made me reach for his hand.

"It doesn't matter, sweetheart. I wouldn't want anyone's kidney unless they were sure." I said, smiling.

Compassion bubbled from my lips. I forgave my brother his limitations. Drug-fueled, I was elevated above judgment, surfing a divine crest of unconditional love. Then I wondered if Kevin was suspect of my tender tone. He knew forgiveness was uncharted territory for me.

"Well, I will be your match," he said, squeezing my hand. And between Dilaudid and Kevin and his romantic declaration, I believed everything would be all right.

Later, we walked the hospital halls long after the soft chimes of visiting hours' end had faded away. Dragging my unruly IV pole beside me, I tried not to cry. My husband never cried, and hated it when I did. I called him my robot, and he called me The Roller Coaster of Hen. He didn't understand how I could cry so much, and I could count the times he had cried on one hand. As he stepped inside the elevator, my tears began to fall as if on cue. *Drip, wipe. Drip, wipe. Drip, wipe.*

"Don't cry, sweetheart."

"Drive safe." I whispered. The elevator doors connected with a hush, and all went silent. Shuffling down the hallway, I wiped the lingering wetness from my eyes. The fluorescents went dark and the night-lights flickered on like electronic fireflies. My room stood in shadow as I climbed back into bed. I shifted beneath my pile of blankets, restless.

Will I lose my kidney?

The muted TV flickered overhead. I squinted against its light, reaching over the tray table to search through a pile of discarded dry-ice packs. All done. Pain sliced across my forehead. My neck began to throb. Scanning the room for more ice packs, I noticed the patient dry erase board.

Patient boards are updated several times a day with vitals and medication changes. *Patient: Henriette Ivanans-McIntyre. D.O.B: 10/29/1968. Medications: Dilaudid q.2.h.* My heart thudded. I knew what that meant. I could have a pain shot every two hours. Could this be true? Fumbling for the call button, I pressed its red center firmly.

"Yes?"

"Can I have a shot for pain?"

"I'll be right there."

Holy shit. Or was that holy shot? All I had to do was ask. God Bless America.

As I waited for the nurse, I pictured Kevin driving home. Did he exhale upon watching Cedars shrink in the rear-view mirror? My stomach flipped. Was there a gap growing between us? He got to leave, and I had to stay. He got to hold a bobbing balloon and I had to watch.

The nurse entered the room, medical paraphernalia in hand. "How're doin,' honey?"

"Not so great." I mumbled, eyeing the syringe.

"This will help."

Moments later, Dilaudid had saturated my soul and I was falling, falling, falling into the gap, not caring if I ever crawled out.

A few days later, Kevin and I drove home in silence. The second round of steroid therapy had failed. My kidney transplant was in chronic rejection.

The plan was simple and anti-climactic after a twelve-night hospital stay. I was switched to the hottest immunosuppressive, Prograf. Less nephrotoxic (poisonous to the kidney), the hope was that Prograf could sustain the transplant's life longer than my current medications could: A year. Maybe two. Regular blood work and appointments would continue, but eventually, I would lose my kidney.

I watched the buildings fly by in their insulting ordinariness. Nothing on the Los Angeles streets had changed, but everything inside our car had. When we married thirteen years earlier, the idea that I would ever become a medical problem when presented against my radiant health seemed unimaginable. Yet, the possibility had always existed, right from the moment Kevin acknowledged his vow with a prophetic squeeze of my hand.

...in sickness and in health...

My husband was willing to give me a kidney. Yet, how could he ever understand my world? Those who can unwind themselves from the IV tubes can never understand the medical ties that bind the rest of us to stay. He wanted to give me a kidney, but I needed one. The idea that Kevin could be just as devastated as me did not seem possible.

Tucked between my legs was a CVS bag holding Prograf and Fiorinal. Upon discharge, I had joked with Dr. D. *As long as I have my Fiorinal, I'll be fine!* I took in Kevin's stern profile as he piloted us home. I did love my husband.

Sitting on the edge of our bed, I rubbed my face between my hands. Kevin was already prepping for a photo shoot. Just like that, he had returned to his old life. Head spinning, I flopped backwards. When would I start to feel sick? Where did I go from here?

Through the wall I heard him laughing with his client. Opening the CVS bag, I placed Her on my bedside table. I had no headache, but heartache. Pain is pain, right? I poured several pills into my palm, and swallowed.

Then I curled into a ball and waited for Her to tell me that everything would be all right.

6. ACETAMINOPHEN

"Til Death Do Us Part" are the words exchanged by two people when they commit for life and marry under God. I know Kevin and I exchanged those vows. Yet, at some point over the next two years, Fiorinal became the one I was committed to.

On the heels of my rejection diagnosis, The Perfect Storm landed in Shadow Hills. With the biggest economic crisis since the Great Depression, the housing market crashed. Our $600,000 house was worth $275,000. Actors lost their Joe-jobs and, without disposable income, hung on to their headshots. Kevin's business plummeted by 30%. Because I was sick, my SAG (Screen Actors Guild) health insurance, which carried both of us, threw me onto Disability for a year ('08), followed by a year on Cobra ('09), then out the proverbial door. Now with separate group health plans, our monthly premiums skyrocketed from $100 to over $800 a month. By the summer of 2010, our old life had vanished.

From February 2008 to June 2010, my kidney function worsened, and edema, headache, anemia, and nausea developed. But curating the identity of Rejecting Transplant Patient consumed me long before the symptoms ever did. Fiorinal helped me see that. I was sick.

That was all We needed to know. We gave up on my kidney long before it ever gave up on me.

I dropped my agents. I told myself it was because I had trouble memorizing my lines, but it was relief to let go of a career that had not panned out. I stopped volunteering at animal rescues. I was immunosuppressed! I couldn't pick up dog poop! I gave up my gym membership half a year before I was confined to bed.

She made sense of these decisions whenever they felt like excuses. I knew people with cancer got to the gym and immunosuppressed patients could volunteer in other ways. But She had a way of playing my Sick card so that it never felt like Carte Blanche behavior. *You're not giving up on Life,* She would coo. *Just accepting your destiny.* Her strategy made sense. I could be successful at being sick.

She exercised tough love reminding me, *You are a loser. You are chronically ill. You are a waste of space.* Kevin kept saying I was not any of these things, but what did he know? He had everything: His health. A career. Hobbies. His empty words bounced off my soul. She filled me up, understanding me in a way my husband never could.

Kevin got in sync with Our monthly trysts, and tried to tear us apart. As I lay stoned, he would storm in and yank open the bedside table drawer. Rifling through books and facemasks, sometimes he would find Her and separate Us. I'd just smile and roll away knowing I had cleverly hidden some of Her elsewhere.

While Kevin slept, I'd hunt. I'd stumble around the house in my clogs, my head deliciously thick with Her, rooting through every pocket of every bag. Some nights I'd trip on the uneven floorboards and crash to the ground, laughing all the way there. I felt no pain. Quick swigs from the wine bottle hidden behind the water heater primed me for the night's scavenger hunt, while drowning all fear I might not find Her.

Under a black sky, I would tiptoe outside and unlock the car, holding my breath at the sharp electronic beep. My heart raced as I scoured through the glove compartment. In the air, nocturnal chirping grew frenetic, warning me morning was almost here. My greatest fear, for dopesickness to lick the sides of my body the way the sunrise strokes the cold canyon awake into a scorching burn. Slowly, then completely.

After I found Her in a pantry drawer, Kevin would sleep with Her stuffed between the mattress and box spring. Impossible to liberate. During those nights, need consumed me. Unsteady, loaded, I would crawl into bed and stroke my husband's back, whispering only one word over and over again.

Please.

My hot lips trembled as I placed my mouth directly over his ear. Kevin lay still, his eyes wide open like a corpse. I pulled at his arms, his legs, shaking him like a toy that wouldn't play right. I'd crawl on top of him, my tears dripping into his eyeballs. Deep into a desperate night I would beg, but once he had a hold of Her, like me, he never let go.

Bingeing on Fiorinal often resulted in a rebound headache from withdrawal. This occurs when your body has ingested an insufficient amount of the medication you were taking to dispel your headache in the first place. For relief, I'd ceremoniously drape a washcloth over my forehead. It was my steadfast prop, a deliberate reminder. *Don't forget, sweetheart. I am sick. I am justified in lying here all day long.* He could question whether or not I had a migraine, but he could never dispute that I had renal failure. Lying alone, delirious, beneath a wet washcloth, I was the clear winner.

Curling naked with Her beneath the sheets was all I wanted. I had given up my career, hobbies and health. I would forget to eat and drink. To dress. To bathe. I was totally committed. Shedding every part of myself to get closer to Her. When wrapped inside this drug-addled burrito, I was whole.

Butalbital (one of Fiorinal's active ingredients) suppresses the Central Nervous System (CNS). Excessive use of Fiorinal presents as ear ringing, mild sedation to total anesthesia, and diarrhea. Overnight, I wore Kevin's underwear stuffed with maxi pads and / or additional pairs of underwear in anticipation of the night's release. Stuffing them was nothing but a practical inconvenience. It just made good sense.

On the toilet, I'd convulse. My anus burning hot, the back of my neck drenched as I gripped the seat. Then I would collapse, my head lolled over like a wilted flower, my soul lost inside the buttery-smooth high. Leaving behind my shuddering body, I felt nothing but Her. I was Her. I had become the high. I was a double-blue plastic capsule sprinkled upon an aching soul. As I wiped the unruly drip from my upper thighs and slinked back into bed, I believed She was worth it.

FRIDAY JUNE 4TH, 2010.

IN THE DARKNESS of the bedroom, We lay together. A thin line of light from the TV flickered beneath the door, but I heard nothing. I slept with a fan as white noise to cancel out tinnitus from a car accident. The whirring sound also came in handy for drowning out life beyond bedroom walls.

Suddenly, the door flew open. The strip of light exploded into a rectangle framing my husband's raging shadow.

"We're going to the hospital!" he yelled, flicking on the light. My arm flew over my face.

"What are you doing?" I screamed. Kevin had just destroyed the delicate balance of light and sound I'd created to complement my narcotic frequency.

"How many pills have you taken?"

"Turn off the light," I whimpered. How many pills? I didn't know. Well, I had some idea, but fuck him if he thought I was going to check. I wasn't born yesterday. Tonight, She was in a baggie, taped to the backside of my bedside table. I rolled away, pulling the covers over my head.

"You can overdose on too much acetaminophen! You could destroy your liver!"

My liver? What was he talking about? My liver was fine. My kidney was the problem. I jammed my fingers into my ears. Some creature kept screaming. Then I realized the sound was coming from Kevin.

"GET UP! GET UP! GET UP!"

He pulled blanket after sheet off the bed until it was stripped. Each furious tug of the fabric burned my bare skin. I went to grab at the final sheet. Back and forth we pulled, engaged in a surreal marital tug-of-war, until with one humiliating yank I was completely exposed. Then he wrenched the mattress up and down, up and down. Flapping it about as though it weighed no more than a piece of paper.

"Stop it!" I shrieked. "I have a headache."

"You have a HEADACHE?" he jeered. With an unfamiliar roar, Kevin heaved the mattress onto its side, spilling me onto the ground. There I lay, a 41 year-old woman naked but for a pair of my husband's underwear. Kevin swooped down to retrieve me with a claw-like grip.

"Stop it! Let me GO!" I spat. He turned the corner into the living room, striding through the foyer and out our front door like a marital threshold in reverse. He was holding me in the same position as our wedding photo, the one he had just passed on the dresser. Instead of my arms like wings taking flight, I pummeled my husband's chest. Instead of beaming into the camera, I screamed into his ear.

"NO! NO! NO!"

Kevin stared straight ahead, navigating the uneven cobblestone patio that runs the length of our house and out to the car. Somehow, he plopped me into the passenger seat and slammed the door. The skin on my arms burned from the release of his grip.

"Stay in the car! You have overdosed!" he raged.

Why was he acting so crazy? As Kevin walked around to the driver's side, I sobbed. I couldn't stop shaking. Why? Why tonight of all nights? Why was he trying to take Her away from me? I had to get out. Kevin hated a scene, so I flung the door wide and screamed louder than I ever have in my life.

"NOOO! HELP MEEE!"

My howl ricocheted through the canyon. Our neighbors might have heard my disturbing cries the way I caught wind of their parties, but I knew no one was coming to my rescue. Screeching, I tore toward the house. Hysteria was my only protection against the man but a few steps behind.

"FUCK YOU! FUCK YOU! FUCK YOU!"

As I bolted down the patio, I did not feel pebbles or twigs scratch my bare feet. I felt only panic that I would lose Her. Slamming the front door behind me, I charged into the bedroom, pounding the door into its frame over and over again. *Leave. Me. Alone.* Locking it, I threw myself onto our shipwrecked bed. We had but seconds. I scrambled for the hidden baggie and palmed a couple tablets, swallowing them dry. Panting, I began to rock. How would it go down?

Sometimes Kevin would surprise me. He'd reach for his guitar and awkwardly strum John Denver songs as I lay on the couch, tears sliding down my cheeks from pain.

One time, he guided me into a soapy bath and washed my back in circles. *Why are you being so nice?* I had asked, surprised he would play the game. He knew I was high. Maybe he had been so tired of being alone that he was willing to share me.

Sometimes he would make love to me, the shadow over my body. But She was the One who filled my senses. My ears would ring with Her voice, unable to hear his moans. I'd trail my flaccid tongue around his fingers, his cock, unable to taste him percolating with salt and strain. My limp arms would collapse, unable to pull his thrusting torso towards me. I wanted to feel my husband, but She was coming between us, even as I could not. She was fucking my husband.

I would grunt against Her, aching to come. Those nights it was not a violent release, but slow like the ripples of a slightly disturbed pool of water. To achieve orgasm, I would airlift out of this twisted threesome, and insert myself with someone else, unable to bear my betrayal. When Kevin drifted off to sleep, I would stare at his back for long minutes. *Something is wrong with this.* Then I would turn away and swallow more pills. To forget what I could not feel, and what I could.

Scratch, scratch, scratch. There it was. One of my hairpins followed by the click of the doorknob. This wasn't Kevin's first break-in.

"I'm calling 911! I'm calling the police!" he towered over me. His eyes glowed like black marbles.

"SO WHAT! Go ahead!" I spat, as he walked away. Please. I knew what reverse psychology was. There was no way Kevin was actually going to call the police. He hated attention, maybe even more than he hated me in that moment.

But what if the police did come? They couldn't make me go anywhere. Could they? I shut off my fan, straining to hear. Stumbling over to the doorway, I peered around the corner into the living room. Kevin was on the phone, pacing the narrow stretch of our kitchen and dining room area.

"I need help at my home. My wife has attacked me. She's taken a lot of pills."

"That's a lie!" I shrieked from the doorway. "You attacked me, you ASSHOLE!"

Then I heard him use his sister's name. What! When had that happened? How dare he! This was none of her business! My throat swelled in frustration as I staggered around, struggling to form words.

"GO TO HELL!" I screamed. Bile flooded my mouth as I spewed my poison towards the receiver. Kim needed to hear how I was suffering! Dying of renal failure, with a migraine and an asshole husband who won't. let. me. sleep! Sobbing, tears flying off my cheeks, I charged towards him, feral.

"We have to go the ER!" Kevin lunged for my arm.

"NOOO!" I wailed, twisting away from his grip. Suddenly, I was spiraling through the air. I landed on the couch, bounced up and then down onto the coffee table, smacking my face against its wood corner.

I gasped. It hurt. Really hurt. Even through my body's narcotic sheath, I felt pain. I struggled to take a breath, the wind knocked out of me. My body lay wedged in the crack between the couch and the coffee table. I couldn't move.

I knew this had been an accident. Kevin would never deliberately hurt me. I also knew how guilty he was going to feel about this. In that post-thwack second, I understood all the focus had shifted to his transgression. Now he had fucked up. This was my window. I didn't want him to feel bad. I just wanted this to be over so I could be alone with Her again.

"Ow. Owww!" I cried. Then. "Help me."

As Kevin bent over me, I floated back into his arms, his willing bride once again. Leaning against his chest, I surrendered. Together we walked away from the battlefield and into the bedroom, restored to its pre-war state. When had he done this? The lights were off, the mattress lay flush to its frame and the sheet was pulled tight, welcoming me with its cool smoothness.

Kevin laid me down, and then leaned over to turn on the lamp.

"No!" I cried, turning my head. "It's too bright."

"Let me see your face," he insisted. I could barely see him through my exhausted tears. He studied me sternly, touching the area above my left eye. It was a gentle graze that normally sprang goose bumps. I flinched.

"You're going to have a bump." His eyes trailed my stringy hair to swollen slits for eyes. For long minutes neither of us spoke. The only sound our breathing as it deescalated from panting into extended breaths of calm.

"I'm sorry, sweetheart. I didn't mean to throw you. I meant to get you on the couch." He said this over and over again as if a magical incantation that when repeated, could unthrow me and undarken this night.

"I know, sweetheart." I murmured. My eye was beginning to throb. "It hurts."

"You might have a concussion."

"I'm not going to the hospital!" I wailed. Kevin's face dropped.

"Fine." He knew. This fight had to be over. This night had to be over. "Have you taken your pills?" He meant my immunosuppressives.

"I don't remember." I lied.

As Kevin slipped out of the bedroom, I reached behind my bedside table and liberated another couple of pills. Possibly 3. Probably 4. *Take a few extra. Preventative. For the pain to come,* She whispered. Although Fiorinal had sedative properties prescribed for neurological pain and not anti-inflammatory for muscular pain, Her illogical logic always made perfect sense to me.

Kevin returned with water and my prescriptions.

"Inderal? Once a day?" He held up a blue pill. I pushed myself up to sitting.

"Yes."

"Did you take it this morning?"

"No." Now it was Kevin's turn to flinch.

"Cell Cept. How many?"

"Three. Twice a day."

"So, three pills now?"

"Yes. Three." I slurred.

Kevin turned away to assemble my meds. His profile was etched in quiet horror, the shocking realization that under Her spell I would not take my immunosuppressives.

She was rolling over me now, pulling me down into Her hypnotic undulations. I longed to sink into the pillows and succumb, but after the fury of the night, I wanted to give my husband something. Every line on his face read as worry. My peace was surging through my veins. I could give my husband his. For him, I could take my pills.

Kevin handed me three tablets of Cell Cept. Hand shaking, I took a small sip and swallowed. I sighed against the headboard; grateful for the tender way he was attending to me. The lamp cast a triangular shaft of light over us. Under the room's strangely romantic glow, we relaxed into our roles: Kevin the fixer, and me, the fixee.

"I know this is Cyclosporine," he said, presenting me with the last pill.

Cyclosporine is an older immunosuppressive: a gelatin tablet encased in a tin-foil-esque packet. It cannot be exposed to air until you are ready to take it. Kevin popped the backside of the bubble and removed the enormous pill. Its chemical smell wafted out and our eyes met.

"It still smells like skunk," he offered with a half-smile.

When I was 23 and Kevin was 18, I agreed to have dinner with him in the Toronto home he shared with four roommates. After an endearing dinner of pasta from a mix and instant pudding from a package, we moved downstairs to his basement bedroom. I always carried my meds with me whenever I suspected I might not make it home. Swallowing my pills, I tossed the Cyclosporine packet into the empty bag that lined his garbage can. I suppressed a grin. Had he changed the trashcan for little ol' me?

Jammed together in his twin bed, we talked long into the night. Kevin lay with his back pressed up against the wood-paneled wall, his arms wrapped around me. I faced outward, scrutinizing a room dotted with the markers of a young man who had just left home: flannel sheets, a battered poster of a Broadway show, and a catch-all box containing sheet music, and ceramics painted by his mother.

He held me with a confidence that belied his age. Every square inch of his body pressed against mine, and yet he made no move to kiss me. *Should I turn in towards him? Should I try to kiss him?* His breath was warm against my neck, as we meandered through an all-nighter of firsts. We giggled. We sang. My skin blazed with the desire to be touched, but he made no move.

"Are you comfortable?" he asked.

I wasn't really. The way we were positioned it was impossible for me to relax and fall asleep, but I didn't want him to let me go. Plunged into a pool of feelings so fresh I could barely breathe. How could a 19-year old boy make me feel so safe?

With anyone else, I would have turned and taken what I wanted, but what Kevin offered was enough. Holding me with such certainty it now feels like that was the moment he stepped into his lifelong role. Three and a half years later, the words "to have and to hold" would be mere formality.

Nineteen years later, he was even more handsome. He had certainly aged, having lost all his hair, and at 38, his skin already had a roughness about it. But he was a man who had arrived. The way he passed me my pills and the washcloth. Assuming control of what his arms had promised on our first date. *I will take care of you.*

Years later, Kevin would tell me he had wondered about the

stinky silver package in his garbage can. The medication, and the woman who had to swallow it intrigued him. Why did she need to take it, and why did it smell like skunk?

Kevin removed the glass from my hand. I sank into the pillows, my glassy eyes rolling back to white. When they flickered open, Kevin was frowning.

"You haven't had enough to drink."

He was right. We can go without food for almost a month. When you go without water for two or three days your kidneys are in danger of shutting down. I knew this, but it was hard to care when She was inside me. She didn't want anything to come between us anymore.

"I bought you apple juice." Kevin presented me with a frosted glass of the golden liquid. I gave him a weak smile. For me, apple juice was cold-pressed nostalgia in a glass. It reminded me of my first hospital stay at 13 where it stood all night on the tray table, ready to comfort a scared girl with its familiar sweetness.

Managing a few sips, my stomach burbled. Fiorinal had me. The six pills I had swallowed since our fight were pulling me into Her swell.

"That's all I can drink." I croaked. Kevin took the glass away, and placed a cold washcloth over my eye. The cool shock of it burned my skin.

"Can you hold it there?"

"I can try." Kevin eyes grew dark as my limp arm struggled to hold on. He sighed. "I'm sorry, sweetheart."

"I'm sorry, too. Did you really call 911?"

"No, I was just trying to scare you. Try to rest." Then he slipped away, leaving the door cracked behind him.

Alone at last, We drifted away to the television's murmurings. The epileptic flickers of light did not bother me from beneath the wash-cloth. I liked picturing Kevin watching the screen. He had his comfort, and I had mine.

The nights I thought Kevin was watching television, he was researching drug toxicity. That night, it had been acetaminophen. The recommended daily dose of acetaminophen (Tylenol) is 3,250 mg or 10 regular strength tablets. 20 Fioricet tablets (a kidney-friendly version of Fiorinal which contains acetaminophen, caffeine and Butalbital) have twice the recommended daily dose of acetaminophen. Poor Kevin. He didn't understand that this information didn't scare me at all. The only thing that would have scared me was hearing She was gone.

She was the Perfect Drug. With later-discovered opiates, I would nod off into blissful detachment, then unfortunate unconsciousness, sleeping through the best part of the high. With Her, whenever I began to glide away, Her caffeine component jacked me up so I never dropped into total anesthesia. As a CNS depressant, She would cross the near impenetrable blood/brain barrier that prevents most drugs' entry from the blood into the brain, and my thoughts would no longer be my own.

It wasn't so much that I wanted to kill myself. The idea would just surface as a suggestion. Her suggestion. *You should take all your pills.* Not all of Her commands made sense anymore. Confused, I would answer, *I don't think I have enough pills* or *Maybe in the morning,* then roll away from this twisted call and response. Why would She suggest that? I didn't want to die. I couldn't imagine life without Her.

I awoke to whirring. Loud. It was so loud. Where was I? My eyes fluttered open. It was pitch black. Then I made out the shadowy lump of the covers. Bed. My ears were ringing. My fan was humming. Was it the dark hours of early morning or post-dinner night? I tried to turn my face to check the time. My limbs felt restrained, as if buried under damp clumps of soil I could not shake off. I reached up, up, up from inside this coffin of sleep, towards the cold blue glow from the clock.

Something was holding me in a ferocious grip. I felt wetness on my cheeks. Was I still crying? Was it from the washcloth? Hot drops plopped onto my skin as if from a gentle rain. Kevin. He was crying. His arms held me in the womb of his nook. My skin warmed against him. His cheek was smushed, hot and damp, against mine.

"I don't want you to die," came his whispered droplets of prayer.

My heart soared, shaking off Her anesthetic weight. Kevin was holding me the way he had on our first date nineteen years ago, my body embalmed in unconditional love.

I will take care of you.

"I'm not going to die." I slurred.

That night, we slept together inside the eye of Her tornado, savoring the elusive elixir two halves of a couple make when they become one.

I did not know until years later that on nights like this Kevin would set his timer to go off every two hours. To make sure I was still breathing.

7. FIORINAL 2010

I *will never be able to raise my head.*
My eyes flickered open, then shut against the bright light of day. I squirmed. My entire body ached with a flu-like fierceness. The storm of dopesickness was rising inside of me.

Kevin. Where was Kevin? Even behind closed lids, I could feel he wasn't lying next to me. Bracing myself, I cupped my hand across my eyes, and then opened them against a lightning strike of pain. Through spreading fingers came white light, and then the hazy shapes of our bedroom.

As I shifted, a whiff of Tiger Balm filled my nose. During the desperate night, I had slathered it beneath my nostrils, trying to clear the congestion that prevented me from sleeping with my mouth closed. Open–mouthed breathing was the only option when I gorged on Her. Rattling snores that made Kevin shake me awake. Not because he was a light sleeper, but because breathing like that—too loud and deep—means your central nervous system is shutting down.

I had also smeared it on my forehead, temples and jawbone. But this obsessive distraction never quelled the Rebound Headache. As I slept, Fiorinal had withdrawn from my system. Euphoria had devolved into bone-searing pain. My ears began to ring. Even over my fan, and the A/C wall-unit, Her frequency grew increasingly shrill. I hated this side effect. As if She was screaming at me. I reached for the bedside table and then remembered.

Oh, my god. She's all gone.

A skunky sweat pooled in my armpits. There was only one way to survive withdrawal from Her. More of Her.

My cracked lips smacked open in disbelief. The sour stink of dehydration wafted from my mouth. Oh, my god. I had to do it. I had to move.

Reaching over my head, my hand skillfully crawled through the obstacle course of half-finished glasses of juice and a crusted lump of washcloth. Her plastic side brushed my finger and I grabbed on. Lifting Her up, I read—*1 refill*—but there was one more thing to check. My eyes zipped across the label. *Date filled: May 30th, 2010.* What was today's date? I wracked my brain, my blood vessels angrily surging with the effort.

The house was still. Even over the electronic rattling, I sensed I was alone. No photography clients fluttering about. Was Kevin shooting a wedding? Weddings were almost always on Saturday. Yes. It was Saturday. Saturday June 5th. Kevin had mentioned something about staying overnight in a hotel. San Diego. The wedding was in San Diego. *Thank God.*

That it was Saturday also meant in four days we would be attending my kidney transplant evaluation at Cedars-Sinai. This half-day seminar includes a PowerPoint presentation on types of dialysis and the projected wait list times for a kidney if you do not have a living donor. I, of course, did. We hoped.

Together, we would meet my transplant coordinator, who, much like a conductor, was responsible for synching up all the instruments in my medical orchestra pit: Surgeon, urologist, social worker, financial counselor, dietitian and one of the four attending kidney transplant physicians. I would be evaluated for heart disease, hypertension, and ulcers, undergo screening for blood and tissue type, and psychological soundness.

My head pulsated as I slid upwards against the headboard. Then I punched in Rite Aid's phone number, by heart.

Press 1 if you would like to refill a prescription.

Yes, yes, yes. I would like to refill a prescription. I pressed "1."

If you know your prescription number please enter it now, followed by the pound sign.

I punched in the first five digits of the pharmacy code, also by heart. My finger throbbed with every jab. Ow. Ow. Ow. Ow. Ow. My hand shook as I squinted at the label. I couldn't see the last portion of Her code. Tears collected in the far corners of my eyes. It was agony to find the tiny number. I blinked and the sticker came into glorious focus. 1-2-3-4-5-6. Each electronic cheep pecked away at my eardrum like a swallow I wanted to smash beak-first into the wall. Then the automated voice clicked away into silence.

I knew this phone call would go one of two ways: 1) In a minor-chord tinged tone, she would sadly inform me: *There are no refills left on your prescription. We will contact your doctor on their next business day with authorization to refill.* 2) In a major-chord tinged tone, she would brightly declare: *Your prescription will be refilled.* After only a week since pick up, I knew the odds of a refill were slim to none. Insurance almost never approved the refill of a controlled substance like Fiorinal until 30 days had passed.

There was a brief pause on the line, and then a series of clicks. I swiped at my armpits. My chest seized up as the automated voice clicked in.

Your prescription will be refilled.

Fat tears of relief dribbled off my chin. *Did she really say your prescription will be refilled?* How had this mini medicinal miracle occurred? This was clearly a computer glitch. *Oh my god, oh my god, oh my god.* Goosebumps of delight sheeted my skin.

A few minutes earlier, I had been loath to ever leave the uterine comfort of my bed—my cotton batten protection against a world in which I had no interest in participating. The idea of breathing without Her was unbearable. With five unexpected words, my body was shot through with adrenaline. I could sit up. I could button my jeans. I could trudge through this physical hell with the soul-stitching knowledge that I would soon be holding Her.

The harsh light peeking over the curtains told me it was after-noon. I squinted at the clock. Did it say 11:38 am or 1:38 pm? I squinted again. The "1" was a "3." It was 3:38 pm. She would be ready at 4:08 pm. I could almost taste Her plastic shell melting on my tongue; feel Her acidity drip down my eager throat.

I swung my legs over the side of the bed and hoisted myself to sitting. Nausea gripped as I eyeballed the jeans that lay at my feet. I could do this. I could slip them on, grab the car keys and...my heart stopped. *Motherfucker.* Kevin had the car. I would have to walk.

To get there, I would have to navigate the extreme driveway down from our cabin to the street, traverse two roads, a busy thoroughfare, and walk beneath a freeway overpass. Then continue on to the strip mall where my sanctuary would be waiting like a random crucifix in the desert, its neon-sign flashing its message of salvation.

I sat for a moment with my head in my hands, trying to still my uneven breath. Swinging my legs over the side of the bed had been a Herculean accomplishment. The idea of using them felt impossible. In my dopesick haze, it never occurred to me to taxi my mission. I would have to walk for nearly two miles roundtrip in the blazing sun. I had no choice. I needed Her.

Unwittingly, I had been entered into an extreme sports competi-tion for which I was utterly unprepared—dehydrated, with no time to carb-load, and no sports therapist to help me visualize the finish line. I sighed. There was nothing a trainer could tell me that I didn't already know. All I had to do was focus on Her beautiful blue-on-blue self, knowing She would be cheering for me at the end.

I would make a mental "To Do" List! The obsessive lists I had been compelled to make throughout my life would help me now: 1) Slip on jeans. 2) Keep on Tiger Balm-stained t-shirt (this conserves energy.) 3) Skip brushing teeth (brushing motion too jarring, will trigger head pain.) 4) Skip brushing hair. (see: Reason #3.) 5) Place baseball cap on head (reason is twofold: cap hides unbrushed hair and protects head from sun.) 6) If possible, pee. (renal failure and dehydration an unexpected bonus!) 7) Slip on clogs (how serendipitous that clogs are shoe of choice—will expend no energy bending over to tie laces!) 8) Grab house keys (hide on property, do not waste energy carrying.) 9) Walk.

Out the window, it looked like your typical California day: 72 degrees and sunny. But when I opened the door, I walked straight into a wall of heat. California summers are dry and intense. Not like East Coast heat, and its mummifying humidity. This heat is focused. It brands your skin with its hot-knifed edge.

I leaned against the doorframe and steadied myself. My brain was spinning, my ears buzzing with those Barbiturate bugs. I plugged my nose and swallowed hard, attempting to clear a head so clogged with phlegm I could barely breathe. Then I closed the door and began to walk.

I slipped my keys behind one of Kevin's backdrops, and then walked across the asphalt where we parked our car. When I reached the swinging metal gate that marks the top of our driveway, I unhinged the chain link ring that keeps it closed. Down the steep slope I shuffled, bracing my body against ribbons of sand that threatened to take me down.

The afternoon sun pummeled the back of my neck. As I stumbled over pebbles, sand filled my clogs, but I never stopped to empty them. Every time I raised my foot, I wondered if I would be able to complete the step. I didn't think about the long distance to pharmaceutical salvation. I focused only on lifting my leg and placing it a few inches ahead on the road.

Head down, I noticed things I couldn't from the temperature-controlled comfort of our car: the glint of a flattened soda can or triumphant succulents sprouting from the cracks in the cement. Against all odds, life. No one passed me on this sidewalk-less stretch of road. For this I was grateful. I was conserving all my energy for five words: *Picking up for patient Ivanans.* I was loath to waste it on "How are you?" when I really didn't care.

Our street ends in a fork, a chain link fence and the roaring freeway beyond. To the left, the road circles up a hill into a loop

dotted with McMansions. I turned to the right, doddering down the
street, my t-shirt drenched. Arriving at the busy thoroughfare that
would take me to Rite Aid, I stopped, swiping at salty beads beneath
my sunglasses. If I had been protected by residential obscurity, my
cover was about to be blown. The city was about to assault.

Around the corner, a freeway off-ramp ended in a traffic light and
three lanes. Occasionally, there would be a man begging at this intersection, armed with cardboard Armageddon signs and messiah
beard, but on this day I was the singular act in this urban freak show.
Swaying in the heat, I pressed the *Walk* button and stepped away
from the curb. The cars roared by, barely gearing down from their
speedy freeway flight. I glared at the digital hand. Willing it to morph
into the neon-white strides of the walking man. My stomach
rumbled, hollow from days of not eating. I had to keep moving.

The light changed and the cars began to slow. Engines revved in
angry protest, anxious to reignite their wild ride home. The drivers'
judgmental stares pierced my body as I passed. *Why is this woman
walking by an off ramp?* I tightened the elastic band that held back my
shoulder length hair, and then pushed my sunglasses up with my
middle finger. *Fuck You.* I could have been anyone. A woman whose
car had broken down. Looking for the bus stop. On a reality show.
Why did they need to know I was en route to salvation?

Along the next stretch of road, there was no relief from the triple-
digit sun. No buildings, just ribbons of cement tying into the freeway
above. I must have stood out like a wild animal traversing a desert
plain, as I limped toward the underpass.

Shuffling into its shadowy relief, I sighed as the cooler air hit my
skin. My nostrils twitched at the stench of piss. Someone squealed to
a halt at the light up ahead. My heart leapt, already thudding a frantic
beat. Inside the graffiti-covered walls of the cement cavern, the
freeway above roared like thunder. I wanted to collapse on the urine-
kissed sidewalk, and even if I had, I would have crawled every last
foot to get to Her.

At the final light, I paused. On the other side of the intersection
was a Sizzler, and beyond that, the strip mall.

Although Kevin and I had lived in Shadow Hills for four years, we had never eaten at Sizzler. Joints like Sizzler or Coco's (which lay at the far end of said strip mall) just weren't our bag. By no means foodies, Standard American Fare like iceberg lettuce and poor cuts of red meat held little interest. But the restaurant, or more specifically its sign, had long been a source of entertainment. Over the years, the lights of the Sizzler sign had been fading. We would mock the partially darkened sign, as we waited on the off ramp for the light to change.

Hey, wife. Want to go to ...ZLER for dinner? Hi. Yeah, I'm wondering if ...ZLER has a take out menu? No, not SIZZLER, but ...ZLER. Could we make a reservation for two at ...ZLER, please?

From what marital adventure had we been returning while idling on that off ramp? A night at the movies? An uncomplicated day of errands? It didn't matter. I reveled in my husband's company for its own sake. Once Kevin got on a roll, I would double over with laughter, grab at his arm, and like a child, tell him to do it, *Again! Again!* until I was wiping away tears. As I shuffled by the restaurant, my eyes watered from the flecks of dirt kicked up from the cars whizzing by. I did not look up at the sign. There was nothing to see. Over time, the letters had faded from "ZLER" to "LER" to "ER" to "R" to black.

I wondered if Kevin had responded to my text, praying he would crash overnight in San Diego. *Are you staying?* Having a husband was painful when I was dopesick, and a nightmare while being high. Either way, I didn't want him around.

I wobbled down the mall driveway into the parking lot, my stomach churning at the cars' exhaust. I stopped and spat. The jaundiced gob glistened. I shivered, disgusted. Spitting in public is one of my biggest pet peeves (along with deliberately misspelled signs and people sweeping trash underneath my table while I eat). Who had I become? I didn't know or care. I just wanted to get inside, get my pills and leave me behind.

Rite Aid's doors whooshed open with a welcoming sigh. The cool blasts of chemical air soothed my trembling skin. Breathing in the familiar antiseptic aroma, my shoulders softened. I removed my sunglasses and wiped at my face repeatedly. My hairline was soaked. As I secured my glasses, I could see my hand was shaking. I swallowed several times, my sandpaper throat catching on itself.

I shuffled down the store's main corridor, passing the laxative, rubbing alcohol and analgesic aisles. There was only one item on my list today. At the back of the store, gleaming white letters spelled out my deliverance: PHARMACY. Turning the final corner, I gasped.

The pharmacy area was deserted. The uncluttered tile floor gleamed. It was like the scene in *The Shining* when Jack Nicholson walks through an empty ballroom and up to a fully stocked bar with a bartender ready to take his order. No one stood waiting in line, tapping his toes in the throes of detox. My heart soared. All I had to do was walk up to the counter and ask.

"Picking up for patient Ivanans," my voice splintered as the words came out. The pharmacist turned away and began to sift through the hanging bags.

I leaned against the counter, suddenly dizzy. The walk, the heat and the nausea were catching up with me. Rifling through the plastic bags, she came up empty-handed. My palms sprung leaks.

"When did you order this?" She stared at me.

What if the computer had caught the mistake? What if they were out of Fiorinal? How would I walk back home? How would I survive this? I would not survive this.

I stared back from behind my sunglasses and baseball cap. Covering my face like this felt rude and obvious I was hiding something. My cap and glasses like the arrow of a roadside motel pointing towards my neon-bright desperation. This get-up was my poker face, and I wasn't ready to fold.

"Uh, about an hour ago?" I guessed. I wasn't fibbing. I really had no idea what time it was. I had left my cell phone and keys at home. My I.D. and ATM card were tucked into my jeans' back pocket. My outfit streamlined like a spy's for maximum efficiency in completing this mission.

Her eyes narrowed as she read the computer. I withered against the counter, my breath leaving my body. I wanted everything to disappear. The harsh lighting. Her explorative pecking. My cramping gut. Why was this happening? I had come so far. I would have done anything. Stripped naked. Pawned my wedding band. Anything.

"Oh!" she laughed, her eyes relaxing. "We haven't filled it yet! Give me 15 minutes!"

Fifteen minutes! Was this a joke? Why would it take that long? There was no one else here! I grabbed at my chest, my breath coming back to me in choppy bursts. At least She was back there. I could do this. Just a few more minutes. How would I kill fifteen minutes inside a Rite Aid? Peruse the Aisle of Random Items with turkey basters and Chia Pets? Lie down in the middle of the floor and die?

Despite the Freon breeze swirling around the store, I couldn't stop sweating. I had to get something to drink. Rivulets of sweat streamed from my hairline as I scanned the coolers. Nothing appealed to me: from milk to juice to iced tea to soda to water. Especially water. The idea sent my stomach into violent waves. It was too pure and clear, too shocking for a system clogged with drugs. I needed something to soak up the bile. Tomato juice! Yes. That would hydrate and fuel me with much-needed calories.

Slumping into one of the chairs, I brought the tomato juice up to my cracked lips, daring a small sip. As the clumpy liquid moved down my throat, my stomach lurched in protest. Bracing the container against my mouth, I forced myself to take another couple of sips. I didn't care that I hadn't paid for it. Arms crossed, my Entitlement and I sat scowling in the waiting area as the pharmacists took their sweet, sweet time.

They were having way too much fun, laughing together the way friends do. Maybe they were friends. Why were they so happy? They were working on a sunny Saturday afternoon, surrounded by a bunch of pills they couldn't have. Trapped. Yet, I sat unencumbered by responsibility, ostensibly free, and was miserable. I stared at the shelves of pills behind them, wondering what they were for and wishing I could get my hands on them. I didn't realize inside this prison thoughts, I was the one who was trapped.

I spotted a tiny clock on the pharmacy wall. Although

approaching 6 pm, I wasn't worried about getting home to check my phone for Kevin's response. Wedding receptions were at night. His standard contract was for eight hours of shooting, usually beginning at 1 or 2 pm and ending at 11 pm. Kevin being Kevin, he would always stay longer than contracted. Above and beyond the call of duty was his MO and San Diego was over two hours away. Kevin wouldn't be home for hours, and hopefully, not tonight at all.

But any thought of my husband was random and fleeting, like a rare cloud that might pass through on an otherwise clear summer's day. My thoughts were focused on Us, and how hard the pharmacists should be working, not how hard I knew Kevin was working. He was running around in brutal heat, contorting his body into crazy positions to get the perfect shot. Putting money in the bank, bread on our table, and pills in my pocket.

"Ivanans!" I walked up to the counter and plunked down my tomato juice. The pharmacist placed an extra-tall container beside it, slipping it into a white paper bag. *They must have run out of short containers.*

This pharmacy had made mistakes in the past. One time, they had doled out 90 Ambien instead of the 30 tablets Kevin had been prescribed. Another time, I had been all the way home before realizing I had someone else's antibiotic and not my Vicodin. Seething, panicked, I had raced back, terrified that although the antibiotic was untouched, I would be denied the 30 Vicodin I would gobble in just over a day. After that scare, I checked my medications before leaving. Especially today. Today was a return trip I would not survive without Her.

I thanked the pharmacist and stepped away. Ripping open the bag's stapled top, I plunged my hand inside and grabbed Her. Through the plastic I saw the familiar double-blue capsules heaped on top of one another in a playful mound. It was Her all right, but the pile looked enormous. I turned the bottle on its side and read the label: *Henriette Ivanans-McIntyre. Fioricet (Acetaminophen/Butalbital/Caffeine). No Refills. 120 capsules.* My breath caught. 120 capsules! My prescription was for 60. I glanced up at the pharmacists, but their heads were down, giggling. This was bad. Shockingly negligent on their part. I couldn't even begin to imagine how this had happened.

I looked around. No one was watching me. My knees wobbled. I had hit the jackpot! I wanted to shout with melodic jubilation the way a slot machine jangles when it hits three 7s in a row. Blood rushed to my head as I fought the charge for home before the pharmacists realized their horrendous mistake.

An agonizing tug-of-war pulled at my gut. I should be responsible, walk up to the counter, point out their mistake and hand Her over. I knew I should do this, but I could not make myself move. I could not return this Accidental Prescription. I wouldn't be able to control how much I took or how often. I would take all of these pills in four or five days. I would become dopesick, but I could not let Her go.

Holding Her high beneath the florescent lights, I triple-checked the label. A halo flared around Her, spotlighting what would soon be my salvation, airlifting me out of purgatory, and then dropping me straight back down into hell. She rattled as if to say, *You are mine.* I would not return Her. I would consume Her, every last pill.

I did not take a pill right away. She could alleviate my symptoms, but in just walking with Her, I felt restored. Her power to transport me was something to be revered. I would honor Her in the quiet isolation of our bedroom. Far away from any sight or sound that might detract from those first blissful moments of relief. She would release me from nausea, ear ringing and throbbing temples. These moments were too profound to share with the dregs of humanity. In a way, having Her dangle from my arm was like pharmaceutical foreplay. Now that She was in my possession, I could hold out. Euphoria would arrive at home.

I do not remember the trek home, but for the walk up our driveway. It was a hurdle I would have sprinted up four years earlier. Or barely elevated my pulse two years prior, post-rejection diagnosis. Today, my heart was racing as I closed the metal gate in triumph. I planted my feet on the asphalt plane the way a climber stakes his claim atop his Everest—with exhilaration and pride. The walls of our cabin glowed with the shifting orange light of the evening sun. I had only been up for four hours, but my day was already coming to an end. I had completed the mission. I was home.

I entered the cool of our living room, all four A/C units blasting. I loved the clatter. It reminded me of sitting in a plane on the tarmac, its engines whirring in anticipation. Ready for take off.

I swiped the dampness from my neck. My blood sugar was dropping the way it often did when I starved myself for days to feel Her effects more acutely. This insane deprivation was easy to justify. Fiorinal's instructions clearly stated She was more effective if taken on an empty stomach. Shaking, I stumbled into our bedroom, fearing I might faint. Yet, I would not eat or drink a thing.

Our bedroom was now dark. I switched on a lamp. Removing Her from the bag, I cracked open the lid and swallowed four capsules with warm tomato juice.

Instantly, my stomach constricted in that familiar way. My body jerked back on itself, but there was no time to run. Red projectile spewed everywhere, splotching the walls, floor and my feet with a watery thud. Thick red liquid dripped down our pale green wall. *The pills!*

I fell to the floor, scooping up the dissolving capsules from the puddle. I didn't think there was anything odd about a 41-year old woman on her knees rescuing pills from a pool of bile, while 116 capsules of the same medication stood right above her head.

Popping the melting capsules back into my mouth, I knocked them back with another slug of the warm juice. Bringing my fist to my mouth, I suppressed the impending gag, and swallowed. On the table, my cell phone was blinking. It was Kevin.

I don't know if I am staying down here tonight.

An hour later.

Where are you?

I collapsed onto the bed, sinking into the mattress as cool currents of air soothed my aching body.

I was sleeping. I have a migraine. Stay. Treat yourself to a nice hotel room.

Everything would be so much easier if he stayed away.

I rolled over and placed the phone next to Her. Even as my head began to swirl with relief, I told myself they weren't working fast enough and palmed three more. Seven in twenty minutes.

Faster, faster. It's never fast enough...

Night was falling on Saturday June 5th. On Wednesday, I was to meet the professionals who would decide my transplant eligibility. I had to show up. I had to be sober. This meant at some point soon, I had to stop.

I could do it. My bones' fierce flu-like ache had been tamed. My limbs were now marshmallow-soft. Euphoria had arrived. I was not worried about urine tests that might screen for drugs, or showing up dopesick. I had no worries at all. It was only Saturday. Wednesday was four long days away. I would stop. Now. Soon. Tomorrow. Yes. I could do this. I would be fine.

I swallowed five more pills.

And then III more.

8. NORTRIPTYLINE

A couple of months earlier, I survived my worst night of dopesickness. Unable to sleep, I had pounded at my shoulders with my fists, pressing my head up against our headboard so hard, it left a deep indentation. I thrashed about all night, finding not one second's peace from the crippling pain that consumed me.

As the sun rose over the canyon, the front door had creaked open. Through a slit in the bedroom curtains, I watched Kevin rummage through the back of the car, retrieving something from the pocket behind the front seat. *Oh, my god. That's where he hides them!* My body shuddered with relief as he walked back towards the house. Everything disappeared but his clenched fist.

On the edge of the bed, my husband appeared like a merciful angel holding 7 Fiorinal. He had seen me endure the hell of withdrawal enough times to know he needed to give these pills to a body dying with, and without Her.

He opened his palm. With a crude grab, I gulped them down.

"Thank you," I whispered.

Why he'd made me suffer all night, as I moaned through the bedroom wall, is something only my husband can answer. I felt no anger. Never speculated about when he may have stolen them from me. I felt nothing but a full-body rush of gratitude for his dysfunctional decision. Especially when he gave me the remaining 4 a couple hours later.

~

"Look, everyone! This is Henriette! This is Henriette begging for pills!"

It was Monday afternoon, June 7th. It is the next thing I recall after Saturday June 5th.

"STOP IT!" I screamed into the wide lens of the 1995 state-of-the-art, Hi-8 video camera we purchased to record our wedding.

Kevin had chased me around the house with the camera, and I was now cornered in the bathroom. In the mirror, I caught a glimpse of my madwoman state: naked, hair matted from damp washcloths gone dry, and dark eyes caked with the sands of a restless sleep. Enraged, I began to flick water at him from the bathroom sink. He jumped back, but continued to film.

"Are you an IDIOT?" I screamed.

Did he really think shoving a camera into my face would get me to calm down? I would calm down when he gave me back my pills. I dove to yank it from his hand. He dodged away easily, laughing. Every hair on my skin sizzled. Kevin stuck the camera deeper into my face. Piece of shit.

"I'm going to put this on Facebook."

"GO AHEAD!" I scoffed.

Please. As if. Kevin would never make himself look bad by posting something that made me look bad. Did he really think recording my hysteria would work like some magical mirror to get me to change? Right. Like I'm suddenly going to stop, calmly watch the footage, turn to him and say, "You know what? You're right. I really am crazy." He was the fucking crazy one. I tore up into his face.

"They're MINE! WHERE DID YOU PUT THEM?"

Suddenly, Kevin's face went dark. He set the camera down and marched out the front door.

"What? No. No! NO! NO! NO!" I stumbled towards the bedroom window watching the car disappear down the driveway.

"KEVIN!" I screamed into the glass. I threw myself onto the couch, sobbing, clutching at my head, until through a tiny lucid window I realized Kevin was no longer here to witness my hysteria. Precious time was a-wasting. Hands shaking, I grabbed my phone and commenced with harassment by text.

Where are they? [Send.]

I know you have some. [Send.]

Please. [Send.]

Refresh. Refresh. Refresh. Nothing. Pursing my lips, I pounded his number repeatedly. The call went straight through every time. I raised my arm to whip my phone against the wall, and then raced into his office instead.

His narcotic charity from two months prior was confusing me. Like a child who one time hears *Yes* out of a million *No's*.

Where are they?

My eyes narrowed, scanning every corner of the room, flickering like a flashlight from his desk to the bookcase to the filing cabinet. Savagely, I yanked open his desk drawers, rifling through papers. I plunged my hand deep inside the front pocket of his guitar case. Nothing. I whirled around. She had to be here somewhere. Rivulets of sweat streamed from my scalp. I dropped to the floor, dumping a manila envelope full of receipts everywhere.

BAM. My breath caught. I looked up, holding the zipper to his bagpipe case taut in my hand. Was he home? Droplets fell from the tip of my nose and onto the floor. *Drip. Drip. Drip.* I ran to the window, whipping the curtain wide. The car was still gone. I wiped at the back of my neck, smearing my clammy palms on the curtain as I let it drop. Nothing. It had been nothing. Where the fuck had he gone anyway? Fucking asshole.

I dumped the pen container upside down with an unapologetic slam. The front door banged shut. He was home! I whirled around, banging my leg against the desk's edge. Pens, pencils and highlighters went clinking onto the ground. Holding my knee, I limped into the living room, and charged right up into his face.

"WHERE ARE THEY!" I bellowed.

Kevin didn't move. His arms were not crossed in front of him, in their familiar McIntyre stance. They hung limply by his side.

"SAY SOMETHING!" I roared, shoving him hard.

Exhaling, I realized this wild-eyed, sweat-drenched, buck-naked wife wasn't building much of a case for getting her drugs back. I had to rein it in. I scraped at my tongue, at the thick coat of dopesickness that caused words to trip from my mouth. Inhaling, I articulated slowly.

"Sweetheart. Could I please have my pills back?"

I inched closer to him. So close to his face, I could see his gray beard hair dotted with my spit. His mouth began to move, to form the words I knew would save my life.

"There are no more pills."

My mouth opened to scream when something rattled. Someone was trying to get inside. Through the glass of our front door, I saw the outline of a thin woman. My head exploded. It was my girlfriend, Melissa. Although eight years younger, we'd cultivated a deep friendship forged in the fires of rock star crushes and health tragedies. She had shown up for every hospital admission and was one of the few friends whose eyes did not glaze over when I discussed my transplant.

How dare she! Fuck them. FUCK. THEM. I knew what this was. I had to get out of here, but there was no escaping our 1000 square-foot cabin, two against one. I clenched and unclenched my fists repeatedly. Cocksuckers. I was trapped in my own episode of A & E's *Intervention.*

It was Kevin's fault. If he had just given me the pills he had stolen from me, this never would have happened. Melissa and Kevin stood poised, ready to pounce. No one said a word. Every breath shredded my throat. I was out of ideas. Across the living room and into their faces I screamed with everything I had.

"FUCK YOUUUUUU!"

Melissa's eyes widened as the words splattered across her face. I bolted for the bedroom, locking the door behind me. Quickly, I pulled on a t-shirt and sweats. Seconds later they were both standing in the doorway, watching me with their dumb blank eyes: The sane regarding the insane. My blood surged with hate. Overcome, I pounced onto my husband. My fingers clawed at his t-shirt. It tore easily, splitting right down the middle. Even in my insanity, I could appreciate how cinematic the moment was. Unmoving, my husband sustained my physical fury, but his eyes went dark, boarded up against the storm of his wife's rage.

Then Melissa and I were squatting on the floor. A lucid thought flew by: *I wonder if she'll notice I'm wearing the sweats she gave me.* It fluttered away awkwardly, like an injured bird, unable to sustain its flight path for very long.

Head bent, tears streaming down my face, I refused to look at Kevin. I had to convince Melissa to convince him to get my pills. My husband would do the right thing. He had given me pills once before. He had to have some hidden. He just had to.

"I just need a few more. I'm going to be sick."

Melissa's voice was calm. "Hen. There are no more pills."

Her eyes were clear, shining with truth. I dared to look at my husband. Kevin's shoulders were slumped, the ripped t-shirt falling from his frame. In a flash, I saw him standing over the toilet, a water-fall of tablets plip-plopping into the water below and my ear-splitting scream that had drowned out the flush. *No. NO. NO!!!*

"Henriette. They are all gone." Kevin repeated.

Melissa explained to me what Kevin had explained to her. All the pills were gone, and I was in real danger of an acetaminophen over-dose. I had to go to the ER.

"Hen. Will you go?"

My will began to crack. There was something about her tone. Kevin never lied. I believed them. There were no more pills. My body began to convulse with a bone-rattling terror. I could barely see my husband through my watershed of fear. Tears, endless tears. Under the harsh lighting, his face looked gray. Destroyed. My heart, like his t-shirt, ripped in two. Yes. I would go.

"Will they help me? Will they help me?" I sobbed from my knees.

"Yes, Henriette. They will help you."

Which I now know was Kevin's way of admitting he no longer knew how.

~

THE CEDARS ER WAS OVER-CAPACITY. I lay on a gurney in the hallway. Rapid-fire sounds of a hospital under siege shredded my ears: screeching IVs, a PA system belching with Codes this-and-that, and the self-important stampeding of medical personnel. I flipped back and forth, never once finding more than a fresh minute of relief on either side.

With nowhere to sit, Kevin hovered. No one brought me anything for pain. Not even ice water. Irritation gnawed at my bones. I glared at my husband. He had promised me they would help me.

Then I was given 16 oz. of a bitter tasting liquid poured over ice for my nausea. I could take my time, but I had to drink all of it. I powered through it, hoping, like in *Alice in Wonderland,* if I followed instructions—*Drink me*—I would shrink and disappear from this hell.

Kevin left to report to Melissa in the waiting area. My flesh burned. Why did he get to leave? He had made me come! I wiped away an angry tear. Where was my fix-all injection? The one I had seen administered on the big screen? With a quick plunge, patients slump into grateful bliss. Rolling onto my stomach, I reached for the metal bar that protected me from falling onto the ground. Burying my face into the sheet I inhaled, praying this mouthful of cotton would take me out.

And now the math: The half-life of any given medication is the amount of time it takes for a body to get rid of half the dose or half its strength. The medicinal components of Fioricet (kidney-friendly Fiorinal) are: Caffeine (40 mg), Tylenol (325 mg) and Butalbital (50 mg.) Acetaminophen's half-life is 1.25 to 3 hours. Caffeine's half-life is about 3 hours. Butalbital's half-life is 35 hours. This means, although Butalbital's acute narcotic buzz is gone after a few hours, it lingers exponentially in a body over days.

Again, one Fioricet tablet has 50 mg of Butalbital, and a half-life of 35 hours. This means, after 35 hours, 25 mgs of Butalbital remained in my system. After another 35 hours, 1/2 of 25 mgs—or 12.5 mgs—would still be there. After yet another 35 hours, 1/2 of 12.5 mgs—or 6.25 mgs—would linger, and so on. This means one tablet of Fioricet loitered in my body for over 140 hours or 5.8 days.

Each time I took another Fioricet in that first 35-hour period (or let's face it, tens upon tens), another 50 mg of Butalbital was added. After the first 35 hours of this binge, I had taken at least half of the 120-tablet Accidental Prescription—or 60 tablets. 25 mg (half-life) x 60 Fioricet equals 1500 mg of Butalbital still in my system. This math does not take into account my continual popping—several tablets every hour—of fresh Fioricet. Although I was never very good at math, I am not sure how anyone could properly calculate the results of such abuse. The end result was always the same: multiple days of unbearable withdrawal.

Or in other words: Her high was long gone, and Her low interminable.

There are three options for withdrawal: 1) Cold Turkey. 2) More of the same drug, or "Hair of the Pharmaceutical Dog." (You can see by the above math, that it is nearly impossible to solve Her equation. (Keep taking Fioricet and its half-life marches onward to infinity) or 3) Different drugs that ease the symptoms of withdrawal.

I remember her face over mine: An opaque stare from between two curtains of straight black hair. She introduced herself as the ER psychiatrist. I was unclear on why I needed an emotional assessment. I had come to the hospital for a physical detox.

Kevin stood next to her. His folded arms seemed to be holding his torso together. Over the ER's insulting cacophony, I strained to answer her questions. Each time I spoke, my lips collapsed upon themselves. She kept asking me to repeat myself. My stomach clenched in annoyance. Yeah. Fine. I was slurring, but seriously, why was my answer so hard to understand?

"Why did you want to kill yourself?"

I did not. Why did she keep asking that? God, it was hard to talk.

"Get lot hea-th-aches," I managed, my flaccid tongue unable to support the "d." Kevin and I locked eyes. *Help me.*

"Henriette gets a lot of migraines." The psychiatrist looked at him.

"It's important that Henriette answer for herself." Kevin crossed his arms tighter. My body was up on its side, straining to participate. When was she going to bring the drugs?

Inside the vomit-stenched, antiseptic air, I smelled something darker lurking on the hospital horizon: A reason for my obsession with Her. She needed a reason why I would kill myself.

"I don't want to lose my kidney," I slurred.

A woman losing her 23-year old kidney transplant would be depressed, if not despondent. Yet, this was but a half-truth, a gurney-side manipulation. I certainly did not want to lose my kidney, but depression over its rejection was not the reason I had swallowed all of the Accidental Prescription. Taking 120 tablets in 2 ½ days for a migraine was also not the truth.

My truth was I had no idea why I had taken all of Her in 2 ½ days, so I had to offer the psychiatrist a lie. Of course, this lie corroborated suicide attempt. Why else would you take 120 tablets of anything unless you were suicidal?

Offering no reaction, she walked away. Kevin followed her.

While I lay there waiting for the magical injection that never came, Kevin would corner her. The psychiatrist considered this event a suicide attempt, and wanted to implement a 5150.

In California, a 5150 is an involuntary psych hold, placed by a county clinician or peace officer on a patient suspected to have a mental disorder. The patient must meet three of the following criteria, she must be determined to be: 1) a danger to herself—in imminent danger of harming herself: 2) a danger to others—in imminent danger of harming another person; or 3) gravely disabled—with no means of food, shelter or clothing or is unable to keep herself safe. A

5150 permits a patient to be held for up to 72 hours against their will for assessment, crisis intervention and possible treatment.

This day, Monday, June 7[th,] 2010, I would be admitted to Cedars for a suicide attempt, but not a 5150. My husband would talk the psychiatrist out of it, understanding something I had zero ability to comprehend. Patients who have been 5150'd rarely appear on transplant lists.

When the psychiatrist reappeared gurney-side, she stared at me for a moment. Her forehead furrowed with deep lines.

"Are you sure you took all those pills?"

I wanted to laugh, but all I could do was stare back.

"Your blood tests came back normal," she continued. "You have no liver toxicity. You registered a normal level of acetaminophen."

She could not explain it. Neither could I, but I had the answer.

My body just loves drugs.

~

EVERY INPATIENT ROOM at Cedars has a push-button phone. Mine was ringing off the hook. Usually, it's Cafeteria Services calling about a menu or someone from Admitting chasing down a copayment. It was now Tuesday, but my temples still throbbed to the insistent beat of withdrawal. *Ring. Ring.* Why wouldn't it stop? No one knew I was here. Sighing, I grabbed the receiver, my IV tubes dangling like eerie plastic fingers.

"Hello?"

"Ms. Ivanans? This is the transplant clinic. Wednesday's evaluation..."

Perfect timing! I needed to talk to them about the appointment. Coincidentally, I was already at Cedars, dealing with "headaches issues." Could they push back Wednesday's evaluation to Friday? Yes, Friday. That would work better for me.

In that moment, a measuring tape that spanned Earth's girth would have been too short to calculate the size of my ego. I really believed a team of seven specialists: Transplant Coordinator,

Surgeon, Urologist, Nutritionist, Social Worker, Financial Advisor and Nephrologist were like the easy ingredients of a tossed salad that could be thrown together at a moment's notice. My ego was so blind it could not even see that, *D-uh*, of course she knew I was there for "headache issues." She had just called my room.

"Your transplant evaluation has been postponed. You have been red flagged as a suicide attempt. In six months, you will be psychologically evaluated and it determined whether you can be listed."

To be "listed" means your name is added to the UNOS (United Network of Organ Sharing) directory. On this list, patients wait by seniority for a kidney. The last one added endures the longest wait— 5-9+ years depending upon blood and tissue type. My "suicide attempt" meant the transplant clinic would revaluate in November whether I could be added to UNOS. If my name had already been on the list, it would have been deleted.

My first thought was: *It was not a suicide attempt.* My next thought was: *Fuck you. I don't need your list. My husband is going to give me a kidney.* My head spun. This was so inconvenient. Kevin wanted to give me a kidney, but we had no idea if he was a match. Now, testing would be postponed until November 19th, 2010.

"I get a lot of headaches" had become my mantra, but no one was buying it, including me. "Suicide attempt" did not sit right either. On paper, I saw it. Yes. Swallowing 120 pills in 2 1/2 days looked like a suicide attempt. That I had done it five days before my transplant evaluation, well, a psychologist with a degree from a matchbook cover college could have figured that out on his first day: I had sabotaged my transplant evaluation.

I was sure I hadn't. I had not tried to kill myself. I did not want to die. This binge had gone past chasing a bigger and better high. I had been unable to stop taking pills, and had no idea why.

∼

ON WEDNESDAY, Dr. D. came to see me. Twelve years my nephrologist, his face bore a complicated expression: Shock beneath sadness. His typically twinkling eyes unbright.

"What happened?" was all my beloved physician could muster.

There was no point in feeding Dr. D. the party line. *I get a lot of headaches.* He had to have read my report: Took 120 Fiorinal in 2 ½ days. Suicide attempt. 5150 recommended, not implemented.

As he moved in from the doorway, my tummy fluttered with the truth. Yes, I had been chasing a high. Fiorinal was awesome, with or without a migraine! But that still didn't explain why I would binge to overdose.

Confused, my willingness to confess disappeared as he reached the bed. Still, I wanted to offer him more, a more refined manipulation than the ER psychiatrist. Even as they tumbled from my mouth I understood my words were constructed to look good on a psychiatric report.

"I feel like I am losing everything."

Being the great doctor that he is, Dr. D. seized upon the kernel of truth. If our lives are made up of those pie-like graphs divided into varying-sized slices like: Marriage, Career, Family and Health, my entire pie was now consumed with Health.

"You have so much more to offer than this."

Dr. D. was not scolding me, but offering an observation he believed I could not make for myself: I was more than my kidney failure. I offered him a weak smile, liking that he believed this for me. Yet, being sick was not why I had swallowed 120 pills. I was alone in understanding that.

As he left, I turned stiffly onto my side and scanned the patient dry erase board: *Henriette Ivanans-McIntyre. Age 41. 10/29/1968. Renal transplant patient. "PAIN MEDICATION D/C."* I sighed. What a contrast to two years earlier when I'd chanced upon the bright blue pronouncement that I could have Dilaudid every two hours as needed for pain.

God, I missed Her. In that moment, I would have betrayed Her entirely. I would have accepted any other pain medication. Writhing on over-washed sheets without repeated injections of hard-core detox drugs had not been my idea of help when I agreed to come. Shattered upon our bedroom floor, I had been unable to connect the pharmaceutical dots. Looking at the board, reality bit hard. This hospitalization was the end of Us. As every cell in my body screamed for Her, I was far more traumatized about the dissolution of Our relationship than the postponement of my transplant evaluation.

~

ON THURSDAY NIGHT, a tiny man in a tweed jacket slipped into my room. His laminated tag read, "Dr. A. Neurology." An enormous file was tucked underneath his shoulder. I ran my fingers through my snarled hair. His kind eyes gleamed in the shadows.

"Hello. I'm Dr. A. Is this a good time to speak with you?"

"Yes," I mumbled, surprised by his adorable politeness. He pulled up a chair by the head of my bed.

Dr. A questioned me well into the night. How often did I get headaches? How long did they last? How often did I get migraines? How long did they last? My skin tingled. Oh, I adored him already. His questions were like medical foreplay! I could love a man who understood the difference between headaches and migraines! With gentle swirls upon the page, he recorded my answers, pausing to glance up at me with soft, crinkled eyes. With endless patience he waited as I still struggled to form words. He knew I was categorized a "suicide attempt," yet with each look radiated nothing but empathy.

"I'm going to put you on a non-addictive muscle relaxer called Xanaflex. This will relax your neck and shoulders. I want you to try Imitrex for your migraines. It is a non-narcotic, Triptan drug. Take it at the onset of migraine. Finally, we'll try an anti-depressant called Nortriptyline. It is found to be effective as a preventative treatment for headaches."

My pulse raced as I heard myself agree to a non-narcotic regimen. *Wait! I'm not ready!* Fiorinal and I had been together for 19 years. Longer than Kevin and I had been married. My breath came quickly as I watched the neurologist gather up his papers. What had I been thinking in coming here? That someone could teach me how to take Her as prescribed again?

Yet, another part of me was exhausted. Ready to let go. Shaking, still barely able to sit up, the idea of treating my migraines with something else felt like a cool breeze upon the back of my neck. I was willing to try.

A nurse entered with my first round of DHE (Diphydroergotamine): intensive non-narcotic IV therapy that would finally relieve my withdrawal symptoms. She stood at the computer typing new chapters into my already long story. The plastic bag swayed as she dropped the medicine onto the pole.

"This will make you feel better."

I watched the clear liquid flow through the plastic tubing. Over a couple of hours, the DHE—like a medicinal Roto-Rooter—would blast the rest of Her from my veins. I rubbed my bleary eyes. I had barely slept in five days. Above all else, it was sleep I craved. Sleep, thus, escape from the paralyzing reality that I would never know Her again.

I turned towards the nurse. "Am I allowed anything for sleep?"

"Let me check."

The glow from the computer highlighted her focused face as she scrolled away. My heart was pounding, my breath arrested.

"Yes, you can have Ambien. And Xanax."

Ambien is a highly addictive medication prescribed for insomnia. Xanax is a highly addictive medication prescribed for anxiety. Both are intended for short-term use, as they take you to an altered state.

"Can I have those tonight?"

"Sure, honey. I'll go get them." I exhaled. I had lost Fiorinal, but in Her wake, found two new friends.

The nurse was right. I did feel a whole lot better.

~

"BLLLAAARRRGGGHHH!"

My husband does not like to talk about bodily functions, never mind experience them. We looked after our seven-month old godson every Wednesday for a year, and Kevin never once changed a diaper (feigning his trademark dry heave every time). I, on the other hand, revel in being the girl who is super-cool about poop, pee and the like. I am the Anti-Princess who worked as a janitor to put myself through theatre school, cleaning blood, vomit and feces off Toronto's subway platforms. Yet, there my Prince Charmin stood, watching me hurl into a kidney-shaped bedpan.

"You OK, honey?" the nurse asked.

I nodded weakly. "Yeah, I think that was...BLAAARGH!!!"

Even in chronic rejection, a transplant patient must maintain that 12-hour, twice a day balance of immunosuppressives to sustain the kidney's life for as long as possible. As I wiped at the strands of drool dangling from my chin, Kevin and the nurse swooped in to eyeball the pan's steaming contents.

"Did she swallow the Cyclosporine?"

Kevin leaned in. "This one is Cell Cept, for sure."

"Is this one Cyclosporine?" the nurse squinted.

"No, Cyclosporine is a gel capsule."

"What about this red stuff?" she said, pointing.

"That's the tomato soup she had for lunch."

My heart flipped as my husband exhibited a new watermark in protection. During my '98 kidney biopsy, he had trembled observing the single-packing semi-automatic needle plunge into my abdomen. With my '08 rejection diagnosis, his valorous wings had sheltered every fear. Post-overdose, Kevin soared over me, circling, assessing every situation, pecking away at anything that might cause me harm: from a 5150 neither of us understood, to a big pile of puke. The man who hated bodily functions was practically submerging himself in mine.

As the pungent stank of Her remains ribboned up from the plastic pan, we locked eyes. His shone with purpose. My pulse quickened. How could I have ever forgotten? The love of my life was standing right in front of me, not lumped, regurgitated, in a plastic trough on the bed.

I was in, all in. And just for today, grateful She was on Her way out.

～

AFTER NINE NIGHTS, I was discharged. Along with Xanaflex, Imitrex and Nortriptyline, I was sent home with prescriptions for Xanax and Ambien. My heart fluttered as I folded the script in my hand. Part of me knew I should say something. Having overdosed on 120 tablets of a controlled substance and a suicide attempt on my record, should I be going home with two highly addictive medications?

But Fiorinal had been my obsession. The love of my life. Kevin had been prescribed Ambien, and it never occurred to me to try any. And Xanax? Well, I had already swiped my mother-in-law's and never sought my own prescription. Ambien and Xanax was just a couple of lower companions I'd hang out with. If Cedars wasn't worried, neither was I.

Leaving Rite Aid, I shamelessly popped the Xanax cap and swallowed one pill as I strode through the sliding doors. No problem. I was taking it as prescribed—1 pill, not 120. My eyes glazed over with gratitude as Xanax hit my bloodstream. It was no Fiorinal, but I could not deny how happy I was to have made its acquaintance again.

～

IN JULY, I got my first post-Fiorinal migraine. I took an Imitrex and a Xanax, and curled into a ball on our bed. Dr. A. was a genius. They worked. The combination caught the migraine, but there was something too pat, too straightforward about the pills' effectiveness. I missed Her chaos, Her soul-sucking madness. Staring at our ceiling, I sighed. Giving Her up had been the right thing to do. Then why did I feel so empty? Pondering this, I reached into my drawer for another Xanax.

Over the summer, I took Nortriptyline every morning, and had to admit it was working, too. Nortriptyline was keeping the storm of my migraines at bay. I noticed something else. Into autumn, my nightly glass of wine evolved into two, and then from one to two vodka/sodas. Yet, on Nortriptyline, I never got a headache. Or more accurately, I never got a hangover. Nortriptyline was magic.

In Her absence, I turned more and more to the thing that had deepened Our bond—alcohol. For me, alcohol was to Fiorinal as Skipper is to Barbie—at first glance, sloppy seconds. Alcohol was not the obvious star, but every once in a while the understudy comes along and steals the show. I gave it a chance. Pills they could take away from me, but alcohol was everywhere.

My mother once schooled me that, "Certain friends fulfill certain needs." Why could this not be true of pills? Pills had always been my friends—from immunosuppression to migraine relief to a multi-purpose antidepressant that prevented me from ever feeling hung over. How friendly was that? Yes, Fiorinal had been the one that got away, but Nortriptyline became the rebound pill that introduced me to an untapped world I had only just uncorked.

9. ALCOHOL

By November 2010, I entered Stage 5 CKD or End Stage Renal Failure (ESRF). ESRF is when your GFR is less than 15% kidney function. Just so we're clear here, the only options with renal failure are dialysis, transplantation or death.

Dr. D. was now treating me with 19 medications for symptoms of ESRF, while I treated myself to a daily dose of Codeine from the several bottles I had smuggled home from an October trip to Toronto. When I opened my meds drawer in the mornings and saw Codeine lying next to my ever-expanding pharmaceutical crew, I could breathe. I longed for Fiorinal and our forbidden weekends, but Codeine and her two pals, Xanax and Ambien, were at least like having a good friend come over and play.

My kidney was barely filtering, which meant toxins were clogging my bloodstream. My symptoms had devolved to the extreme, the list you scroll to the bottom of your computer screen to read: hypertension, bleeding gums, facial rash, nose bleeding, constipation, canker sores, confusion, insomnia, nail fungus, vomiting, loss of appetite, and depression: To name a dozen.

For every symptom, there was a pill, but for every pill, a side effect, and yet another pill to treat that side effect. Dr. D. was now strategically prescribing to secure me a pre-emptive transplant—

avoiding dialysis by any medication necessary. There were phosphorus binders to lower my spiking phosphorus, NephroVite, a dietary supplement for renal patients, and three blood pressure medications. Building a dam of pills against the rising tide of symptoms and inevitable flood that would send me down the river to dialysis if I could not find a match in time. I was willing to take 200 pills a day if it meant avoiding dialysis, but never thought to put down the drink.

Alcohol and I had been acquaintances for most of my life. Nights of blackout drinking in high school and theatre school, and the subsequent hangovers left me disinterested. When Kevin and I began dating we enjoyed binge nights, guzzling beer after beer until the early morning hours. When we awoke, disheveled, Kevin would whisper "booooozehound," into my ear, and we would laugh.

I would take Codeine with wine, but it was Fiorinal that changed the drinking game. So obsessed was I with the effect this winning combination produced, I obsessively repeated the rhyme in my head —*Fiorinal and Alcohol*—the way a teenage girl scribbles her crush's name in her notebook. Yet, Alcohol and I remained distant cousins. Kevin and I maintained an untouched stash in the house for guests and my use of it was periodic.

In a post-Fiorinal world, vodka would be my savior. I was discontinued from the headache/hangover-preventing Nortriptyline after only three months due to a side effect where my mouth burned when eating anything. Yet my hangovers did not return. Vodka was perfection. My new drug of choice.

No, alcohol is not a pill, but it is defined as a drug in Merriam-Webster's dictionary: *a substance that is used as medicine.* ESRF's debilitating symptoms required treatment. In my 24-7 state of nausea, Alcohol took the edge off. No matter what pill Dr. D. prescribed I was enslaved by toxins, except when I took a few swigs. With Alcohol, I was reinvigorated, part of the world around me, even if it was just the slog of a loop between Cedars and our cabin. Alcohol was my new medicine, and I had been schooled to take my medicine every day.

As we watched late-night sitcoms, it stood on my bedside table instead of in a baggie taped to its back. Double cans of Corona waited in the fridge in plain sight, not hidden inside my Secret Cupboard. Kevin no longer insisted I was drinking too much, as he had when I picked up the alcohol pace that summer. For him, these fights were unwinnable; inevitably ending with *You should have been a lawyer.* With CKD on my team, there was no argument I could not win: *It's legal. Everyone drinks. It makes me feel better.*

Into fall, I caught the odd troubled look when he noted a beer in my hand, but no jealous rages as had been with Her. Alcohol was my steadfast friend, not the hysterical backstabber She had been. We were still living in an open marriage, but my husband was tolerating Alcohol the way a French wife condones her husband's mistress—with patient scorn.

I drained the dregs of our alcohol cabinet from Cointreau to Bailey's to port. I polished off the staples: half-full bottles of gin and rum that had traveled with us from three homes over a decade. I loved my husband as much as I loved my new medicine and did not want to see him worried, so I began to hide multiple drinks not unlike the way I had hidden Her. I would keep one drink out on the counter and another hidden behind the water heater. It never occurred to me that this behavior was alcoholic, just thoughtful.

I would come to learn my increasing obsession with Alcohol is called cross-addiction. In the fall of 2010, it just made good sense. For me, Alcohol was not pushing me closer to total kidney failure, it was smoothing out the ride there.

In those last few months before the transplant, we existed inside a surreal medical limbo. In November, I had not yet been approved for transplantation, and Kevin had yet to be tested. Blood tests, Epogin injections and procedures anchored us to Cedars. She was the mother ship around which everything in our life orbited. We existed inside suspended time, something Unnamed ticking in the air. We could hear it, the way IV droplets echo inside a hospital room. They do not actually make a sound, but your life is consumed by its ominous metronome beat.

· · ·

FRIDAY NOVEMBER 19TH, 2010. 139 days pre-transplant.

JUST UNDER SIX months after my Fiorinal overdose, Kevin and I attended a half-day event at Cedars' Comprehensive Transplant Clinic. The day's objective was to determine whether or not I was medically fit to be listed for a kidney transplant. It began with a group PowerPoint presentation on types of dialysis and estimated wait times for cadaver vs. living donor transplants.

"Are you OK?" he whispered, as I rubbed my eyes.

"No." I whispered back, as the fluorescents flickered back on. Estimated wait times for second-time kidney transplant patients, because of potential antibodies developed towards their first kidney was 7-20 years. Kevin squeezed my hand under the conference table.

"I will be your match."

The transplant coordinator showed us to a tiny room. We each clutched our preferred hit of caffeine: Kevin with his Coke Zero and me with an Earl Grey tea (in lieu of now verboten coffee). One-by-one, I met the potential members of my team—nephrologist, social worker, financial consultant, nutritionist, and surgeon. They whirled in and out the way sitcom characters do—with high energy and plot-twisting questions. Except no one was laughing.

I fidgeted in the hard-backed plastic chair as my first interviewer, the attending nephrologist, opened my big fat file. After a long line of questioning, he glanced down, and then cleared his throat.

"So. This suicide attempt. What was that all about?"

My heart skipped a beat. Kevin's eyes met mine. It had not occurred to me that they would bring this up. Once again, I would have to lie about the events of Monday June 7th. I swallowed lightly, feeling Kevin's body tense. He too, understood the significance of my answer. I still believed calling it a "suicide attempt" was an overreaction, but this doctor didn't. So I pulled out all the tricks: Unblinking eyes. Unwavering voice. Finally, I had a use for my acting abilities in LA, except this performance would not win me an Academy Award, but rather a kidney.

"I was really struggling with migraines. Now I treat them with a non-narcotic regimen. I would do anything for a new lease on life." I folded my hands in my lap, proud of that last statement. "A new lease on life" is mantra in the world of organ transplantation.

"OK. Good enough." The doctor smiled and closed the file. I smiled back.

I passed the test that day, and was medically approved for a transplant. I was unsurprised. I never believed I would be denied. Was I cleared because of the money Cedars makes on a transplant? Or maybe something nagged at them the way it nagged at me. That no one was willing to deny me a transplant because of something they couldn't quite put their finger on.

SUNDAY NOVEMBER 28TH, 2010. 130 days pre-transplant.

KEVIN and I were sitting beneath a trellis threaded with wine grapes. The flirtatious afternoon sun darted behind the odd cloud, cooling the air for me to reach for my sweater, only to emerge again beaming with warmth.

We were at the Kendall Jackson Wine Center in Central California. Visiting a winery was on my California bucket list, up there with spotting dolphins in Big Sur and visiting Hearst castle. We had combined this Santa Rosa trip with a wedding Kevin had shot the day before.

We had been pulling into the winery, when I received a call from Social Services Disability. Unable to get service inside our car, I'd paced in the leafy shadows of an old knotted tree as Kevin stood nearby, ready to help me answer any question. With less than 13% kidney function, I often struggled to remember what day it was, let alone vital financial information. They advised me that on appeal, I had been awarded $830 a month with a back payment of $2300.

We sat alone, waiting for our wine and cheese sampler. The silence was dotted with faint chirping upon a soft wind. Lavender, melon and orange blossom from the sensory garden perfumed the air. My heart bobbed in my chest with the welcome news.

A long cheese platter was placed on the table. Lined in a neat row on another plate were ten mini wine tumblers—five for Kevin and five for me. A sunbeam glinted off one of the glasses like a wink.

"This looks great, sweetheart." I thanked Kevin.

"Which one do you want to try first?" he asked.

His voice was soft, imbued with relief over the award. Our expanding financial burden was like a knapsack my husband strained to carry every day. When I stopped acting in 2008, our monthly health insurance premiums had increased 700%. I had not been able to lift the bag off the floor for the last two years. This money would allow Kevin to set it down and catch his breath. We each chose a glass and raised them high.

"Well, this is good news." Kevin smiled.

We laughed. It was. As we clinked glasses my heart inflated, proud to once again contribute something to our little family of two. My eager lips wrapped around the tiny glass. Tilting my head back, the golden current singed my throat. My insides warmed. Kevin never made me feel less than equal in our marriage. I sipped again.

A voice began to rise inside my head. *You are a loser. You are chronically ill. You are waste of space.* Our monthly health expenses far exceeded this financial award. I was financially benefitting from 13% kidney function with a 67-year old kidney. This was no accomplishment. My stomach flipped. Kevin had not even been tested as my living donor, never mind approved.

My husband reached his hand across the table to grab mine. For a moment, we did not say anything.

"I will be your match, sweetheart."

He couldn't say it enough. With those six words my soul shivered the way it did when he stroked my hair at night as we lay watching mindless sitcoms. I knew the odds of us being a match were slim. Many siblings—considered the best possible fit—are unsuccessful matches, never mind non-related living donors.

The fruity notes tickled my tongue as I took yet another sip. In the dying afternoon light, his features softened. I loved him so much. Today, we were just like any other couple in love on a romantic adventure. I was not collapsed into my chair. My eyes were no longer teeny slits disappeared into the swollen hills that were my cheeks. I knew Kevin had no way of knowing he was a match, but relinquished to the wine and wonder of the kindly shadows, I believed him.

"Aren't you going to finish yours?" I nodded towards his unfinished samples. All five of mine were empty. Kevin had sipped at but two. We were getting on the road soon, and my husband never drank and drove. He couldn't stand it if he had any alcohol in his system. It had the opposite affect for him. He hated not being in control, squirming in his altered skin, when others melted into theirs.

"That one was my favorite." I pointed to the empty glass on the far right. Not a drop glistened in the sun, whereas Kevin's glass stood full, unsmudged by greedy fingerprints.

"I'm good." he insisted.

I tilted my face towards the sun. My head was swimming with relief, our problems floating downstream on this alcoholic river. Pushing the wine on Kevin was my gift to him. *Share in this solution with me.* Alcohol was a gift for me, separating me from the very thing we had sat down to celebrate: I was finally sick enough to be awarded money. I wanted to give Kevin the same gift. After urging him several times in a row, I paused then asked,

"Can I have yours?" When he did not accept my gift, I took it for myself.

TUESDAY NOVEMBER 30TH, 2010. 128 days pre-transplant.

"WHY DID you want to kill yourself?"

What? Still with this?

Two days later, I was at my psychological evaluation. I sat opposite Dr. C., Cedars' transplant psychiatrist.

"I was really struggling with migraines. Now I treat them with a non-narcotic regimen. I would do anything for a new lease on life," I parroted exactly what I had said two weeks earlier at the medical evaluation.

In Canada, they don't psychologically assess transplant candidates, I thought, picking at my jeans, genuinely inconvenienced by the whole affair. I scanned her office from the crookedly drawn blind behind her big doctor desk to the floor-to-ceiling wall of pretentious books. *There's nothing in those books that can tell you anything about me.* Dr. C. leaned back into her fancy armchair, a pad of paper balanced upon her crossed legs. *Why does she get a comfortable chair? She isn't sick.*

I had been wrong about the medical evaluation. This was the performance that would win me a kidney. This woman had the power to expunge "suicide attempt" from my record, or at least override it. I took a sip of water. With each question, I brought out the thoughtful pauses and meaningful head tilts. Then Dr. C. asked me something, the answer to which seemed so obvious it had to be some kind of a trick.

"You've already had one kidney transplant. Why would you want to go through it again?"

My face burned. What kind of question was that? Her unwavering look enraged me. I looked away. Suddenly, I got why everyone kept asking me the same question: *Why did you want to kill yourself?* Everyone believed I had attempted suicide, so why would they list someone who wanted to die? Why would they waste a kidney on me?

My head spun. I had no time to sort out this thinking. She held all the psychological cards. All I knew was that I did not want to die, and I wasn't willing to gamble away a kidney. So I pulled out my emergency quote, and recited Gloria Steinem:

"Even if I'm 90 years old with one eye working, I want to be around to see what's going on." What I really wanted to spit out was, *You try life confined to bed for one week and see how you like it!*

She scribbled something on her pad. I hated her—her gyrating pencil and the deep furrow in her brow. What was she writing? Living with renal failure was different from memorizing highlighted sections in textbooks. Who was she to believe she knew anything about me? Finally, she asked for a current list of my medications.

"I take Xanax three times daily, and sometimes Ambien. But only when it's like 5 am and I still can't sleep." This was all true.

"Yeah, you really need to get off the Xanax." she mumbled, but nothing more. Again, I looked away. Who cared what she thought? She wasn't the one prescribing it to me anyway. *Let's see you suffer from renal failure with no relief,* I thought as I crushed one between my molars in her adjoining bathroom before the long ride home. Did she ask me if I drank? If she had I would have answered the same way I had for my entire medical life: *Just socially.* For that was truly what I believed my nightly vodka-sodas to be.

A few days later, I was approved for a transplant—medically and psychologically. Dr. C.'s final assessment was that the Fiorinal over-dose was a suicide attempt, but that I had my addiction under control. The woman who had taken 120 pills in 2 ½ days was considered psychologically sound. On January 3rd, 2011, I received a letter stating I had been added to the Cedars-Sinai transplant registry and UNOS (United Network of Organ Sharing).

Dr. C.'s hand had been stronger, but I had won the game after all.

SUNDAY DECEMBER 5TH, 2010. 123 days pre-transplant.

SLUMPED AGAINST THE PASSENGER SEAT, I stared at my chauffeur husband. My energy level had now deteriorated from exhausted to uncharted. Rarely did I drive. Rolling my head to the side, I took in the flickering lights as we zoomed along. U2 came over the airwaves, and I sighed. Kevin reached for my kneecap. Only three years earlier, I had seen U2 ten times on their *Vertigo* tour.

"Did you know Bono had back surgery in May?" I asked.

"Maybe he broke his back carrying all his money around."

I burst into giggles. Kevin knew about my major Bono crush. It felt good to laugh, and to be out.

Yet, as the car clicked away the fifteen-minute drive, I found myself fantasizing about slipping back into bed. Even though once there, I'd squirm all night in skin-crawling discomfort. As we pulled into Burbank's Target, the neon-red letters beamed its homage to regular life.

"Here. You push the cart." Kevin winked.

I meandered down the main aisle, grateful for the rolling walker. Kevin whirled in and around the offshoot aisles tossing items into our cart with casual energy. My shoulders softened as I watched other shoppers do the same. The cart anchored me inside this swirling sea of normalcy.

"Woo-hoo! Woo-hoo!"

I turned around at the curious, glottal stop disco beat coming from my husband. Kevin was strutting towards me sporting an effeminate multi-colored designer jacket, one arm on his hip. For the man whose daily uniform consisted of plaid shirts and jeans, he looked ridiculous. I burst into loud laughter. For a moment, I felt the turning of the heads toward us. Then they all disappeared, and everything was Kevin. Unable to stop giggling, I began to hack, my stomach cramping in protest. Then I burst into tears.

Kevin pulled me into his chest—a huge move for a man who breaks out into a rash at public displays of affection. Then he whispered those three little words that every woman in chronic kidney transplant rejection longs to hear.

"Let's go home." He wiped a tear from my face.

Once home, Kevin dumped the four Target bags on the kitchen counter. It might as well have been forty.

"I'm just going to sit down for a minute," I said.

Kevin went into his office to work. I collapsed into the living room recliner, my breath coming in shallow bursts. I pictured yanking the chair's lever so the footstool section would pop out and I could stretch out my legs, but the idea of reaching down felt akin to a five-mile run I used to conquer with ease.

Across the room, our overstuffed chair was submerged in rumpled sheets, jeans and underwear. The unfolded laundry stared at me. I stared back. The mound seemed to taunt me, the OCD freak, with its casual disarray. *C'mon. Fold us.*

I sank further into immobility with every passing second, as if cement was setting in my bones. On his way to the bathroom, Kevin crossed between the laundry-laden chair and me. We said nothing, but he saw. It was the way he noticed everything—with a barely discernible flick of the eye and a brain catalog that would, more often than not, translate into some later action. We no longer needed words. Kevin knew I wanted to fold that pile of laundry but could not get up.

An hour later, I was sitting with a vodka-soda next to my laptop. Invigorated by my nightly medicine, I was detailing our Adventure in Targetland for my blog: *Hey, Buddy, Can You Spare a Kidney?* (After my 2008 diagnosis, Kevin had set up me up on Blogger and instructed me to: *Write about it.*)

My fingers danced upon the keyboard. The bobbing cubes tickled my lips as I sipped. Suddenly, pinpricks of discomfort shot up from my feet through my calves. Twisting my head beneath the table, I saw my ankles had burgeoned into four fleshy sections, not unlike the Michelin Man. They looked like they belonged to a dangerously obese person, the kind who struggles to walk. A cold sweat broke out on the back of my neck.

My symptoms were endlessly fascinating to me. The random bruise no longer impressed. ESRF had pummeled me with so many blue-black markings I played connect-the-bruises. My nails had always broken off because of my immunosuppressives, but now they no longer grew at all. This gradual battering of my body was happening over time, but this blow right before my eyes. This was proof. I was dying. I took a huge gulp of my drink.

"Look how bad my swelling is." We were bent over, staring at my ankles.

"I think it might be the alcohol."

"Kevin. My creatinine is 4." A 4 creatinine translates to 12% kidney function.

My husband looked at me for a brief second, and then returned to his office. I snapped a photo of my eerily distorted ankle planning to post it on my blog with a caption like, *13% kidney function!* or *This is renal failure!*

I knew part of the reason my ankle was swelling up was Alcohol, but I didn't care. I considered being as open about my drinking online as I had been about my Fiorinal overdose until I remembered the last time I had been honest about my salvation, it had been taken from me. And besides, the kidney was shot anyway.

A few minutes later, along the short walk to the bathroom, I noticed the pile of laundry had been folded. I burst into tears once more, grateful to my husband for this small kindness, but even more grateful he had not called my bluff.

THURSDAY DECEMBER 23ʳᵈ, 2010. 105 days pre-transplant.

THE FOLLOWING IS an excerpt from my blog.
so, this is christmas.

COME. TAKE *my hand. let's spend a day together...*

having always been night owls, lights are out around 2 am. so i rub my legs together for a while (restless leg syndrome), toss and turn (insomnia), read and finally pass out around 4 am. i wake around 7 am to pee (attempt at urination / edema) and find i can't get back to sleep (anxiety). this is when i hit up facebook and suddenly i'm dead to the world. (turns out i don't care what you had for dinner). rise and shine after my requisite 10-12 hours of sleep (fatigue) around 2 pm. thank god, for our teeny 1100 square foot house, as i barely negotiate the downing of 19 medications (nausea) from drawer to fridge. now, we make the most delicate of decisions. remain in pajama pants or slip on kevin's old clothes (edema)? i usually go for the former. forgoing coffee for herbal tea (hypertension), i volley between washing my hair or doing the dishes (exhaustion). dare i try both? forget to eat (no appetite). the day passes into night. sometimes i sprawl lifeless in the passenger seat, as kevin quietly swoops in and magnificently shepherds our life. and sometimes i just lie in bed and play connect the dots (bruising). time for a bath and attempt at relaxation (headache). then it's a final game of "to ambien or not to ambien?" as i stomp out a charleyhorse (muscle cramping), tape up my fingers with band aids and antibiotics (changes in nails) and scratch my skin within an inch of its life (pruritus/itching).

JANUARY 20TH, 2011. 77 days pre-transplant.

SOMEONE WAS STROKING MY HAIR. Then gently shaking my shoulder. Over the whir of my fan, I made out Kevin's voice calling *Sweetheart* from a faraway land. I cranked open my eyes to see my husband's face beaming over mine.

"We are a match."

He bent over me, his lips meeting mine with the gentlest of brushes. My heart ballooned. I reached up to touch a cheek vibrating with joy.

Camera in hand, he said, "I have to go back to work. " Then, like magic, his apparition vanished. I turned over, my skin warming with the realization that I was not surprised.

I drifted back to sleep and to the first moment we met. We were standing outside his basement bedroom. Kevin was just 18 years old. I was 23. Sinking into one hip, I scanned his face from his shaggy blond hair to the endearing smattering of pimples on his chin. I ran my fingers through my long red mane—a lioness primping for attack.

"So, when's your birthday?"

As it popped out of my mouth, I was baffled. I never asked people this question, did not ascribe meaning to dates, names or astrology. If I had paid attention to our signs I would have bolted. Kevin is an Aquarius: honest, intelligent, inquisitive and spontaneous. I am a Scorpio: jealous, passionate, determined and secretive. In relation-ships an Aquarius-Scorpio match has the lowest survival rate.

Maybe I asked because he was so distractingly gosh-darn cute.

And so young! Not even Ontario's legal drinking age of nineteen. Maybe I wanted to know how long before society would declare him a responsible adult—or at least responsible enough to buy me a drink. Or maybe the twitch between my legs rendered me so nervous I didn't know what else to say.

"January 26th," he said.

I grinned at him, warm all over. This was cool. Goosepimply cool.

"Oh! That's the day I had my kidney transplant!" Kevin's eyes lifted in surprise. "This means we are going to be special friends!" I gushed, and then cringed.

Oh my God. Lame. It was something my pragmatic mother might have suggested I say. What a corny response to this lightning-bolt piece of information I could not yet decipher. It had to mean something—but what?

As I drifted off into another toxic afternoon slumber, I smiled at the memory. Yes, the surprise would have been that we were not a match.

MONDAY FEBRUARY 7TH, 2011. 59 days pre-transplant.

BY FEBRUARY, I clutched a homemade sack of rice and lavender seeds to my stomach 24/7. When nuked, it retained heat for hours at a time. I scratched at my skin constantly. At night, two space heaters and an electric blanket forced Kevin out of our bedroom-turned-sauna and onto the couch, while I, always cold, shivered watching sitcoms long into the night.

I kept my cell phone on silent mode because I didn't want to talk to anyone who wasn't sick—which got me out of talking to everyone. I just didn't have it in me to pretend to care about anyone but myself. But I still checked my messages.

This afternoon, I clicked off the remote and wiped the television coma from my eyes. With a sluggish arm, I reached for my phone. My transplant social worker had called. She had emailed me a form I had to read, sign and fax over. The form stated I would abstain from all illegal drugs, prescription drugs (not prescribed by my doctor), marijuana, alcohol, nicotine, and all over-the-counter medications (e.g. cold medicine) that contain alcohol. By signing, I would agree to random drug testing before and after receiving a transplant. If I tested positive, I would lose my place on the transplant registry and be required to attend to a substance-abuse treatment or relapse-prevention program.

WHAT! Angry tears stung my eyes as I scanned the document. My heart battered against the walls of my chest. Stop drinking? Were they insane?

"KEVIN!" I screamed, bolting out of bed, my swollen feet pounding the short distance to his office. I burst into the room, laptop in hand. Kevin flinched as I waved my computer in front of his face. Nothing, nothing was more important than fixing this.

"Look what they want me to sign!" He stood up and removed the laptop from my hand. I circled him. "I mean, what? I can't have a glass of wine with dinner?"

He looked up from the screen. "Henriette. Let me read this."

I plunked myself down, arms folded across my chest like a petulant child. Whenever Kevin called me Henriette, and not "Sweetheart" or "Mouse," it signaled his discontent which was my signal to back off. Especially when I needed something from him.

"Let me call them," he conceded.

With an audible whoosh, I exhaled. "I mean this makes no sense! What? They can just randomly test me anytime? And rehab! What are they talking about?"

Kevin held up his finger by way of a scolding parent, a firm signal that I needed to shut up. He was now talking to Dr. C. and had stepped away, distancing himself from my combustible state. My brain was whirling. *The last time I checked, alcohol and cigarette smoking were legal! Sugar is poison! Why isn't there an abstinence clause for that?*

Kevin turned around, his expression unreadable. "She wants to talk to you."

"What! Why?" I frowned.

"Henriette. It's your transplant." He passed the phone to me.

Cheeks burning, I scowled at my husband. The way I saw it, any argument concerning drugs and / or alcohol would seem more reasonable coming from my husband. I explained to Dr. C. that my problem had been with Fiorinal only, and it didn't seem fair that they could dictate whether or not I could have a glass of wine with dinner. Back and forth it went, our flaccid game of Frisbee, neither side catching on.

"Honestly, Henriette, we've just never had anyone question this." My chest swelled with pride, as if she had just pinned me with a 1st Prize blue ribbon with the words "ARGUMENTATIVE" emblazoned in gold.

"I guess people don't read it. Everyone has just signed it."

To point out the obvious to a psychiatrist, *If everyone else was jumping off a bridge, would you?* would not serve me. Instead, I tossed the phone back to Kevin. Match point.

My husband walked into the bedroom and closed the door. He knew I had a terrible habit of talking in the background when agitated. I paced the living room, my hands shaking. Kevin would fix this. He always fixed everything. The door cracked open, and my heart flipped. Kevin emerged, tight-lipped, the phone hanging from his hand.

"The form will be amended."

"Thank God. Seriously, what the fuck."

"Uh-huh." Kevin walked back into his office and shut the door.

Every offending word on the form was removed, but for one statement. "I, Henriette Ivanans-McIntyre, will not abuse the use of prescription pain medications or use medications/drugs that are not prescribed or approved by my Cedars-Sinai physician/surgeon."

Kevin's play had been the same as mine, to focus on my problem with Fiorinal, and that it was none of their business if I wanted a glass of wine with dinner. Lumping my struggle with migraines together with other substances was unfair. As I had wagered, hearing this plea from Kevin had somehow swayed Dr. C.

If there was ever an example of Kevin's love for me it was this call, because he had to lie. The man with The Golden Soul had to lie more fluidly than he had ever lied in his life. While reading the form, in a protective flash, Kevin had seen a much bigger picture than the single image I glimpsed of a vodka bottle being removed from the frame of my existence. He knew I was an addict. He knew that when they tested my urine, I would test positive for drugs and/or alcohol. I would be delisted, ordered into a substance-abuse treatment program, and suffer on dialysis for what—months? years?—until relisted.

But Kevin had two sides to play. He was also lying to me, pretending to agree with me—that they had no right to deny a pending kidney transplant recipient, alcohol. He told me later, he believed everything would change when I had a transplant. It was this hope that enabled him to lie to Dr. C., and his wife. If we could just get a kidney, the booze would evaporate and the pills would dissolve from our marriage. By amending the form together, I had secured my right to drink and Kevin had secured my right to a kidney.

In the end, those fuckers never tested me once.

FRIDAY FEBRUARY 18TH, 2011. 48 days pre-transplant.

"THIS IS CEDARS-SINAI." Kevin's transplant coordinator had called. "Congratulations! You have been accepted as Henriette's donor! We are hoping your surgical date will be April 5th, but we won't know for a couple of weeks."

That day, I, too, got a voice mail. "Hi, Henriette. It's Dr. D. Your creatinine is 4.3 (11% kidney function). We have to talk about dialysis. Let me see you next week."

It was official. Renal failure had stormed my shore and D-day was upon me.

For months, Dr. D. had valiantly swept in to my pharmaceutical rescue with tens of pills, but by March 10th, my creatinine was 5.3, or

9% kidney function. I would not be strong enough for surgery without every-other-day cleaning of my bloodstream. Surprising both of us, I blurted out my acquiescence.

"Yes. I want dialysis."

On March 13th, a tube was inserted into my Subclavian Vein (which is located directly underneath your Jugular Vein) in my chest and threaded around the right atrium of my heart, which leads to the blood vessels. The other end of this tube hung down, several inches long, over my right breast. This PermCath was the portal where I would be connected to the dialysis machine, as I had been at 19. On March 14th, I had my "first" dialysis session, 22 years after my "last."

SATURDAY MARCH 26TH, 2011. 12 days pre-transplant.

DESPITE ALL OF Cedars-Sinai's bells and whistles, it turns out there's just no way to dress up a dialysis center. It was an almost mirror image of the Toronto unit I had spent six weeks on before my first transplant. The room held 20 dialysis machines and accompanying beds. The beds are a combination of a hospital bed and dentist's chair, although patients who are too sick to sit up receive treatment on gurneys. The machines' repetitive churning had not changed. It clanged the same ominous mechanical lullaby, hypnotizing patients into a sleep just one breath above death.

Length of dialysis sessions is calculated by: age, gender, weight, height and GFR. In March 2011, I was 42, 5'3" and 53 kg (115 lbs). My dialysis sessions calculated to three hours in length, with a half-hour prep time on either side. By comparison, a 6', 200 lb man would most likely dialyze for four and a half hours. Finally a reason to be grateful for my stunted growth!

On this particular Saturday, when other married couples might have been driving along the Malibu shoreline or relaxing at the movies, Kevin stood across from my machine, studying the nurse as he hooked me up for the sixth time. After just five sessions, my husband had turned pro, identifying what would make me more comfortable throughout my three-hour sentence.

Strategic dressing was key. Today, it was a scoop-neck blouse so the nurse could easily access my PermCath without chance of infection. Changing its dressing was time-consuming and painful—like someone taking half an hour to rip off a Band-Aid. The nurse flushed tubes, input information, and discarded what seemed like innumerable piles of packaging, gauze, needles and plastic. As the pile of hospital waste on the table grew, I shrank into helplessness, unable to look down at the tube springing out of my chest like a giant plastic worm. The raw skin around it throbbed. I tried to ignore the tugging when the nurse connected the final tube, programmed the computer to remove several kg of fluid and then, anti-climactically, pressed, "Start."

My shoulder-length hair was always pulled back: 1) I had no energy to wash it, and 2) so it wouldn't get caught in the tubing. With my braids and swollen face, I didn't look much older than I had at my first dialysis rodeo. I also dressed for the unit's Siberian cold: Thick socks. Skullcap. Several cardigans. Even PermHot Kevin wore a sweater. My hands were clamped around a large cup of tea Kevin had purchased from The Ray Charles Cafeteria, but when there's a dead organ inside of you, there's just no way to warm up.

Dialysis units are kept at low temperatures for the active staff. Patients suffer the brutal cold for two additional reasons: 1) another symptom of renal failure is anemia. My kidney was barely producing the protein EPO necessary to produce hemoglobin, which feeds red blood cells, which provide oxygen, thus energy, and contain iron. Low iron = Shiver me timbers! 2) As my blood passed through the dialyzer (dialysis filter), waste was filtered out and clean blood sent back into my body. When my blood left my veins, it cooled. Before it was returned, a warmed dialysate solution was added to the filter, but sometimes this process was not controlled well and cool blood would slither back into my body, an icy alien creature.

"Are there any more blankets?" my teeth clattered against each other.

Kevin took in the three blankets and parka piled on top of me. "No. That's all we brought."

I studied the machine to my right: its robot-like body, knobby eyes, and flat-screen computer face blinking information about me. It chortled away as my bright-red blood began to swirl through the serpentine tubing. Shivering, I pulled the blankets all the way up to my chin. Perhaps there was a fourth reason I was always so cold—the surreal knowledge that all my polluted blood was leaving my body, and then returned cleaned. I couldn't deny my resentful reverence for dialysis. I understood it was the thing keeping me alive, but hated its emasculating power. I was its bitch.

Glassy-eyed, I stared at the overhead television. Carrie Bradshaw was silently oooh-ing with erotic appreciation over a pair of Manolo Blahniks. I never wore earbuds as the intrusive sound scraped my ears. I never bothered to bring a book. Paragraphs spread out on the page like complex computer code I could no longer decipher. Instead, I dozed inside a toxic restlessness.

Suddenly, a wailing electronic cry filled the unit. Kevin's head whipped up from his phone. A swarm of nurses swooped in, and an oxygen mask landed on my face. My eyes darted around, tracking my husband inside this sudden sea of scrubs. One nurse adjusted the tubing around my ear. Another pushed the table away. A red light flashed in inauspicious time with the feedback-like screech that filled the room.

"Sit very still," the nurse instructed. My eyes bugged, imploring Kevin for information.

"What's going on?" His eyes cycled from me, to the nurse, to the machine, back to me.

"Her pulse is 145. Her BP is 190/121. She needs to sit here for 15 minutes and not move."

Coldness gripped the back of my neck. Chronic illness had overwhelmed and depressed me, but in 29 years as a patient, I had never been terrified. An ideal blood pressure is 118/72. Anything above 130/80 is considered hypertension. At 190/121, I had landed in stroke territory.

Blood pressure measures the force of blood against the walls of your blood vessels. When your kidneys fail, your tissue retains too much fluid (edema), including your vessels, and the kidney's ability to regulate blood pressure is compromised. Your heart pumps harder to compensate, which elevates your blood pressure. In ESRF, excessive fluid becomes life threatening to your other organs. This is why dialysis machines are programmed to remove fluid and clean your blood.

Kevin sent me a small smile. I closed my eyes and breathed in and out through my nose, trying not to picture a blood vessel bursting in my head.

My kidney could no longer clean my blood. My kidney could no longer regulate my blood pressure. My heart was pumping too hard, and I could not, for the next 15 minutes, breathe on my own.

Kevin sat next to me, stroking each finger for equal lengths of time in a kind of meditative trance. Slowly, I turned my head to look at him terrified the oxygen mask might slip off. What did he see? I knew what I saw when I looked in the mirror. My skin was now a chalky yellow. When loose, my hair hung in frayed strands, its strawberry-blond sheen tarnished by medications and stress. My eyes were dimmed by fear. The oxygen mask fogged and defogged with each shallow breath. With my eyes, I tried to communicate to my husband, what I dared not speak from behind the mask. *Thank you.* In that moment, I could see Kevin was a victim of illness too, unable to lay claim to being destroyed by it, but being destroyed by it just the same.

~

LATER THAT AFTERNOON we arrived at Rite Aid. Legs still trembling from my session, all I wanted to do was go home, but Dr. D. had phoned in another prescription, what would be another failed attempt to temper my nausea. To kill time at the pharmacy, we often snapped photos for my blog. My photojournalistic postings included all kinds of medical images: getting my blood drawn, posing with Dr. D. and Kevin and I recording our blood pressure with Rite Aid's public machine. I would caption these photos *Today my BP is lower than hubby's!* or *She gives good veins!* Kevin would grab a cane and role-play Martin Crane from *Frasier*. We craved these laughs created from the black comedy of our circumstances. But today, we were silent, spent from the afternoon's close call.

It is sometimes difficult to spot Kevin's faults. He is loving, but not gushy, loyal, but not demonstrative, and he is always, always on his phone. Morning, noon and night, it went with him everywhere, into the bathroom and beyond. Unlike me, he always had his ringer on, were Cedars to call.

We were loitering at the intersection of Energy Bars and Tampons when it rang. As the conversation devolved into a back-turning situation, Kevin began gesticulating toward the maxi pads. This was not good.

"It's just that Henriette is really sick right now."

Leaning against a wall of vitamins, my freshly cleaned blood drained into my stomach. Oh, God. What now? Kevin had already registered a false positive for opiates back in February when tissue tested. We had endured our own not-so-funny version of the classic *Seinfeld* Poppy Seed episode—when Elaine tests positive for opiates because she has consumed a poppy seed bagel that morning—which, it turned out, was exactly what Kevin had done. (*Kevin! Seriously?*) His transplant evaluation had been postponed for another nightmare week until his blood panel could be cleared.

"So it's not going to change again?" I peeked at his profile. His already pinkish skin flared an angry red.

"Fine." If he could have, Kevin would have slammed down the phone. Instead he delivered, what was for him, a furious goodbye. He turned around to face me. "They changed the date."

"To when?" I held my breath.

Today was March 26th. April 5th was our scheduled date. All we had to do was hold out for twelve more days. I placed my hand on his taut arm. His voice rumbled, "April 8th." I laughed. "Sweetheart. That's only three more days."

It was his clenched jaw, those arms tucked up into his armpits. I was not the only one hurting. Kevin was suffering renal failure right alongside me—from every twitch of my PermCath, to each wave of nausea. Every miserable molecule shaking inside of me was shaking inside of him. This would not be over for him until his kidney was inside of me.

"I'd like to see one of those doctors wait three extra days for their paycheck, never mind a kidney."

I laughed loudly and then soft-shoe shuffled around his rigid frame, poking at him until his arms gave way. His face relaxed into a reluctant smile, as he swept me up into a hug.

"Remember when your phone rang off the hook with auditions? Now we get excited about approval for surgery." For a moment we did not speak.

"I have to stop at Ralph's," I confessed into his chest.

The misconception about dialysis is that it makes you feel better. Dialysis "replaced" my kidneys for as long as I was on the machine, but the second I was disconnected my veins began to fill with toxins. All night and into the next day I would shake, my bloodstream too quickly taken from poisoned to pure. This is the horrible irony of the dialysis experience—not unlike the novice alcohol drinker. One who has not built up a tolerance for alcohol will get sick. I had no tolerance for a clean bloodstream.

When your kidneys can no longer balance minerals, they must be removed from your diet or it can be fatal. High levels of potassium can cause heart failure and spiking phosphorus leads to osteoporosis. My diet consisted pretty much of tomato and mayonnaise on white bread sandwiches. Celery sticks smeared with Philadelphia Cream cheese. Limes. And Corona.

Corona's bubbles helped Alcohol hit my brand-spanking clean blood faster. With those first crisp sips, my nausea vanished. Anxiety softened into waves of calm. Corona transported me from the electrical shocks that shot through my heart all night long. It saved me from startling drops in blood pressure that sent me falling through space even as I lay flat on my bed.

Kevin didn't ask why we had to stop at the grocery store. He knew what was on my stunted list and no longer raised an eyebrow. We had gone to war over pills, but he had lost the desire to battle over booze.

"OK. Last stop Ralph's." He kissed the top of my head.

We were in this illness together. We had amended the abstinence form together. We had endured dialysis together. In twelve days, we would have a transplant. Together.

My husband would give me his kidney, and everything would change.

10. XANAFLEX

pril 2nd, 2011. 6 days pre-transplant.

IT HAD BEEN the longest day. Kevin and I sat through a one-hour briefing on what to expect pre, during and post-transplant. We then peeled off into separate rooms and met with our individual social workers, transplant coordinators, financial consultants, nephrologists and surgeons (me once again, and Kevin for the first time). I endured my third to last session of dialysis. Finally, we picked up his nephrectomy medications, including pain medication, curiously prescribed ahead of time.

During our dual briefing his coordinator confessed, with a perplexed scrunch of her face, that many donors burn through their pain meds before surgery. Seriously? Did she really not understand why that happened? Dispensing pain medication early was just about the most idiotic thing I had ever heard. Then I wondered why I didn't get my pain meds ahead of time.

Back at home, Kevin stashed his prescriptions inside his office cabinet and retreated to the bathroom. For Kevin, it is like a second home. In this man-cave, he spends hours scrolling on his iPhone, squatting in a few inches of neurotically self-restricted water. My husband loves baths so much we spent $265 on a custom-designed spout that allows you to regulate the flow of water from a trickle to a full-on torrent.

In the kitchen, I turned on some music and gulped half a glass of white wine. As I chopped vegetables for a tomato/iceberg lettuce-dialysis-approved salad, I heard water dribbling into the tub. Kevin was descending into his grotto. Taking another nip, I tiptoed across the living room in that stealth-like way I had mastered during the apex of my relationship with Her.

Cracking open his office cabinet door, I scanned the containers he had just put away: Three 10 oz. bottles of Magnesium Citrate, a bottle of Colace (stool softener) prescribed in anticipation of post-surgical constipation, and a bottle of 20 tablets of Tramadol.

The bathwater was still trickling. I lifted the Tramadol. The pills rattled slightly. There was a deep creak and then a click. I froze. Leaning backwards, I peered around the corner. Kevin often made last minute, mad dashes back to his office, streaking naked and wet, to retrieve something like ear buds, or a Coke Zero. All clear. He must have locked the bathroom door. The unsettling click now a reassuring sign he was settled.

Kevin had discovered an allergy to opiates, manifested as migraine headaches and nausea, back in 2009, at age 38, when diagnosed with shingles. Back then he had been prescribed Vicodin, and then Norco for the intense pain, until he voluntarily discontinued their use. When Kevin voiced his "distaste" for opiates, his surgeon's compromise had been the mild-to-moderate synthetic opiate, Tramadol, for his nephrectomy pain.

My heart beat steady. I cracked the lid open, being careful not to shift the pills. I peered inside. The tablets were white and oval-shaped, like rounded-edged diamonds. They looked so familiar. Oh! My brain pinged with joyous recognition. They were almost identical to the non-narcotic muscle relaxer, Xanaflex, Dr. A. had prescribed after my Fiorinal overdose.

Curling my index finger, I slid a single tablet up the side of the container and popped it into my mouth.

Against his cocooning waterfall, I slipped into our bedroom, being careful to avoid the floorboard that creaked. From my bedside table drawer I withdrew one Xanaflex tablet from its bottle. Back in his office, I dropped the tablet into the Tramadol container, and shut the cupboard door.

As I was sweeping discarded lettuce into the garbage can, it hit me. My limbs wilted with pleasure. The seductive elixir of events had me by the balls: An empty stomach sloshing with cold wine, the sparkling pop beat, the intangible pre-transplant magic swirling in the air, and Tramadol. *Hell, yeah.* I was going to swipe the rest.

I wiped my hands, preparing them for a pristine swipe. Head spinning, I tiptoed back towards our bedroom. The more my brain churned with rationalizations, the more my decision made sense. *I mean, what if he notices that one of the tablets is imprinted with a different code? He could go on pillfinder.com and discover it's a Xanaflex. I did not think this through. I have to take them all.*

Opening the drawer again, I palmed 20 tablets of Xanaflex from my prescription bottle. *The doctors prescribed him such a mild pain med. They can't be anticipating he will be in much pain.*

Passing the bathroom, I paused for the sound of splashing. *I'm going to be in the hospital for 4 nights. He's only going to be there for 2. Obviously my pain will be much worse.*

Inside his office, I cracked open the Tramadol bottle and poured out 20 tablets (19 Tramadol and 1 Xanaflex) into the palm of one hand, then silently funneled my 20 Xanaflex into the empty container. Then I turned away, being careful not to let the cupboard door bang shut with a revealing thud. *Xanaflex is a muscle relaxant. He will get some relief from that.*

I swaddled 18 Tramadol and the random Xanaflex (no time to separate!) inside the cleaning cloth in my glasses case, and then stashed that inside my purse. *Kevin doesn't even like pain meds. He barely took any for his shingles. Shingles! More painful than childbirth!*

Slipping a second tablet into my mouth, I returned to the kitchen, drowning any memory of The Great Swipe with my final drops of wine.

~

THURSDAY, April 7th, 2011. 1 day pre-transplant.

ON WEDNESDAY, April 6th, Kevin and I checked into the Ramada Inn on Santa Monica Blvd. in West Hollywood. This motel is a 5-minute drive from Cedars unlike our home, which is always a two-hour+ roundtrip slog. Kim was coming to LA for two weeks to help us. It made no sense to have her navigate the clogged cement arteries of Los Angeles. It also made no sense for Kevin to endure that drive post-nephrectomy. If all went well, he would be discharged after two nights and I, after four. The story was writing itself. My Prince Charming would bestow me with his kidney as Glass Slipper, and in the Ramada Inn as palace, the final chapter of this post-modern fairy-tale would unfold.

It was about 2 pm on Thursday. I had just completed my final session of dialysis. Kevin had consumed two of the three bottles of Magnesium Citrate to clear out his intestines pre-surgery. No longer allowed to eat, he was in the loft bedroom taking a nap before Kim's arrival. In 24 hours, Kevin and I would be post-operative, recuperating from the transplant.

Limbs still trembling from dialysis, I leaned against the bathroom doorway and crunched a couple of Xanax between my molars. Almost ready to join my husband upstairs in a nap, I scanned the room as the lovely bitter taste flooded my mouth.

The simplicity of hotel existence thrilled me. Life slowed to Present tense. For a few glorious hours inside the walls of a hotel room, the Past was erased, the Future of no concern, and Life reduced to us, and whatever bottle lay inside my purse. Even today. Even on the Night Before Transplant.

The room's decor was an L.A. take on your typical Ramada Inn.

The main section of the space was long and narrow: white walls, dark wood and silver accent lights. A chrome banister bordered the open-steps staircase that led up to the loft. Kim would sleep on the pullout bed downstairs.

This modern décor was a radical departure from our cabin's wood floors and infusions of color: from the bedroom's leafy green, to the kitchen's butter-yellow to a glittering gold for the dining room. Yet, our palette had begun to wear on my nerves. The cheaply framed renderings of autumnal glory that hung in our bedroom had been chosen to remind me of better days in my hometown of Toronto. Nourishing shades of pumpkin and squash no longer struck me as Mother Nature "showing off," but trees on the verge of giving up, like the woman whose existence had been reduced to a 7' x 7' mattress. I sighed. This room's sterility felt like a fresh start.

My tongue dug into the corner of my molar, freeing the last crumbles of Xanax. I dug through our suitcase, pulling out a bottle of champagne. (Veuve Clicquot—our wedding champagne.) A bar fridge stood neatly slotted into the space beneath the staircase. We hadn't stocked the fridge with much. There was so little I could eat, and Kevin's last supper had been Wednesday night at 9 pm. There were a handful of energy bars, some apples and a six-pack of Corona. I attempted to slide in the magnum, but the fridge was too short. Grabbing the ice bucket, I embarked upon a return trip to the ice machine. Dumping a mound of cubes into the bathroom sink, I twisted the magnum this way and that, until it stood tall inside its icy mountain.

Returning to the fridge, I cracked open a Corona, chastising myself for not remembering to pick up limes. After a few healthy gulps, my heart powered down, dialysis' intense shocks subsiding. The detox palpitations feeling less like sticking a finger into an electrical socket and more like annoying pinpricks. I added a few Coronas to the bathroom sink.

With tired fists, I rubbed my eyes and began to make my way up the staircase, one hand clutching the chrome railing, the other, just as firmly clutching my beer. With each labored step, Kevin's deep breathing coaxed me forward. My heart expanded. Cinderella making her way up the royal staircase to greet her prince. Like fairy dust, the promise of something new floated in the air.

Setting my Corona down, I leaned over my husband. With my finger, I trailed the smattering of freckles atop his pinkish shoulders, and then scanned the Celtic tattoo of two angry dogs facing each other on his right shoulder. Then I kissed the top of his head, feeling the smooth skin of his baldness transition into a fine carpet of gray fuzz.

"I love you, sweetheart." I murmured.

His eyes barely flickered, so drugged was he by the satisfying heaviness of his nap. I reached for the beer and took another sip before sinking into bed beside him. I wondered if he could smell it on my breath. He said nothing, but shifted.

"I love you, too."

Burying my nose into his back, I wrapped my arms around him. There was nothing bigger than this. I drew him closer to me, driven by a ferocious need to consume him, unaware that I, myself, was being consumed by something neither of us understood.

For three hours we curled together in perfect slumber, already joined by love, and in less than 24 hours, by kidney. Like the Glass Slipper, his kidney would be the perfect fit, and we would find Happily Ever After. At least, inside the four walls of The Ramada Inn with Kevin, Xanax, Corona, and Veuve Clicquot on ice, it felt like we would.

FRIDAY, April 8th, 2011. Transplant Day.

"YOU CAN GO down and see him now." A shriveled woman with the word *Volunteer* embossed on her lab coat stood in front of me in the surgical waiting area. My heart leapt.

Surgeries at Cedars begin at 7 am. An earlier rotation of surgeries had finished, and the volunteer's arrival meant my pre-op bed was now available. Kevin had been brought down an hour earlier. His nephrectomy was scheduled for 9:00 am, and the transplant for 10:00 am.

I plowed through the double doors the way a cowboy struts into a saloon. The hospital was my world. My jam. Concentrated urine, the reek of feces, the tang of splattered blood and the sour stank of vomit. I could identify them all beneath the disinfectant cleanser drifting up in ribbons from the floor. These smells invigorated me the way sea spray tingles your face. In here, I was comfortable, but I knew my husband wasn't. My skin quivered with expectation. For years, Kevin had been helping me. Now it was my turn.

I pumped at the wall sanitizer and rubbed my hands together, scanning the room of fifteen hospital beds. A large computer monitor hung above the nurses' station, identical to the one in the waiting area, not unlike an airport Departures / Arrivals screen. Updated patient information hopped from *Pre-Op* to *Surgery* to *Recovery* columns depending on whether the patient's gurney was rolling toward surgical takeoff, cruising through the OR, or had landed back in the recovery room.

"He's in bed number nine."

The volunteer disappeared into the swarm of scrubs buzzing around the station. The anticipatory din thrummed in my chest. Through the chaos I spotted Bed #9, and Kevin. He sat upright, rigid, almost as if he was afraid to move. His electrified eyes darted from the nurse at his bedside computer to the screen flashing above me. We locked eyes. My face stretched into a wide grin. His head was covered in a blue surgical cap. A plastic tube wiggled down from the IV pump into his left arm. *Oh, he must have hated that.* His eyes flickered with relief as I approached the bed.

"Here she is," his nurse smiled at me.

"How are you, sweetheart?" I said, leaning in to kiss his lips.

"Better now that you're here."

"Have they given you anything?"

"No."

My blood boiled. Not only was I obsessed with my pain management; I was obsessed with Kevin's.

I was a native of Hospitaland. I understood the language (The Pain Scale). I was comfortable donning the customary garb (The Hospital Gown). I had permanent status. Kevin was just here on a temporary visa. He had not mastered the lay of the land. Like a tour guide, I could show Kevin how to get what he did not even know he wanted. I glanced down at the top of his bandaged hand, its skin flaring red from the recent needle insertion. I pursed my lips, annoyed.

Inserting an IV needle is more painful than a simple blood draw. Kevin would not have known how to breathe in and out through his nose. He would not have understood the delicate timing from the sterilization of the skin, to tying off his arm with a rubber hose, to a needle that sometimes danced a painful hokey pokey before the vein was securely accessed. He would have forgotten that in Hospitaland this ritual is required before gaining access to popular tourist attractions like Morphine and Dilaudid. He did not know that painful seconds could drag on for what seemed like hours, but that it would all be worthwhile.

I frowned at the nurse. "Is he getting a sedative?"

"Yes. We are taking care of that right now."

We didn't speak as the nurse prepared the vial. Kevin wanted quiet when he felt out of control. As the nurse injected Valium into his IV, his body shuddered ever so slightly, and then relaxed against the stiff sheets. I looked into his eyes and smiled.

"Are you scared?"

"A little." His blue eyes shone. "I love you."

"I love you too." I kissed the top of his head one last time, the paper hat scratching my lips. And then they rolled him away.

Don't let anything happen to him. It was not a prayer. It was love. And I sent all of mine with him as the gurney clickity-clacked around the corner and out of sight.

"Now it's your turn, honey."

I laughed, wiping my eyes. "That's right."

I hopped up onto Bed #1, my legs dangling over its side. I wasn't nervous. It was my turn.

When would I get my sedative?

~

As DIFFICULT AS it is to get a kidney, with wait lists from 3-20+ years, the kidney transplant is not considered a complicated operation.

In the mid-90's, surgeons began to remove donor kidneys laparoscopically. Kevin's nephrectomy was conducted through four small incisions in his abdomen. Narrow surgical instruments and a laparoscope (a long, thin tube with a camera at the end) were inserted. His blood vessels were tied up and the kidney freed. A short incision, just over three inches long, was made above his pubic bone—the same place as a C-section, only shorter. This location causes the least pain of any position, heals extremely well and gives a good cosmetic result.

Then Kevin's surgeon simply put his hand into the abdominal opening and removed the kidney. After it was flushed and placed in a pan, the kidney was walked through an adjoining door into my OR. An incision on the right-hand side of my abdomen had just been created—a mirror image of the one on my left for my Mum's kidney.

The second Kevin's kidney was placed into my abdomen and attached to my ureter (a long duct that passes urine from the kidney to the bladder) urine sprayed everywhere. Peeing on the table is not a bad thing. It is the messy, miraculous thing you want. *She peed on the table!* My new kidney was a urinary rock star.

SATURDAY, April 9th, 2011. 1 day post-transplant.

FOR THE FIRST 24 hours post-surgery, I was profoundly susceptible to infection and kept in isolation. Every time a doctor or nurse entered my room they had to wear a mask, gown and gloves they would strip off upon exiting, and toss into the medical waste bin stationed right outside my door. Post-op, I had an allergic reaction to the antibiotic Clindamycin administered intravenously to ward off infection. Long into that first night I scratched, my skin aflame, but this was like a light breeze compared to the maelstrom Kevin endured.

Kevin's catheter had not fit easily when inserted, and it had been forced. No one was ever upfront about what really happened, but we later deduced that they should have immediately tried a thinner catheter. This mistake explained why the first thing Kevin said to Kim in recovery was, *My penis hurts* followed by, *How's Henriette?*

When the catheter was withdrawn in his room, his penis was so irritated he simply could not urinate. His nurse inserted a second catheter, waited a few hours to see if my poor husband could pee, and when he could not, withdrew it. He suffered through five catheters in two days. Another nurse tried to reinsert a catheter multiple times in one sitting, and then dropped it crying out, *I don't know what to do!* My husband was caught inside a horrific medical Catch-22. He would not be released until he urinated, but with each new catheter, his penis, ureter and bladder became so inflamed, this became nearly impossible.

Later that first day, Kim wheeled Kevin down from *The Elizabeth Taylor Suite* on the 8th floor into mine two floors down. (This room is assigned to all living donors as a compensatory gesture, along with a kidney-shaped pillow autographed by his transplant team.) She stood behind his wheelchair, eyes crinkling with joy from behind a mask. My husband looked pale, his body stock-still, self-paralyzed against the pain.

"Are you in pain now?" I growled.

"Yes," he mumbled from behind his mask. His penile predicament made me want to punch someone.

"Sweetheart! Ask for drugs. They will help you."

"I have to go. I just wanted to see you," as he slumped over said pillow.

"Tell them!" I insisted.

All he had to do was pick up his bedside remote and call the toll-free number. Ask and he would receive the pain-free Hospitaland experience. As Kim wheeled him away, I barked *Make sure they give him something!* Then I turned over and squeezed the PCA Hydromorphone IV pump that released a dose of bliss into my bloodstream every nine minutes. Blotting out my physical pain and the worry that two floors above me, Kevin was suffering through his. I did not understand his resistance. Why? Why would anyone choose to suffer through pain?

TUESDAY, April 12th, 2011. 4 days post-transplant.

"WE'RE GOING to send you home with Percocet."

Two residents stood at the end of my bed preparing me for discharge. My creatinine was spectacular: 0.9. Did I feel ready to go home? Nope. Not if I was going to be in pain.

For two days post-surgery, I had been on that Dilaudid pump, and then switched to Percocet tablets (Oxycodone 5 mg and Acetaminophen 325 mg). My eyes flickered between the two doctors. Here in the hospital, my pain had been managed perfectly: I never hurt or felt high. What about when I was home and moving around? Would one Percocet be enough? What if I tolerated six pills the way someone else tolerated one?

These doctors didn't know my secret: That I had been taking Tylenol 1 with Codeine every day since 1988, and that I had abused Fiorinal for years. Even I no longer knew where the watermark of my pain tolerance level hovered. I gnawed on a cuticle. Pain medication abuse karma was coming around to bite me in the ass.

"What about when the Percocet is wearing off?" I asked. My heart flipped. This brazen query surprised even me. One of the doctors scrunched his brow.

Percocet is taken *1 to 2 tablets every 4 to 6 hours* because it contains acetaminophen, which in excess is toxic to the liver. The doctors felt Percocet 5 mg would be safe and enough to control my pain until the next dose. I was not concerned with enough. I was concerned with more. The brow-crunching doctor was tilting his head at me. I directed my attention to the other. Undeterred by anyone thinking I might be trying to score, just moving on to the next person until I did. This doc nodded, willing to throw me a narcotic bone.

"Sure. We can prescribe you some Dilaudid for in between doses of Percocet." Dilaudid does not contain any acetaminophen.

My soul soared. Not for my impending release into the world with my new kidney. Not for my reunion with my savior husband. I had scored two different Class 2 narcotics. The only level stronger than Class 2 is Class 1 and the only opiate in that category is heroin.

~

KEVIN DID EVENTUALLY PEE, and had been discharged back to the Ramada Inn two days earlier. As soon as I got to the motel, brother and sister went to pick up some of my once verboten foods: nuts, cheese, and pumpernickel bread. I opened the bar fridge. My mouth watered, not in anticipation of the delicious items being purchased for me, but at the sight of a Corona. Had Kim had one or two? Not that I cared—you can always buy more alcohol—but I didn't remember drinking five before the transplant.

I cracked the bottle open, savoring the sigh that follows the quick twist of its cap. The bubbles scraped my throat as I gulped several times. With a satisfying pop, I suctioned the glass from my lips and sighed.

Wandering into the bathroom, I peered into the mirror. My eyes sparkled. My skin was restored to its peachy glow. Gone was the jaundiced shade that not even makeup could cover. Although I was on 10 mg of moonface-inducing Prednisone, my face looked almost sculpted. I appeared reborn.

Squatting on the toilet I peed easily, no longer running the tap for countless minutes to trigger my body into squeezing out a few drops. From the way my jeans hung from my hips, excess fluid was no longer loitering around. Life with edema had been a punishing costume I had been consigned to wear by the Luck of the Draw. Today, my flesh lay comfortably against my bones.

Muscles softening, I glided into the living area, restless, craving something I couldn't name. Eyeballing the near-empty bottle I mused, *I wish I had more.* Inside a large brown bag on the desk were my new medications and an Adult Transplant Wellness Kit—a thick brochure outlining Everything You Always Wanted To Know About Kidney Transplants But Were Afraid To Ask.

I couldn't have our basset hound, Maggie May on the bed for a month post-surgery, swim for six months or eat raw sushi for a year. I was banned from picking up dog poop for life. My PermCath would continue to dangle from my chest for another month, while my ureter stent would protrude from my vagina in case the kidney rejected and I stopped urinating. These temporary science fiction-esque appendages were eerie reminders that no transplant is fool-proof. Dialysis lay in wait for me—that computerized monster ready to siphon my blood, gargle it around in its metallic mouth and spit it back out into my bloodstream.

Prying open the paper handle, I pulled out 13 medications—five familiar and eight new. Now that my kidney was up and running, most of the 23 medications prescribed during my final days had been discontinued.

The Old-Timers, my immunosuppressives, remained, but at increased dosages: Cyclosporine, Cell Cept, and once again, Pred-nisone (I had not been on Prednisone for nine years). Added to the roster were the following Newcomers: 1) Omeprazole (for upper gastrointestinal complications post-transplant). 2) Sulfa (an antibiotic taken for one year to prevent pneumonia). 3) Acyclovir (an anti-viral taken for six months to prevent herpes-like viruses). 4) Flagyl (another antibiotic taken for three months to prevent infection). 5) Nystatin (an anti-fungal swish-and-swallow liquid). 6) Colace (a laxa-tive prescribed for constipation post-surgery), and 7) Phos-Nak (dis-solvable tablets prescribed to balance my phosphorous). For a short period of time, the kidney ironically works too well at removing phosphorous, depleting the body of this important mineral and it must be supplemented back into the bloodstream.

Then I pulled out the Dependables: Xanax and Ambien. They had not been ostracized from the pack because of new blood. My heart fluttered, grateful to see them standing tall next to The Old-Timers on the dark wood stage of the desk. I plunged my arm one last time into the bag and extracted two containers: The Breakout Stars: Percocet and Dilaudid. I could not think of a better way to break in a new kidney than with a cold one chased by a couple of opiates.

Corona streamed through my crystalline bloodstream. I was revived, like a withered plant come back to life after the neglect of dehydration and dark nights, but I wanted more.

I cracked opened the Percocet and a single pill tumbled into my palm. With a hearty swig, I swished it down. Then I held the thin container of Dilaudid up to the light. Only 12 tablets at the lowest dose—2 mg—but man, had I scored. I rolled out one of the tablets and stared at the tiny pill, fascinated. One powerful speck of white. Rumor had it the smaller the opiate pill, the more punch it packed. *Here's hoping.* Pinching the pill in between my forefinger and thumb, I placed it inside my mouth. Then I guzzled the rest of the beer down.

Transplant patients are told to drink in strict moderation. Alcohol affects the body's ability to absorb immunosuppressives. New transplant patients are not supposed to drink at all. I was not supposed to take the two opiates together, especially with alcohol, yet the potential of this combustible combination—Corona, Percocet and Dilaudid on an empty stomach spoke louder to me than any medical anecdote.

It's just one beer. You're taking them as prescribed.

Yet, I knew enough to hide the finished beer. Clutching the bottle, I twisted this way and that. *Should I hide it in my suitcase?* No. Better to leave the evidence at the scene of the crime. What if the bottle broke? How would I explain the alcohol-splattered shards of glass in my clothes? *I should hide it down by the ice machine.* Too risky. What if I ran into them in the hallway before I hit the vending area? There would be no explaining away the empty bottle of beer in my hand.

The solution had to be hiding it in plain sight. The bathroom garbage can. I placed the bottle inside the empty container, and then crumpled long reams of toilet paper, piling it on top of the bottle. Not my best work, but I was pressed for time. Why would Kevin think to look inside a garbage can for anything?

Endless, euphoric waves lapped upon the pristine shores of my bloodstream. I really did feel like Cinderella. My Prince Charming had come to my rescue, restoring me to good health with his kidney as the Glass Slipper, unchaining me from a life of illness. My thoughts drifted through the perfection of this moment: Opiates on the desk, a new kidney in my abdomen, cheese and nuts on their way and a final night in a hotel. It was storybook perfect.

I stepped away from the bathroom not a moment too soon. The door buzzed and then clicked open. Kevin and Kim entered with two brown bags full of food. Kim placed them in front of the bar fridge underneath the stairs.

"Hi, guys! Whad'ya get?" Did the lilt of my voice land a titch too sharp, ringing discordant in Kevin's ears? He whirled around to look at me. My blood iced over. Dropping to his knees, he stuck his head deep inside the fridge. "Did you have a beer?"

"No." My mouth went dry. Denial is always the first line of defense. Maybe they will surrender and you will not have to go to war.

"There was one beer left." Kevin was not backing down.

My heart dropped. Fuck. "Maybe the maid took it?"

Weak. I knew my answer was lame the second it clunked from my mouth, but I couldn't think fast enough. Kevin stormed into the bathroom. Kim and I did not move. Two seconds later, he emerged holding the bottle with a satisfied mass of bubbles at the bottom. With one look he had cracked my unsophisticated strategy. I felt a shiver go through me. This was new. He had called my bluff.

"Yeah, so, I had a beer."

His voice shook. "I can't believe you did that. You're on pain meds."

My chest tightened. This was starting to feel ridiculous. It was one fucking beer. Kim, the chattiest person in the world was silent, two expressionless dots for eyes. Kevin looked like he might throw the bottle into my face. What was flaring in his eyes—Disgust? Hatred? I was not sticking around to find out. If I succumbed to my annoyance, I would lose this new and improved high. That was not happening.

Like Cinderella in reverse, I fled up the stairs and away from my Prince. For a few minutes, my heart ricocheted in triple time, anticipating Kevin's arrival and the harsh words that would fly. But for the first time in our marriage, my husband did not follow me. Relieved, I stretched long on the bed. I did not know how to fight with the man downstairs, eyes blazing with something darkly unfamiliar.

Over the next hour, I ignored the murmurings floating up the stairs. Finally, I began to hear the steady plod of Kevin's footsteps. Before he reached the top, I curled in toward the mirrored wall. He lay down on the bed, turning his body away from mine.

My husband and I are affectionate partners, but independent sleepers. When it comes to shuteye we peel off one another and retreat to our separate corners, but this distance felt deliberate. Unlike The Night Before Transplant when we had curled together, two halves of a whole, we now lay with our backs to each other, two fragments of the blissful union that had existed only a week earlier.

"Are you mad?" I asked.

Kevin paused. "No. I'm just in pain. The Tramadol isn't working very well."

My stomach lurched. His "Tramadol" was my "Xanaflex", but his urologist had prescribed Tylenol 3 (acetaminophen and codeine) because of his catheter ordeal. "Did you take a Tylenol 3?"

"Yes," he answered. I paused.

"Do you want a Percocet?" I held my breath. *Please say no. Please say no. Please say no.* "No." My body shuddered, relieved. I had been almost certain Kevin would decline my magnanimous offer, but pain can be one hell of a motivator. He had Xanaflex. He had Tylenol 3. He had declined my Percocet. *It's his fault if he's in pain.* Any weak flame of guilt I possessed, extinguished.

Kevin spooned one of the pillows the way he often held me. "I'm going to take a nap."

"OK."

Somehow I had dodged the accountability bullet. Kevin had taken aim at me over one beer, but did not want to resume firing. He succumbed to a nap, whereas I fought it, this elixir too delicious to sacrifice to sleep. I let the narcotic tsunami-like wave pull me under, far, far away from the husband who had caught me post-guzzle—one beer to celebrate!—and reacted like it had been so much more.

Nothing mattered in this painless state. I was now stationed at the far end of The Pain Spectrum at Euphoria. Inside my happy haze, it was impossible to worry about The Future, and whether or not Kevin and I would discuss The Beer. It was impossible to reflect on The Past. What was done was done. What was stolen was stolen. I had tried to help. I had.

I turned towards my husband and gazed at the tight arch of his back. *He is sleeping. He must be comfortable.* My heart sat heavy in my chest. I thought about Percocet and Dilaudid on the desk and wished I had brought them upstairs. Did Prince Charming ever need a time out from Cinderella after Happily Ever After? This was just a blip. He would get over it.

He always did.

11. PROGRAF

T uesday, April 15th, 2011. 8 days post-transplant.

SOUR CHUNKS of vomit swirled in the toilet beneath me. I scanned the water one last time for a glimpse of white. Spitting, I frowned. *Shit. I lost a Percocet.* Wiping cold beads of sweat from my neck, I returned to the kitchen where Kevin and Kim were preparing dinner. The end of the counter where I had left my drink was empty.

"Where's my beer?"

"I threw it out," he answered, tapered eyes daring me to challenge him. Suddenly, after washing down my evening dose of antibiotics and Percocet with a cold Corona, my stomach had lurched in that undeniable way. I glared at him. *Say nothing.* Arguing wouldn't bring back my Percocet, and well, there was always more beer.

Into June, I passed the one-month mark with but one blip. Transplanted kidneys almost always reject in the first month (as had been my case in 1988). On May 13th, a renal ultrasound ruled out what appeared to be swelling of the kidney, but was nothing. I was urinating. My blood pressure was phenomenal, even without medication.

My immunosuppressives, Cell Cept, Prednisone, and notably Cyclosporine, were working well.

Initially, the doctors had been resistant to prescribing Cyclosporine. It is an old school immunosuppressive, first discovered in 1970, and approved by the FDA in 1983. From Minute One 1988, I took Cyclosporine. From its liquid form inception—droplets added to water—to the gelatin capsule of today. On Cyclosporine, my side effects are almost non-existent. Todays transplant doctors rule with Prograf (Tacrolimus). It is the Queen of all immunosuppressives because it is less nephrotoxic than Cyclosporine. I cannot tolerate Prograf. If Cyclosporine was like my little buddy, Prograf was the playground bully who beat me up.

When I went into rejection in 2008, Dr. D. switched me from Cyclosporine to Prograf hoping to prolong my kidney's life. Prograf's side effects had been instant and crippling: migraines, back pain, diarrhea, insomnia, tingling of the hands and feet, loss of appetite (although with my latent anorexic tendencies, this was one side effect I could get behind) and hand tremors so intense I had been unable to sign my name without holding one hand steady with the other. It is noteworthy that I noticed this while signing for a prescription.

How could this drug be the Queen of Immunosuppression? It had to be The Joker, because the joke was on me. After a month, I called Dr. D., desperate, and he discontinued Prograf. Doing this may have shortened the life of that kidney, but we were unwilling to relinquish my quality of life.

In 2011, I butted heads with top transplant physician, Dr. J. a week before surgery when he outlined Prograf as my primary immunosuppressive. I freaked out, insisting, no way. They could put it on the list, but I was never swallowing it again. Cyclosporine was the only option. I had been right. By June 2011, two-months post-transplant, my kidney was functioning perfectly.

I did have pain. Slicing pain in my very red, nine-inch long incision. This pain was unlike the occasional straining of my 1988 transplant scar, that sensation like a pulled muscle all the way down to my groin. (Canadian Dr. C. had long ago explained that unless these troubling twitches were accompanied by a fever—a sign that elevated white blood cells are fighting an infection and can potentially attack the kidney—these chronic spasms are just an unfortunate side effect of major surgery.) This pain scared me, because I actually needed drugs.

After my April 12th discharge, I took Percocet exactly as prescribed, terrified of running out. On April 22nd, I asked for a refill and was met with raised eyebrows and the curious, *Don't you have a stash somewhere?* My skin had bristled. *Why would I have a stash?* My clipped answer had been, *I took them exactly as prescribed.* Thankfully, my surgeon said he was willing to give me the benefit of the doubt and prescribed another 90 tablets. Back at transplant clinic on May 13th, I insisted I still had pain, but was downgraded to Vicodin. I pocketed the script with more than a vague awareness of an encroaching expiration date on my refills.

My resolve to ask for more drugs had been strengthened by a rare phone conversation with my mother a couple weeks post-surgery. After I confessed to incisional pain, she reminded me I had sustained discomfort for months after my first transplant. Conveniently forgetting that in 1988, I'd never needed anything stronger than Codeine.

FRIDAY, June 10th, 2011. 63 days post-transplant.

I WAS SITTING opposite my least favorite of Cedars' four transplant physicians, Dr. V. In 2008, when Dr. D. switched me to Prograf post-diagnosis, Dr. V. had wanted me to participate in some Prograf trial. I had declined. When he pressed me as to why, he seemed unsatisfied with my answer: Prograf's side effects rendered me bedridden, long before renal failure ever did.

"If you are still experiencing incisional pain, I am going to have to refer you to The Pain Center." He turned to the computer.

I shifted in my seat. Did his eyes narrow? Was it because I had declined to participate in his trial? Was I being paranoid?

If the transplant clinic was not comfortable prescribing me more pain medication, their experiential belief must be I no longer needed them. But I was sure I had pain! Mum had assured me it was possible. For two months post-transplant, this squeaky wheel got the grease, and now Dr. V. was telling me they were fresh out of narcotic oil. My head whirled, scrambling for a play as he scribbled down the name of a referring pain management physician. I bit my lip. I couldn't leave here without drugs.

"Until I get in to The Pain Center, would you be comfortable prescribing Tramadol?"

His face softened with relief. That he could do. This synthetic opiate confuses some doctors. Tramadol doesn't qualify as a real narcotic in their books, like if its synthetic it's not as addictive or something. Thank God Dr. V. was one of The Confused. Once more, I had been downgraded, but narcotic beggars can't be choosers. At least I had drugs until I got into The Pain Center. My future lay within its title. Where there is pain, there must be pain medication. This had to end well.

All I had to do was say I was a recent transplant recipient in significant pain and miraculously a spot opened up that afternoon. First, the newly acquainted Dr. F. prescribed me a Lidoderm patch—a 4" x 5.5" paper patch with a sticky back you peel off and place over the incision. This patch releases anesthetic into the flesh for up to twelve hours, stopping the nerves from transmitting painful signals to the brain. It was perfect! With this patch, I would totally look the part. No one would question my need for drugs now. Then she prescribed me Vicodin. Ah, sweet validation! As the scribble of her pen danced in my ears, my shoulders softened. Dr. F. explained I might sustain incisional pain for six months post-transplant, if not a year. I liked her. I saw a future here.

THURSDAY, June 16th, 2011. 69 days post-transplant.

. . .

"HER BLOOD PRESSURE IS 163/112."

It had been The Accidental Reading. Post-dinner, fueled on a few glasses of wine, I had pulled out my blood pressure machine, eager to engage Kevin in an innocent competition: *Who has the lowest BP with one kidney?* I went last, expecting my result to be applause-worthy. Instead, we hushed at my dangerously high numbers.

"Take it again," Kevin insisted. With each try, my BP rocketed higher until I dissolved into tears. At home, I couldn't blame the reading on WCS—White Coat Syndrome: a real condition where a person's blood pressure runs high within a doctor or hospital environment due to nerves. Kevin then called Cedars' on-call transplant physician.

"It is imperative that she come in tomorrow morning."

FRIDAY, June 17th, 2011. 70 days post-transplant.

"THERE ARE three things that could be happening." I sat with Dr. K., my favorite of the four transplant physicians for his compassion. He began to outline the potential reasons why my blood pressure had spiked.

"One. Your immunosuppressives could be raising your blood pressure and we would have to change them." I furrowed my brow. That made no sense. After 23 years on the same medications, why would my blood pressure suddenly spike?

"Two. Your renal artery could be occluded and we would perform an angioplasty (a balloon-like catheter is inserted to widen the blocked artery). Occlusion? That sounded painful. I closed my eyes and scanned my body for pain above and beyond my incision. Nothing. Protectively, I placed my hand over the Lidoderm patch. Such an obstruction had never happened with my first transplant.

"Three. Your kidney is rejecting and we admit you for a biopsy." My blood ran cold. The car door had barely closed before large tears began to roll down my face. I pressed the speed dial for home.

Not one to loll around the rare times he was sick, Kevin resumed work two weeks after his nephrectomy. Post-surgery, he had sustained testicular pain (possibly a pre-existing condition aggravated by the catheter). Understandably, he declined his urologist's investigative recommendation: a camera up his penis. Kevin did not refill his pain medication and picked up his camera instead.

I knew he had to work, but his absence from my appointment felt deliberate. He had always found time before the transplant. On the drive home, I wailed, *Kevin. I can't lose this kidney.* His calm demeanor irritated me. *Henriette. We don't know anything yet.* But I did.

That afternoon I got a phone call. "Your creatinine is 1.3. You might be rejecting. You need to come back on Tuesday."

At Minute One post-transplant, my creatinine had registered at 0.9. For the rest of this kidney's life, 0.9 will be the targeted baseline when striking the perfect balance between underimmunosuppression and overimmunosuppression. The doctors walk a fine line with immunosuppression. If too little medication is prescribed, a lapse in the protection of the kidney can occur, making it susceptible to attack by my immune system. If too much medication is prescribed, I am crippled by these toxic drugs' side effects and even more susceptible to illness.

Dr. K.'s plan was to track my creatinine with three blood draws over a week to establish a trend. If it came down from Friday's 1.3 into a normal range (0.4-1.2), it was unlikely I was rejecting. If it stayed at 1.3, it was concerning. If my creatinine spiked past 1.3, rejection was likely. A creatinine trend is also established because you never want to jump the gun on a biopsy. A biopsy itself can cause rejection.

TUESDAY, June 21st, 2011. 74 days post-transplant.

THE DAY BEGAN with an 8:30 am blood draw, followed by a 9 am vascular renal ultrasound that would rule out whether or not I had an occluded artery.

"The kidney looks wonderful," gushed the ultrasound technician. They saw veins and arteries pulsating with life. I could never make out anything more than a shadowy, pixilated blob. I squinted at the screen, trying to make meaning of this thing inside of me.

"I'm going to turn on the volume," he said. Kevin sent me a smile.

Usually, this was my favorite part. I could trace a finger along my angry scar, or caress my belly's bulge, but the kidney's gurgling cry had always been how I connected to this life-saving oddity. Today, I vaguely channeled a prayer that its voice would sound strangled, suggesting an occluded artery and not rejection.

An alien-esque surging filled the room. *Wa-ooosh. Wa-ooosh.* My stomach dropped. The rhythmic sound was my kidney asserting regulated blood flow. Strike one.

At 10 am, we went to transplant clinic, but with blood results still pending there wasn't much to discuss other than the disappointment/success that was my ultrasound.

At 1:30 pm, Kevin and I met with my beloved nephrologist Dr. D., whom I had not seen since the transplant. As my gurney had been rolled out from the OR, I seized upon a flicker of recognition for the man loitering by the swinging doors. My arm flew up, his flew out, and our hands locked in a triumphant clutch as I rolled onwards towards Recovery.

Now in his office, Dr. D. bent over me, bedecked in his kippah, trimmed gray beard and tailored suit. He palpated my kidney, eyes smiling beneath a furrowed brow. In his familiar hands, I felt safe. I couldn't be rejecting.

"It does look swollen, but I think it's retaining fluid, not rejecting."

If fluid collects around a transplanted kidney (as had been ruled out on May 13th), there can be damage if the pressure is not treated. Dr. D. is a nephrologist, not a transplant physician. Although he knows a lot about transplants, it is not his specialty. The nagging tug at my gut suggested his opinion was prejudiced by our fourteen-year relationship. He had agonized about putting me on dialysis, and when we finally did, confided to Kevin that he was not certain it had been right to defer for so long. I had endured but nine sessions, and he had been at every one. We both wanted him to be right.

As I buttoned up my pants, I thought, *Swelling is a form of pain.* In front of Kevin, I dared not ask for drugs, but filed the idea away. *Maybe appointments are better without Kevin.* A Cedars' trip without my husband would bear more narcotic fruit than one with him.

At 3:30 pm we met with my urologist, Dr. C. After a pelvic exam, we returned to his office and he analyzed the morning's ultrasound.

"My money is on rejection. The kidney looks inflamed. The tissue around it looks fine."

My stomach flipped. This was the opposite of what Dr. D. had said. Kevin squeezed my hand. Strike two.

The phone call came in just as we arrived home. "Your creatinine has spiked from 1.3 to 1.6. See you Friday for repeat blood work."

FRIDAY, June 24th, 2011. 77 days post-transplant.

KEVIN and I were killing time at Cedars' one sit-down restaurant: The Plaza Café. Here you are handed menus and shown to your table like regular people who do not walk around with hospital bracelets as accessories.

We had arrived at 7am for a STAT blood draw. My overnight bag waited underneath the table in case of another creatinine spike, in which case I would be admitted for a renal biopsy. We were to remain at Cedars until one of my transplant coordinators called.

Hollywood is the definitive theme at Cedars. Myriad celebrities are admitted for heart attacks or "exhaustion" (code for drug and alcohol abuse). Yet from my gurney's perspective, the murals of Old Hollywood celebrities like Gable and Monroe had never been glamorous distractions, rather comforting reminders that everyone gets sick. Everyone dies.

"Did you know Jean Harlow died of renal failure?" I gestured at the photograph behind him, a stunning B&W image of the starlet, all pale skin and black blood lips. Kevin turned around, bleary-eyed. "They didn't know her kidneys were failing until the day before she died. They thought she had the flu."

I stirred my oatmeal listlessly. We were exhausted. One of the many things we have in common is a full-throttle hatred of the morning. Yet, more than fatigue hung inside our silence. There just wasn't anything to say until the phone rang. Our lives suspended once again by a pending blood result.

"She was 26." I added. The age I married Kevin.

My phone exploded with its jangling sound. "Your creatinine is 1.4. Go home. We'll do it all again on Monday."

"Do you feel better?" Kevin asked, his eyes sagging. I looked up at the beautiful young actress. Harlow never had a chance. She never had hope. In 1937, there existed no dialysis or transplantation. My doctors were not yet convinced I was rejecting. I still had a chance. Where was my hope?

"Not really." I excused myself.

Inside the bathroom stall around the corner, I poured 3 Xanax into my shaking palm. One pill no longer worked, my body becoming increasingly tolerant of each prescribed dose. I needed more pills to feel less relief. Agitated, I chomped them quickly, coasting back to Kevin on the instant, mellow wave.

Pre-transplant we had spotted hope on the horizon and driven towards it lead-footed, windows down, tunes cranked high, the dream of a healthy life our high-octane gasoline. Today, we were driving on fumes. I had no use for hope. Hope was uncertainty. Hope was limbo. I needed to be buoyed by something, and my anchor came in bottles of all shapes and sizes. I never wondered what anchored my husband.

MONDAY, June 27th, 2011. 80 days post-transplant.

"YOUR CREATININE IS 1.6. You will check in on Thursday for a Friday biopsy."

As with all four of my prior biopsies, a pathologist would examine the extracted sample and explore three scenarios:

1) White blood cells (WBC) were infiltrating the kidney because I was underimmunosuppressed. WBC account for 1% of your blood. They are immunity cells, continually charging through your bloodstream as if at war. They battle viruses, bacteria and other foreign invaders (like a transplanted kidney) that threaten your health. If I did not have enough medication in my bloodstream, the WBC could be taking over.

2) The opposite: A toxic amount of immunosuppressives—notably the more nephrotoxic Cyclosporine—was threatening the kidney. Cyclosporine in the high doses needed to prevent rejection was too toxic for my kidney and compromising its function.

3) Rejection by Antibodies: I had developed antibodies that were attacking Kevin's kidney. Antibodies are proteins formed in the blood that fight specific foreign invaders. If I had developed these, they could be attacking Kevin's kidney.

Before being approved for this second transplant, my blood had been screened for antibodies developed towards Mum's kidney. I had registered low levels, and did not need desensitization treatment. Many second and third transplant recipients become sensitized to their first transplant and need very specific treatment including IVIG (Immunoglobulin).

4) The pathologist would not consider any hypothesis involving drug and alcohol abuse.

FRIDAY, July 1st, 2011. 84 days post-transplant.

AT AGE 25, after dating Kevin for over a year, I told him I had never wanted children and did not expect this to change. My heartfelt disclosure was his open door to move on. Although only 21, Kevin had felt the same way. Over seventeen years, we remained unified on this decision, almost never hearing the call to parental duty.

Instead, Kevin's kidney became like our child. Born inside my Canadian husband, incubated in an American bedpan as it crossed over from his OR into mine, and then birthed inside my abdomen. The child we never wanted, but the one I could not live without. Its name had been obvious—The Kid—short for kidney and long on irony. This day, that single packing, semi-automatic biopsy needle would plunge into our Kid, and there was nothing we could do but watch.

SUNDAY, July 3rd, 2011. 86 days post-transplant.

THE OFFICIAL CAUSE of rejection would be found behind Door #2: a toxic level of Cyclosporine. The swift reaction to this diagnosis was two days of IV pulse steroids, the same treatment administered in 2008 when Mum's kidney went into rejection. Additionally, Dr. J. removed my preferred serving of Cyclosporine as fish fingers and replaced it with Prograf as spinach. *You will take this because I say so!*

Prograf's side effects were as bad as I remembered: immediate and crippling. All weekend I writhed with nausea and migraine. My forehead became stained an artificial blue from overuse of *Icy-Hot*. My singed skin provided a masochistic comfort, a welcome distraction from the debilitating pain, along with my frequent requests for Dilaudid.

"We're going to send you home." Two doctors stared at me from the end of my hospital bed.

"What?" I looked at them in disbelief. How could they discharge me two days post-biopsy? I could barely lift my head.

"Your renal function is beautiful. Your creatinine has come right down." *So?* My lower back throbbed as I struggled to walk, my muscles heavy as sandbags. Dilaudid worked like a thin shawl blithely tossed to shelter me from Prograf's storm.

"What about my pain?"

"Have you ever had Roxicodone?"

My head whirled like a medical Rolodex flipping through the generic and brand name of every pain medication it had ever cataloged. It came up empty, my brain's pathways congested by the pharmaceutical traffic jam of Prograf, Dilaudid et al. I tried to break the word down. The "Codone" part sounded familiar. "Hydrocodone" is the generic name for Vicodin, but "Roxi?" "Roxi" sounded like "Oxy." I knew the "Oxy" prefix indicated a stronger chemical compound than "Hydro." Wait. I scrunched my face. Why did Oxycodone sound so familiar? I had heard about OxyContin, the high-profile drug often compared to heroin in its addictiveness. But, the doctor had said Roxicodone, not Oxycodone or OxyContin. What was the difference? I collapsed against the bed, unable to put the pieces of this narcotic puzzle together.

"I don't think so." The two doctors looked at each other.

"Roxicodone is a different formula from Oxycodone. There is no acetaminophen, so it's safer for your kidney. It's also an immediate-release formula. Take it at the onset of migraine."

Darkness rolled into the room the way a cloud suddenly covers the sun and hijacks the day's mood. Kevin stood silently beside the bed, arms crossed, undeniably livid.

W-w-wait! I wanted to grab at their lab coats as they turned to go. *I'm not ready!* But the doctors' priority was my kidney's function and not the body it lived in. Prograf's side effects were unfortunate, but renally irrelevant. All they could do was schedule a follow up appointment, and throw me a script for narcotics. (It begged the question, how does a patient with a pharmaceutical suicide attempt, and an averted 5150 on her record get prescribed an incredibly powerful painkiller? But no one was asking.)

My hands shook as I pulled on my jeans. "But I'm in pain."

"I know." Kevin's voice sounded far away. "They think you're ready to go home."

I didn't care about my beautiful creatinine. I cared about my pain. The nurse entered with my discharge papers and placed the scripts for Prograf and Roxicodone I my hands. I didn't look at Kevin, unable to deny the flutter in my chest for this untried drug.

"The hospital pharmacy is closed early because of the holiday weekend. It might be hard getting these filled today."

My husband was standing beside me, but I could not feel him. Could not sense the gentle sweep of his eyes over my body. Could not smell his sweet pine scent that invigorated me when hospital life choked my pores. It was like the soul of him had withdrawn, as if I had been assigned an actor to play the role of husband. Before the transplant, we had been driving towards something together. Now it felt like I was the only one in the car, navigating life with a broken GPS, with no idea what lay ahead on the wide-open medical highway.

For the first time in our marriage, I felt alone.

12. ROXICODONE

On a quiet residential street near Cedars, Kevin and I sat inside our station wagon, the air conditioner the only sound. Exhausted, I ran a trembling hand through my hair, the harshness of my hospital bracelet scraping my face. Kevin scowled over his iPhone, scrolling through a list of pharmacies in the Mid-Wilshire area. Wings of anxiety beat inside my chest. We had already been to two pharmacies and Kevin had called three others. Either the pharmacies did not have the epic amount of 300 prescribed tablets or chose not to carry Roxicodone at all.

"OK. Thank you." Kevin turned to look at me. "They don't have any either."

My stomach clenched. "What! Why doesn't anyone have it?"

From these few phone calls, Kevin had been able to figure out that a Roxicodone script is challenging to fill, more so than its infamous cousin, OxyContin. OxyContin ER (extended release) is commonly used to treat chronic pain. My Roxicodone dosage (20 mg) was uncommon, an IR (immediate release), also uncommon, and without any pesky acetaminophen to diffuse the high. Pure narcotic. With the growing opiate epidemic, the latter reason made pharmacies less likely to carry Roxicodone.

"Everyone is closing at 6 pm. You're going to have to try on Tuesday."

It was Sunday. I had to bite my tongue to keep from spitting into his face *I can't wait until Tuesday!* Was that a smirk dancing around his lips?

"Why are you so happy?" I sneered.

"I'm not."

"I'm in pain. I can't tolerate Prograf."

"I know, Henriette."

"It has to be somewhere. Keep trying."

As we pulled into a Rite Aid on Wilshire Blvd, Kevin turned towards me. "We have to get your Prograf."

"Fuck Prograf."

In a flash of inspiration, I had paged the on-call kidney transplant coordinator, and explained my predicament: I had been discharged post-biopsy, switched to Prograf, but could not tolerate its side effects. I had been prescribed Roxicodone, but could not find it anywhere on this holiday weekend. My coordinator had come to my narcotic rescue and phoned in a prescription for Norco, the strongest pain medication that can be prescribed over the phone without a paper triplicate. Norco, a much lesser opiate, would be like a Band-Aid on a severed artery, but at least I had 40 tablets of something to get me through until Tuesday. Well, 37 now.

A post-apocalyptic vibe descends upon Los Angeles during holiday weekends. Cars disappear. Honking ceases. The abandoned city mirrored the disturbing void inside our car. I rolled my shoulders back as they softened from the Norco. Neither of us spoke. In profile, his face appeared locked. Why was he so angry? He had seen me suffer on Prograf before. He knew I was in pain. I was entitled to pain medication. Looking out the window, I squeezed the pharmacy bag between my thighs. What did he know? He didn't know.

MONDAY, July 4th, 2011. 87 days post-transplant.

. . .

I HAD AWOKEN at 1 pm with a defiant burst of energy. Why the hell should I wait until Tuesday and endure the long drive back to Cedars? Why not keep trying? I propped another pillow behind my aching back. Even with the Norco tablets, I had not slept well. Despite my late rising, dark shadows lingered beneath my eyes. Whatever small amount of food I had managed was streaming through me. Thanks, Prograf.

My hand shook as I scrolled down the list of our area's pharmacies. I had called seven. Five of them were closed, and two of them did not carry Roxicodone. I swiped at my drenched armpits. Suddenly, I saw the list in a new way. Instead of focusing on the corporate pharmacies, the supermarkets jumped out. Of course! Supermarkets have pharmacies! My eighth call was placed to our local Vons.

"Hi. I was discharged from Cedars yesterday with a script for 300 Roxicodone 20 mg, IR. Do you have any in stock?"

"Let me check."

High-pitched music stung my ears as I pressed the phone tight against my cheek. *Please. Please. Please.* I picked at the crusted drool in the corners of my lips. My heart stopped when a series of clicks suggested I had been disconnected.

"I can't fill the whole prescription. I have 268 of the 300."

"I'll take them." My skin broke out into pinpricks of delight. Wait. Shit. I couldn't drive. I could barely sit up. Kevin would have to drive me, but he was still working. I could hear him in the next room, wrapping up his session.

"When do you close?"

"3 pm." I looked at the clock. It was 2:28 pm.

"I'll be there."

By 2:44 pm, we were on our way. When I told him Vons could fill my script, Kevin had dragged his heels, reminding me it was only a few minutes away. Now he was driving the speed limit, always the fucking speed limit. I sighed as we hit another red light.

"Do you really want to lose 32 pills?" Red knuckles clutched the wheel.

"Yes." God. How many times did I have to explain to him I was in pain, and tired of waiting. In that moment, it felt like I would never find this obscure Roxicodone formula anywhere but here.

With sudden energy, I raced inside. Tearing up to the pharmacy counter, I searched the wall for a clock. 2:58 pm. *I made it!* My legs quivered. A pharmacist strolled up to the counter.

"We're closed." she said dryly.

Bitch. You can't be closed. It's not 3 o'clock. It's not 3 o'clock! "But I called. I have a script. I was just in the hospital. I talked to someone."

I knew I was babbling like a crazy person. I had to calm down. Another pharmacist turned around to look at me. I looked down at my wrist. Shit. Why had I removed my hospital bracelet? The official paper accessory would have smashed any doubt I was legit.

The second pharmacist sauntered up to the counter. She looked at my face, but said nothing. I knew I looked like shit. Would that be enough? Would she believe I was a recently discharged patient or an addict trying to score? My hand shook as I held out the prescription. Her eyes narrowed. *Take it. Take it. Take it. Do. Your. Job.* We locked eyes as she pinched the paper triplicate from my fingers and walked away.

~

"Give me the keys." I demanded, and then strode away without a backward glance. *Let him deal with the groceries.*

In the passenger seat, I withdrew the bottle of 268 Roxicodone tablets. On the drive over, Kevin mentioned they sold on the street for between $10-$15 a pill. This meant I was holding between $2,680 and $4,020 worth of narcotics, but you could have offered me a million bucks and I would have walked away.

I turned the label toward me: *Take 1 tablet every 2 hours if needed for migraine.* My breath caught. Inside the haze of Prograf's pain, I had not registered the details of my prescription. One 20 mg tablet was 4 times the strength of one Percocet I had been prescribed post-transplant, and those directions had been: *Take 1-2 tablets every 4-6 hours as needed for pain*. There are 24 hours in a day. This meant I could take up to 240 mg (20 mg x 12 hours) of Roxicodone a day. Post-transplant, I had been prescribed a daily maximum of 40 mg of Percocet. With Roxicodone, not only had I been prescribed the strongest pain medication to date, but the most generous amount—six times the daily amount of post-transplant pain relief.

I cracked open the lid and saw 268 tiny tablets of the prettiest pink color. I rolled one out. It was a stunning shade, the color of a little girl's party dress—bright and hopeful. A unique color so appropriately dazzling in announcing this elite level of pain relief. I had ridden the opiate elevator from Codeine on the ground floor, past Tramadol on the 1st floor, Vicodin, Norco, Percocet, then Dilaudid on the 5th, and had now arrived at The Penthouse—immediate release Roxicodone. The doors were sliding open, welcoming me to the tippy top of this exclusive club. I had not even swallowed it, but already felt on top of the world.

It was unfortunate my kidney had to sustain such trauma for me to be introduced to Roxicodone, but now that I held the drug in my hands, all of the pain—rejection, biopsy, and Prograf's side effects— seemed worthwhile. At the mere sight of it, my back pain, hand tremors and headache dissipated. All my fears buoyed, and then destroyed. Never had a narcotic anchor plunged so deep.

I fondled its hard candy-like shell, mesmerized. How could something so innocuous-looking be powerful enough to deal with Prograf? The doctors had to be wrong. One tablet could not be enough. I rolled out 2 more. And then there were three: 60 mg of opiate and no acetaminophen.

Pain can be well managed when pills are taken as prescribed. I knew this. I also knew that if I did not abuse pain medication, I would not get dopesick. I knew that the IV pulse steroids were still leaving my body, and in a few days, I would feel better. I knew that 20 mg of Roxicodone was plenty powerful. I should just try one first. I could always take more. Yes, I understood all of this, but Roxicodone whispered that doctors only read about pain, whereas I had written the book.

The promising pink tablet had me, manipulating me in a way Fiorinal never had until the very end of our nineteen years together. It wanted all of me. Now. I took a sip of bottled water, and then threw back the 3 pills, swallowing fifteen times the strength of one post-transplant Percocet.

The trunk slammed shut, startling me awake. Kevin slipped into the driver's seat and started the car. I turned my head to the side, wiping drool from the corners of my mouth. My head was swimming with relief, my bones sluggish. I could feel his eyes on me. The prescription bottle tucked beneath my thigh, we began to drive home.

The thick silence between us felt ridiculous. We were both so obviously not talking to one another. What was his problem? The doctors could see I was in pain, why couldn't he? Arms crossed, I matched his silence beat for beat. I had done nothing wrong. I had picked up my legitimately prescribed pain medication. Finally, Kevin spoke.

"Did you take one?"

"Yeah." I mumbled out the window.

"Is it working?"

"I think so," refusing to dignify this question either way.

Lying felt good. It felt necessary. If I told Kevin the truth, that there were 3 pills melting in my stomach, I knew he would find a way to take them from me. I no longer cared about the truth. My truth was that I had to lie.

Kevin is a chatty man. His words were an action of love throughout our years of medical hell. He wielded questions like a scythe, clearing a path for us through the forest of confusing and often contradictory medical information. He poked at the doctors with concerns, sliced through stacks of bills by disputing. His words had been his weapon, his way of fighting for me. The loaded silence felt like he had stopped. His protective sword returned to its sheath.

When we got home, I headed straight for the bedroom. Kevin did not follow me.

It never occurred to me that drinking and pill popping had anything to do with my rejection. Apparently, it did not occur to the doctors either. Nothing ever came of the amended abstinence form I had signed back in February. I was never drug tested for Fiorinal before or after the transplant, nor in the midst of my rejection episode. Rejection is very common in the first year, and the doctors had treated it the best way they knew how: A painful course of immunosuppression and narcotics. A pill for every ill.

Unbelievably, I cannot remember how Roxicodone felt. Opiates, like barbiturates, sedate your CNS. To surf an opiate high is to ride a wave that crests from melted limbs to "nodding off" (to slip in and out of consciousness), and finally, unconsciousness / near death. When I went from a daily maximum opiate dose of 60 mg to 240 mg, I crested over bliss and crash-landed into oblivion.

In the 52 days I was on Prograf, my creatinine would come down even further. Prograf would quell my transplant rejection, but I would lose so much weight—20 lbs in 6 weeks—that on Aug 23rd Prograf and Roxicodone were discontinued. I would go back to Cyclosporine, but I would never go back to Henriette. I would know Roxicodone for 7 short weeks, but I would crave it to the gates of insanity throughout the month of September.

On Roxicodone, I crossed some invisible line and disappeared into a land where narcotics are not only worshipped, they rule absolute.

On Independence Day, 2011, I became 100% dependent on drugs.

TUESDAY, July 5th, 2011. 88 days post-transplant.

I don't remember.

13. AMBIEN

When I met Kevin, he told me he had played the bagpipes as a child. Inspired by his Scottish-Irish heritage, he had studied from age 6 through 17, when he quit to focus on singing. The first time I heard Kevin play the bagpipes was on our wedding day, four years later. In front of seventy-two friends and family members, his ivory-embossed bagpipes tucked beneath his left arm, my new husband nailed *Scotland the Brave* and then, *Amazing Grace* as our guests whooped and hollered in delight.

The bagpipes are the only musical instrument deemed a weapon of war because they inspired troops to battle and instilled terror into the enemy. With his pipes, my 22-year old, hours-old groom proclaimed his entrance onto the battlefield of marriage. Electrified by my young husband's talent, I clapped along with everyone else, wondering whom I had married. He seemed too good to be true. Inside the bagpipes' anthemic swell my soul soared, certain we would be able to tackle any battle to come our way.

It had been an exhilarating surprise, perhaps to no one more than Kevin. His face had lit up, not just from the strenuous breathing required to play such an instrument, but also from the revelatory joy infusing his soul. Yet he did not pick them up for another four years.

In LA, the cutthroat audition scene took its toll on a man who shies away from conflict. He would step away from the actor life he was no longer sure he wanted, and pick up a camera. The shuttering lens served to fill his clients' needs, and our fridge with food, but offered little to satiate my husband's restlessness.

One day, in 1999, the call of the pipes grew too loud for him to ignore and he joined a competitive pipe-band: The Los Angeles Scots (contradictorily based in Orange County). This Grade One level band (the highest ranking a pipe band can reach) happened to be the top ranked band in America. Every August, the LA Scots would compete at the World Pipe Band Championships in Glasgow. This trip became like Mecca for Kevin, an annual refilling of his soul.

The bagpipes are a curious instrument. For me, its initial stirring cry grows old after a few minutes. I never quite understood how the shriek of complicated melodies and harmonies was for Kevin, a spiritual salve. That summer, he must have been craving the bagpipe's brash sound with an addict's lust, if not the claps and cheers he no longer found at home.

THURSDAY, August 4th, 2011. 118 days post-transplant. 30 days on Prograf.

MY EARS TWITCHED at the increasing hum of the 210 freeway. I jammed an earplug deeper into one ear, turning away from the insistent squawk of the crow. The sounds of a new day horrified me. I did not want to get up, wash my face, or brush my teeth. Grooming rituals had become nothing more than a nuisance. I wanted to lie very, very still, ignoring the thin shafts of light peeking around the curtains until they faded to black. That was when I could lie in bed without guilt. In the daytime, people worked. At night, people went to bed, which was where I wanted to stay. The moment I saw the sun, I began to count the seconds until it went away.

Kevin's side of the bed was empty. This was not unusual during a summer we rarely saw each other. We existed like roommates who agree to live together because they have opposing work schedules and know they will never run into each other. I never saw Kevin in the morning because by the time I got up, he was working. I never saw him at night because he was sleeping while I was up drinking. Long after he went to bed, I would surf the Internet, and play pop music, drunk, crawling into bed only after I had passed out on the couch. I preferred this marriage of absentia. Without the buzz-kill that was my husband, the rhythm of our near-miss schedule flowed uninterrupted, like the alcohol I guzzled throughout the night.

As I raised my arm to shield my eyes, a whiff of him whooshed up from the crumpled sheets. My heart squeezed. It had been ages since I had buried my nose into his skin. The musky smell feathered my heartstrings, but not enough to get me to leave the bed.

From the living room, I heard the occasional bump and thought about helping him as I had done so many years past. He loved it when I stood by, nodding, as he vocalized a final check of his packed luggage. As I shifted in bed, I thought, *I could make coffee. Maybe even oatmeal*, but it hovered vaguely in the periphery of my consciousness, remaining unrealized. My body lived in a dream state, as when you are on the toilet straining, and do not understand why you cannot pee. You believe you have risen to carry out the act, yet are so drugged with sleep, you cannot differentiate the true from the false. In August, I was so drugged with drugs I could barely conceive of such an action, never mind carry it out. Also, on this particular morning, I didn't want to make coffee for my husband.

My head throbbed. What had I taken? By summer, my pill consumption had become an improvisational dance with multiple scripts: An uninterrupted opiate stream throughout the day, a few Xanax sprinkled in for my nerves, whatever I came across in people's medicine cabinets, vodka for my late-night, party-for-one and then a single responsible Ambien to help me find sleep through the haze of it all. Since the April transplant, I had been taking six different kinds of opiates: Codeine, Tramadol, Vicodin, Norco, Percocet and Roxicodone. I massaged the dry skin of my forehead, my hand heavy, beyond exhausted. Beyond drugged. Beyond human. Also, I was beyond constipated.

I slumped on the toilet, scraping at my tongue, craving a sharp rinse of vodka to cut the phlegm. My skinny thighs clamped the bowl, quivering as they strained. At 97 pounds, I was 20 lbs. below my average weight. My shaking hands gripped the bottom of the seat. It had been days since I had gone. *Please.* I was desperate to eject the leaden tightness inside. *Push, push, push.* My stomach gurgled. I gasped. *Oh, thank God.* I jammed a finger up my anus and curled it around one rock-hard pebble, yanking out the tiny toxic stone. A feral moan escaped my lips, as two wet globules rolled down my face. The stool's granite-like skin tore at me, and then dropped into the water with a satisfying plop, along with two drops of blood.

Sweat dotted my brow. My gut screamed, on fire. Over the last month, benzodiazepines, opiates, and almost no food had eroded my stomach into a singeing blister. I reached for the Pepto-Bismol and chugged. This pink liquid is forbidden for transplant patients because it interferes with the body's ability to absorb medication. Its sweet chalkiness streamed down my throat, and for a brief second, my stomach calmed long enough to release its protective clench.

Excedrin is also forbidden because its aspirin ingredient is a banned NSAID. Uncaring, I threw back 6 tablets, instead of the recommended 1 or 2. Caffeine is an active ingredient of Excedrin. Often the six pills' 390 mg rush of caffeine—equivalent to three cups of coffee—served as an amateur-hour version of the coffee-enema, widening my intestines enough to yank out a few more marbles.

I knew opiates were constipating, but eliminating them was a non-negotiable. Prograf rendered me in constant pain. So, I just didn't eat. This was easy enough, as Prograf's anorexia side effect, along with my painkillers, had annihilated my appetite. Most days the only calories I consumed were from the milk in my tea. Besides, I loved how scary thin I had become. I had finally achieved the celebrity lollipop-body! Kevin had told me I did not look "good" thin, but "sick" thin, and that I needed to gain 10 lbs., like, yesterday. Nodding affably, I blamed Prograf. Secretly, I was thrilled and had no intention of gaining weight. I loved how clothes hung from my body as on a hanger, without shape or form. Loved feeling my bony limbs touch painfully against each other when I lay down. After how that hellion Prograf was making me suffer, I was claiming my just desserts—even if I never ate them.

As I passed from the bathroom, through the small hallway that opens into the rest of the house, an acidic wave of coffee stung my nostrils. My stomach lurched. I could hear Kevin moving around in the back part of the house. *Is he just going to ignore me?* Slipping underneath the sheets, I let the pills' caffeine buzz electrocute my headache.

Excedrin's rush lasts for 20 minutes at most, but through that brief window, I viewed a world I could stand. My shoulders softened, my head cleared and momentarily, I was empowered. But when the rush dissipated, my stomach would plummet. Puddles of unadulterated fear collected in my armpits. Inside the second skin of my pajamas, I lay paralyzed. Terrified to roll over and find empty bottles I had to find a way to fill. I did not keep track of the amount of pills so much anymore, just whether or not the bottle was Empty or Full. Empty would mean I would have to bathe, dress and make a trip to Hospitaland, or some subsidiary thereof.

I was equally terrified to find pills, because they were no longer working the same way. One afternoon in May, I arrived home with a 30-tablet script of Vicodin. By sunset, I had taken 20, swallowing 2 or 3 every half hour, unable to feel a thing. Taking more pills more quickly, chewing, not swallowing, and desperate to catch the ever-more elusive feeling that everything would be OK. The only time I felt joy was in those brief seconds when I first cracked the lid of a prescription bottle. That first unswallowed pill still held the potential to dissolve my fears. I lived life in narcotic purgatory, one step up from hell only because the potential for escape still rolled around in the palm of my hand. Hell would have been no drugs and alcohol ever again.

Kevin's hand touched my shoulder. My skin warmed. It had been so long since I had felt his touch. Touch was the contact between my fingers and a prescription bottle, or my slippery grip on a frosted glass of vodka. It was clenching the phone when the doctor's office put me on hold, or the steering wheel en route to Hospitaland. Touch in a marriage often means sex. I had no libido for my husband. Pills and alcohol were my lovers, and I have always been a monogamous kind of girl.

His sweet face appeared over mine, flushed crimson with excitement. I squinted at the clock. It was 7:30 am.

"God," I barked. "Why did you wake me? I only got 3 hours of sleep!"

He flinched. "You can go back to sleep after I leave." His sharp, ordinarily titillating aftershave saturated the air. "Ugh, your cologne, " I moaned.

The early morning sun lit a halo around him. His eyes were dancing. My heart pained to tell him how beautiful he looked, but the light in his eyes was not for me. His heart was already on that transatlantic flight. *This is so unfair. He gets to go away for two weeks while I'm stuck in bed? Nice.* He swallowed and a flicker of trepidation flashed through his eyes.

"Can I have a few of your Ambien?"

Suddenly, I was wide-awake. Bitterness flooded my mouth. *You weren't coming to say goodbye. You just want something.*

"No. They're mine." His pinkish skin drained pale. *Good. How dare you ask for pills that aren't prescribed to you!* I didn't care about Ambien. I preferred being altered, not unconscious. Kevin knew that.

"I just need three," he mumbled. Three pills: Two for the flights, and one for the night before the World Pipe Band Championships.

I recognized the look on his face, an expression held against its will. He had no idea how to play this. Being genuine with his request had irritated me. If he had demanded, it would have enraged me. If he tried to negotiate, I would lawyer him to the ground. My head swelled with power, loving that my husband needed something from me.

"They're not prescribed to you." I countered.

I was so full of shit. I wasn't concerned with medical interactions.

I don't remember why Kevin was short, but he had been prescribed Ambien for years.

"You never take them," he offered weakly.

"I might." This was crap. We both knew I could spare some. His shoulders sank. *It sucks to have to beg for pills, doesn't it?* I rolled away from my husband, even as his face crumbled, willing to let that moment serve as our final goodbye. As I heard him slip out of the room, I thought, *Ha. Ha. I won.*

My heart was hurling itself against the walls of my chest. I mean, how dare he? Step. Off. My pills were my business. He had been wrong to ask.

The front door slammed shut. *What? That's it? You're just going to leave?* In a few short hours Kevin's world would span an ocean, and mine would remain the width of our bed. I rolled back towards my bedside table and chomped down 4 Xanax. My hands shook. I could not calm down. I had to calm down.

Outside, I heard a car door slam shut. *Kim.* Kevin's sister and her family were once again visiting LA, and she had arrived from her Pasadena hotel to take Kevin to the airport. He had not even asked me. Soon he would be up in the air, facing one of his greatest fears.

When we first met, Kevin had been terrified to fly. The second time we flew together had been to Winnipeg in 1994, for Kim's first husband's shockingly young death. We were madly in love. Sharing-the-middle-arm-rest-in-love. You-can-have-my-peanuts-in-love. As the plane took off with its ear-splitting roar, I touched my boyfriend's damp forehead. His young face drooping with grief and anxiety, he whispered,

"I don't care if we crash. At least we will be together."

This statement remains in the Top 5 of sentimental things Kevin has said. On that flight, we established a ritual of sorts, albeit unoriginal. Whenever one of us boards a plane we always make sure—whether by phone, email or text—to tell each other, *I love you.* If for some reason we can't, a surprisingly superstitious part of me believes the flight has been jinxed and I'm unsettled until my husband lands and virtual connection resumes. Each time we honor this ritual my heart sings, secure in the knowledge that our heartstrings are tuned to the same corny key of love.

Seventeen years later, Kevin was still uncomfortable up in the air. Staring at the ceiling, I thought about the first time I had heard him play the pipes, and the joy exuding from his young face. Joy I rarely saw anymore. Joy I had just extinguished.

I rolled towards the gaping hole in our bed. My arms ached to hold him the way I had during our first dance—less a structured waltz and more a heartfelt collapse into the safest place I had ever known. Sadness flooded my soul. Why did I act like this? I loved Kevin. I loved him. Something was wrong with me, but I could not stop.

Suddenly charged with adrenaline, I shot up in bed, galvanized to chase after him like a Rom-Com heroine revealing herself to the love of her life before he boards an airplane to Someplace She Can Never Visit. My heart thumped with intention. I felt insane, like a true Jekyll and Hyde. Moments earlier, I had been crippled with anger, now, electrified by love. I could not bear the thought of Kevin leaving without us saying goodbye.

I grabbed my bottle of Ambien. *Go. Go. Go.* With matted hair and pajama pants, I raced into the kitchen and grabbed a baggie from the drawer. Hands shaking, I poured 8 tablets into the plastic bag and raced out the front door. Had they left? This was so exciting! I would rescue him with my pills and save the day!

Chest heaving, I tore barefoot around the corner from the patio. The dazzling morning rays momentarily blinded me. Kim and Kevin were standing opposite each other, backlit. Kim's car was idling, the trunk open as Kevin stuffed a bag inside. When their shadows morphed into focus, I saw they were smiling, oblivious to my sudden appearance.

My chest contracted. What! His body was not slumped from the emotional wreckage of our altercation. He had not been waiting for me. He could have cared less if I had come out to say goodbye! My shallow breathing increased to a furious pant. His shoulders were thrown back. Light. Weightless. He looked happy.

Apologies were hard for me on a good day. They would get stuck in my throat the way my larger pills sometimes did, and my half-measured attempts became indiscernible mumblings. I had planned to throw my arms around him, then when I drew back, eyes sparkling with intention, hand him the Gift of Ambien. But as soon as I saw them just standing there, unaffected by the storm of emotions raging inside of me, I felt the gates around my heart clang shut. The apology dancing on the tip of my tongue fell flat. I ploughed up to Kevin, whipped the Ambien into his face, and screamed,

"YOU ARE A FUCKING DRUG ADDICT!"

Out it came with an inhuman roar, every ounce of poison shriveling my soul. Spit stippled his stunned face, tiny flecks of wet hatred. The bag of drugs slid down his chest and onto the ground. The light in his eyes flickered, and then went out. Storming away, I raged. *Fuck. Him. I am right. He was wrong. He was wrong to ask for medication that is not prescribed to him. I have nothing to apologize for.*

Wiping at the angry tears rolling down my face, I downed 3 Tramadol. *Asshole. Jerk.* Pummeling Kevin had inflated me for a brief second. Now I wanted to crawl out of my shamed skin and disappear.

Did Kevin recline his seat and let the meditative call of the pipes calm him all the way to Scotland? A stirring sound that promised to drown out the angry shrieks of his wife and take him far from a marriage that had become a battlefield after all.

What I did not know then is that Kevin turned to Kim and said, "I am done with her."

I was, too. But how?

14. XANAX REFILLED

M ay 27th, 1995. Our Wedding Day.

"WHY DON'T you pick me up and hold me in your arms?"

We were standing underneath the stone arch doorway of the chapel where we had just exchanged our *I will* s. Kevin smiled and lifted me into his arms, a giggling bundle of tulle and revelation. I was a wife! Spreading my arms wide in a *Ta-Da!* gesture, I turned my face towards the camera. Bouncy tendrils framed my Prednisone cheeks. Kevin turned his face to look at me. His blond hair was cut military short for a show, and his gorgeous profile beamed a kind of "I-can't-believe-I-married-her" look.

It was the final shot of the afternoon, taken in between the ceremony and the reception. The shot that became The One: immortalized in a sterling silver frame of roses and thorns. The One that mocked us from the dresser sixteen years later, on the night Kevin carried me out our front door like a marital threshold in reverse, when he tried to get me to go to the ER thinking I had overdosed on Acetaminophen, while I pummeled him every step of the way.

. . .

THURSDAY OCTOBER 13ᵀᴴ, 2011. 188 days post-transplant.

ON OCTOBER 9ᵀᴴ, Kevin did return from Rite Aid with my Xanax, and then drive, late, to his OC wedding. First, he had delivered me 12 tablets. Then he had returned with 90 more. Four days later, they were all gone.

"FUCK YOU!" Kevin screamed, yanking my cell from my hand and smashing it onto the floor. The phone shattered into tens of pieces, bent plastic and twisted metal flying.

"No!" I screamed back, collapsing to my knees. In the two months since his August Scotland trip, I had become a scrawny woman-child having lost even more weight, sporting pigtails and pajama bottoms a double-knotted drawstring could barely keep up. My life further reduced to nothing but bottles and bed.

"Why, why would you do this?" I whined.

With slow-motion arms, I wrangled the pieces towards me. Gripping the body of the phone, I pushed the back piece against it, but it refused to click. Fingers acting as flaccid sheaths that once supported hard bone. When had all my bone melted away? Had thirty years of Prednisone liquefied them?

"You're not going to be able to fix it," Kevin, my infuriated parent, growled.

"Yeth, I caaan..." I slurred, my arms floating out from my body like scarves on a laundry line. My head dropped over my neck. I jerked it back up. *Why can't I keep my eyes open?* Rocking back and forth, I clutched the broken pieces to my chest. If I could just get this one piece to fit all the others would click into place. I could fix this. This mess could be fixed.

Now Kevin was talking on the cordless phone. When had that happened? He circled the house the way a police helicopter zeroes in on its criminal target—around and around. He was so mean. Why had he broken my phone?

Kevin tossed the cordless onto the couch. "We're going to the ER."

"Nooo. I'm fiiiiiine." I insisted. His eyes went dark. "You're not fine. Dr. A. says you will go into seizure if we don't admit you."

Ignoring him, I kept marshalling the pieces as some surreal game of warped Lego. Holding fast to the wreckage made it easier for me to believe this was all Kevin's fault. *Asshole. I had just been texting.* My zombie brain could not understand, although immediately caused by his hand, the damage was entirely mine.

Over the last four days, I had existed within a void. My brain floated inside my head, separate from my being, as if in a water-filled Frankensteinian jar. Day dissolved into night that dissolved into day again. Time never slowed down so it could never speed up—felt neither long, nor short. I could not feel it at all.

If I had looked up, would I have noticed I was sitting beneath our wedding photo? Sixteen years had passed since those minutes-old newlyweds held each other. Now my husband loomed over me holding fast to nothing. For a second, we locked eyes, and I saw him: a groom destroyed. I was past pain, past euphoria, past everything. Kevin was the last man suffering. If I could make my husband a t-shirt of that moment it would read: *I gave my wife a kidney and now I want it back.*

The next thing I remember, Kevin was pulling up to Cedars' ER. Six months earlier we had walked in together as a team, a willing husband ready to save his dying wife with his kidney. The car idled in the parking dock.

"Get out." He stared forward, waiting for me to climb out and admit myself, by myself, for another overdose. Five years earlier, Xanax had served me well. A single pill that helped me shed my skin and find a place at my in-laws kitchen table. Today, after taking every last Xanax, I could not find a place anywhere. Even in my husband's eyes.

I can't believe I married her.

"Are you coming in?" I asked. Kevin drove away.

I wobbled toward the sliding doors as a male nurse appeared with a wheelchair. He leaned over me as I collapsed into the seat.

"What's going on, hon?"

"My name is Henriette Ivanans. I'm a kidney transplant patient and I took over 100 pills."

15. AMBIEN REFILLED

T hursday October 13th, 2011. 188 days post-transplant.

THAT AFTERNOON, I was admitted to Cedars for an overdose of Xanax and detoxed for three nights from benzodiazepine abuse. It was later explained to me that the amount of benzos I had swallowed in four days (102 Xanax and a hidden bottle of 30 Klonopin I had forgotten about) should have killed me. Not from their consumption, but from the seizures I would have fallen into had Kevin not called my neurologist, and been directed to bring me to the ER. The medical term for this state is "benzo-coma." It presents as ataxia (the loss of full control of bodily movements), psychosis (a mental disorder characterized by a disconnection from reality) and amnesia (the loss of memory).

"You're losing a lot of hair." Kevin said from the other side of the room.

I looked at the brush. Bunches of fine red strands dangled from its plastic spikes. Yes. I was losing my hair. I floated above the comment, uncaring. It was just a fact that landed in the room like: a hospital bed can be lowered or raised. What is there to feel about that? What I could feel was our absence from one another. We sat side-by-side, Kevin in a far-away chair, and me in the bed, existing inside a marital black hole where love had disappeared. What remained were his obligation and my detoxification.

I remember little of those three days and nights. Of Kevin I recall mostly his absence. Gone was the man who dove head first into a pan of my overdose vomit, scanning its contents for my immunosuppressives. In his place, was a man who shot me flashes of cold blue. Eyes no longer bright with compassion, but lasers cutting me down.

"I think I should go to rehab." I was talking to Kim on the phone.

"Yes, I think you should, too."

She did not seem angry or sad. She sounded far away. Everyone was so far away. Like she didn't care. I didn't care. No, less than that. Nothing. I felt nothing. I hung up the phone thinking, *I did take a lot of pills. I guess I should go.*

At this time, Melissa was dating a guy who worked at a for-profit drug and alcohol rehabilitation center in West Hollywood called Klean. While I lay detoxing, my future was virtually drafted over three days between Klean's manager, Jack, Kevin and Campbell, Kevin's father. On Sunday afternoon while Kevin was in his office downloading images mid-shoot, the final email arrived: 30 days of treatment would be negotiated down from $30,000 to $17,000 and I could be admitted that night.

Kevin told me later he had never known such angered helplessness in his life. What did he know of the cost and quality of rehabilitation centers? There was no time to comparison shop. In a few hours, I would be discharged. Kevin felt cornered and unequipped, forced to not only pick up the pieces of his wife's second suicide attempt, but find a way to make them fit back together on a deadline. After agreeing to the reduced amount, he resumed taking photos outside. I can just picture his tight smile as he asked his client about the weather, pets and favorite movies, while recording images of a day he already wished he could forget.

We didn't have the money. Nor had Kevin shared details of my descent into incomprehensible addiction with his parents. They believed our recent trials had been my rejection episode and struggle to tolerate Prograf. I can't even imagine the conversation Kevin had to have with them. What he had to reveal about the woman he had chosen to spend the rest of his life with, and then ask for thousands upon thousands of dollars because he did not have it himself.

I didn't fight the idea of rehab. It felt right to have others make this decision for me. *I did take a lot of pills.* I could not attach the floating tentacles of my brain to the grave nature of my circumstances: Once again, I had almost died.

SUNDAY OCTOBER 16TH, 2011. 191 days post-transplant.

WHEN I ARRIVED BACK HOME Sunday night to pack, it was Melissa who walked with me through the front door. The house was dark. Was Kevin even home? I moved to the kitchen for a glass of water. Suddenly, the air shifted. A chill brushed the back of my neck.

"HOW ARE WE SUPPOSED TO AFFORD REHAB?" Kevin towered over me, the force of his words blowing back the hair from my face. I shrugged.

"Ask your parents." I took a sip of water.

Kevin stepped right up into my face. His was a portrait of hatred: Black eyes glinting as he shook. My brain, thick with detoxification drugs, struggled to recall information I was certain existed. Wasn't it all arranged? His parents had made it clear if we ever needed financial help, to just ask. What was the problem?

"GET HER AWAY FROM ME," he thundered. The ground beneath us shook.

I had never been afraid of Kevin, but flinched as he growled, flinging a fist toward the sky. Water sloshed out of my glass as I jumped back, believing he might punch me in the face, even with Melissa hovering in the shadows.

Jesus. Why was he so mad? I was going to rehab already. I huffed into the bedroom, and began to select my wardrobe. *Which jeans should I take?* Melissa loitered behind me, encouraging me to pack quickly. Apparently, Jack needed to do something called an "intake" before it got too late. In the foyer, I packed up my prescriptions. Kevin leaned against the wall, watching me.

"Cyclosporine. Prednisone. Ambien," I listed.

"They're not going to let you have that." My head whipped up at his caustic tone, almost gleeful.

"Yes, they will. I take it to sleep." I zipped up my plastic case.

An uncomfortable sensation prickled my skin. Why would it make my husband happy if I was denied something for sleep? Was looking at me like, *Are you an idiot? Do you really think they will let you have a highly addictive sleep medication in rehab?* That night I saw nothing through my veil of entitlement I had yet to lift.

It is hard for me to pin down emotion in those first days post-overdose. Feelings flapped around me like sheets whipped high on a laundry line. I could feel change rolling across the canyon and into our cabin, swirling around its wood-paneled walls, an undeniable shift in the air. Kevin said nothing more. For the first time in our marriage, my husband would not take my hand and guide me through the storm. He turned away, walked into his office and shut the door. I would not see him again for a week.

~

KLEAN IS TUCKED AWAY on a small West Hollywood side street, coincidentally just blocks from Cedars. Through a side gate, Melissa and I entered a courtyard twinkling with white lights and palm trees. One section was marked by worn-looking couches and tables clustered together beneath a wood trellis. Off to the side of this common area stood a tiny rectangular building with a wall of glass doors. This was the "tech" room where two or three technicians per shift would coordinate the clients' activities, meals and outside appointments like medical or court. The majority of technicians working at Klean were recovering addicts with years of sobriety under their belts. Around the corner, flush to its back wall, was the "meds" room.

On three sides of the courtyard, stood a twenty-six-bed facility, made up of eight attached Spanish-style duplexes. To access the second-story apartments, one had to climb winding staircases affixed to the outside (ostensibly so residents could not access each other from the inside). My head spun with disbelief. The charming facility appeared almost staged, like I had walked onto the Hollywood set of a treatment center. The decorative lights winked beneath the dark sky as if they knew something I had not even begun to understand. Two techs greeted us, and then escorted me into the first apartment to the gate's left.

It had a kitchen, living and dining area, and bathroom with a spacious shower, no bath. One bedroom had a double bed and private patio. In here, I learned, slept a member of an '80s pop group. As we passed the cracked door to a second and darkened bedroom I peered inside, making out gunmetal gray walls and a blanketed mound on one of the two twin beds. I would sleep in here with another woman in her 40s. My bags were plopped in the living room.

"Let's get you upstairs for intake," said the male tech.

Yawning, I followed him to an upstairs office. Melissa had vanished, gone home with her on-staff boyfriend. A tall and gangly man with Buddy Holly-esque glasses sat behind a chrome desk cluttered with paper folders.

"Hi, I'm Jack. I'm the manager here at Klean." We shook hands.

"I'm Henriette," my voice cracked.

I remember my careful pose at the edge of the chair, a body meek with nerves. He asked endless questions about everything: my kidney transplants, mine and my family's medical history, medications and drug and alcohol abuse—what kind of pills / alcohol I abused and how often. I held nothing back. My body sighed with relief as I spilled almost every secret to a total stranger. Was he shocked by my consumption? His eyes betrayed nothing behind those thick-rimmed spectacles. I, on the other hand, felt like my skin had been peeled away. Every pore vibrated with what? Fear? Gratitude? Both?

As he handed me a copy of Klean's weekly schedule, his face bore a curious look of pride. $17,000 would entitle me to: one weekly private session with a psychiatrist, twice weekly individual sessions with a therapist, group therapy twice a day, the opportunity to go the West Hollywood gym, *Crunch!* five days a week, yoga and meditation classes, a Sunday Target run, and finally, "Sober Fun Day" on Saturdays, when clients were supervised at a movie or The Hollywood Wax Museum for, well, sober fun. My temples throbbed. I wanted to lie down.

His eyes flickered with what—Empathy? Dollar signs? Both? I couldn't get a read on this guy. The tippy-top of the paper quivered in my hand. Day Begins: 7:30 am. It was then that this certified night owl shivered the way I always did when the dreaded sunrise fluttered her radiant eyelashes over our shadowy canyon. I was about to meet the dawn—when there is nowhere left to hide. I exhaled. The schedule felt like punishment. *I deserve it. I deserve to be here.*

Back inside my apartment, my clothes lay in haphazard piles inside my open suitcase. I had been searched. Arranged on the kitchen counter were the confiscated items: Perfume, hand sanitizer, hairspray and dry shampoo. Did they really think I would drink my perfume? Huff my hairspray?

"But I'm a kidney transplant patient. I need hand sanitizer."

"Just come to the meds room," barked the female tech.

What? She expected me to cross the courtyard and enter a separate building just to get a squirt of hand sanitizer? Unsteady, I leaned against the counter for support. I was so tired, but each new and humbling bit of information kept jarring me awake.

Then I noticed my Ambien next to my hair dryer. (A weapon I could electrocute myself with?) Well, wasn't that ironic. The one drug I had never abused, the one I really needed tonight, the one I had lorded over Kevin, had been taken away from me. Well, fuck me. Kevin was right. They had confiscated my Ambien.

In a flash, I saw. The baggie of tablets I had whipped at him. The destroyed look on his face. My defiant self storming away before his long trip to Scotland. I closed my eyes as they filled with tears. *I want to go home.* I would have given anything to turn back the clock just two hours, and tell Kevin how sorry I was, that I did not know why I acted the way I did.

A tear escaped down my cheek. The twinkle lights had come on. I was not starring in an episode of *Intervention.* I was home.

16. TRAZODONE

S ober Night 1. Sunday October 16th, 2011.

SHORTLY AFTER INTAKE, MY CEDARS' detox regimen was revised to include a non-addictive sleep medication: Trazodone. Prescribed in high doses for Major Depressive Disorder, but at its lowest dose, effective for sleep. That first night, Trazodone was the equivalent of being hit in the back of the neck with a Louisville Slugger and I welcomed The Grand Slam.

My body soaked up sleep the way a wilted flower responds to rain. My flesh hummed with relaxation sinking into the tiny bed. On Trazodone, along with my earplugs and white noise machine, I had no trouble falling and staying asleep, despite suddenly being in rehab, and sharing a room with a woman whose acquaintance I had yet to make.

SOBER DAY 1. MONDAY OCTOBER 17th, 2011.

. . .

FOR THE FIRST couple of days, I was to be left alone. I could join group if I wanted to, but was permitted to acclimatize in whatever way felt most comfortable, and that way for me was sleep. I was already addicted. Restorative sleep was my new drug of choice, and one I could have as much of as I wanted.

I slept on without clutching my head in agony, without Tiger Balm slathered everywhere to detract from pain. My torso uncurled around a hot water bottle; my face unsmothered beneath a cold washcloth. Anesthetized to everything but the delicious swaddle of sleep, I have but vague recollections of that first day:

One of the techs knocking on my door, and then cracking it open (to check that I was still breathing?) The fading thumps of footsteps as I drifted away. My roommate slipping in to collect what? A sweater? A book? One time my eyes fluttered open to see her scanning a schedule taped to the wall. I think I mumbled a few words to her as I leaned against the kitchen counter with a glass of water, limbs aching for yet more rest, but I can't be sure. I know I slept on.

SOBER DAY 2. TUESDAY OCTOBER 18th, 2011.

THIS AFTERNOON, I found myself looking at said schedule and realized Klean's clients would be in a group session. My apartment's front doors were in the kitchen and opened directly into the courtyard. I had deduced, from the occasional peek through its glass front, that if the weather co-operated, group was held in the common area directly opposite our apartment—three steps down and ten paces across the courtyard.

I shifted a thin curtain to the side. Wide-eyed, I watched this newly discovered species in their unnatural habitat: Addict. I had never knowingly witnessed them up close. Clients sprawled all over each other like a pack of wild dogs on the ground. Others sunken into the couch, legs firmly planted on the center table. Was I really one of them?

I glanced around at the apartment's modern décor by daylight, and then returned to my odd little bed, moving in towards the wall, my pajama-clad back curled against a sober world I had yet to awaken to.

SOBER DAY 3. WEDNESDAY OCTOBER 19th, 2011.

I SLAMMED the alarm one final time. 7:18 am. 12 minutes to group. I twisted my bony torso up and to sitting, flesh drenched with sleep. I could not remember the last time I'd been up and present for anything by 7:30 am, besides our 5:30 am transplant call. On the Night Before Transplant, I'd had champagne, beer, Codeine, and then popped a Xanax upon awakening, knowing I'd be on IV pain medication by the end of the day. This day, I had awoken stone cold sober, unready to greet the abstinent dawn.

I blinked, rubbing my eyes. I needed some kind of a hit to get me through my first official day in rehab. I shuffled into the kitchen where my roommate—that quirky breed of a "morning-person"—had already made a pot of coffee. (I would later learn she was off somewhere meditating with her dog.) Of course! Caffeine! (At the time I was an occasional coffee drinker.) I poured myself a cup, stirred in liquid creamer, and then took one, two, three giant gulps of the chemical brew. My heart beating triple time, I opened the front door.

The morning light shimmered like fairy dust on the landscaped garden, as if a giant hand from above had cast glitter far and wide. Palm fronds fluoresced. Succulents glowed like neon candy. The colors seemed too artificial to be real, but everything was real. This really was rehab. I sighed. It was a beautiful morning. I clutched my coffee to my chest and clomped three steps down and ten across towards my future.

At 7:25 am I was perched at attention, waiting for "Morning Meditation" to begin at 7:30 am sharp. There were ten other clients at Klean, and the only other person waiting was one of the techs. He was an enormous man of mixed race, wearing sweats and a baseball cap. He uncapped his water bottle and took a quick swig. There was nothing special about him from the outside, but something magical floated off his skin. I wanted to curl up in his lap and go back to sleep.

"Hi. I'm Henriette." I croaked.

"Hi, Henriette. I'm Berry." A winged smile danced upon his lips.

"Where is everyone?"

"Oh, they'll be here."

I shifted, unsettled. Being punctual was a sign of respect, but Berry didn't seem phased by the empty seating area. He took another swig.

Like zombies on the horizon, they began to appear from behind the tech room, straggling towards us in packs of twos and threes. They were dressed head-to-toe in sweats or pajamas. Many of them, like myself, would have been on detox regimens, and thereby walk with a legitimate sluggishness, but these cats shuffled with a calculated gait. I recognized the willful light glinting in their eyes.

If sweats were the unofficial uniform at Klean, cigarettes were the way to accessorize. They were making their way over from the designated smokers' area, located right outside the meds' room door. In order to receive my medications, I had to wait my turn at a table covered in overflowing ashtrays, deep inside a poisonous fog from frenetically puffing detoxers.

One-by-one they plopped onto the couches, staking their pillowed claim. Cigarette smoke drifted over as they took their sweet, sweet time adjusting their hats and limbs just so. I scrunched my nose, picturing their final drags, tilting their heads back towards the glorious morning sky, as they polluted it with an upward-directed cloud of rebellious smoke. I pursed my lips. Smoking was disgusting. (To this day, I have never tried a cigarette. Yes, I see the irony.)

Berry beamed, greeting every client by name. He was acknowledged with the odd mumble, but mostly ignored. Yet he kept smiling as if he possessed some power making him impenetrable to these restless button-pushers. I wanted to slap them upside the head. *Jesus!*

Sit Still! I crossed my legs and sat up even straighter, showing them how it was done. They were rude and defiant. I wasn't like these clowns.

With sidelong glances, I scanned the pack. Maybe I had seen enough episodes of *Intervention* or addiction documentaries to be unsurprised by this motley crew. I noted five men and five women, almost all younger than me, crossing boundaries of age, race, gender, sexual preference and socio-economic-class. Curious, most of them stared at me, arms folded, chins up, from deep inside the couches' protective bosom.

There was the 20-something, pill-popping Vegas DJ princess with jet-black hair and a boob job, who had just lost her mom. The skull-capped, Orange County kid, as addicted to tattoos, as he was heroin, after his older brother shot him up when he was twelve. The down-home Southern Mama who had survived Katrina only to be flown out to Hollywood, California to save her daughter from addiction until it was revealed on national television that they had snorted coke together. There was the gay, bald pharmacist, whose ironic drug of choice was alcohol and who could barely speak when he first arrived. I met the homosexual, mixed race Texan prince, who slammed crystal meth to destroy memories of molestation, the breathtaking Columbia graduate with perfect red lips and an imperfect body image, and my roommate, a single white woman, my age, who seemed to live only for her dog.

What did they see? I was nearly 43 years old. My teeth had yellowed from a summer of not eating and drinking little but tea, and red wine. I had not showered, my teeth and hair unbrushed. About a third of the hair beneath my chin-line had fallen out. Pajamas draped my 97-lb frame.

I was a wife. I was a kidney transplant recipient. I was an actress. I had become the saddest of all Hollywood clichés—an unsuccessful actress now in rehab, but a 10-minute drive from the Hollywood Walk of Fame. Three years ago I had been screen testing for Ron Howard. How had this happened?

"We have a new client with us today. Henriette, would you like to read?"

Berry handed me an enormous soft-covered book. It had to be over 400 pages. Indented into the top portion of its dark cover were the words "Alcoholics Anonymous." I brought the book right up to my eyes, partly because I didn't have my reading glasses, but mostly so I could hide my face. My voice cracked as I began to read the section highlighted in yellow.

"And acceptance is the answer to *all* my problems today…"

The passage was about accepting my alcoholism and nothing in God's world happening by mistake. God? Alcoholism? I mean I knew I had a problem with pills. I yawned. It was all I could do to stay awake. After I finished reading, I handed the book back to Berry. Then we went around the circle, each of us stating an intention for the day: *I will call my son. I will go to court. I will call my sponsor.* I tried to ignore the stomach flutters reminding me I had called Kevin several times and he hadn't returned any of my calls. I had been in rehab for two and a half days and we had yet to speak. It was the longest we had gone without speaking in eighteen years.

On Berry's cue, everyone rose in surprising unison, grabbing hands and bowing heads inside a circle. Then he began to lead us in what I came to learn was The Serenity Prayer.

"God / Grant me the serenity to accept the things I cannot change / The courage to change the things I can / And the wisdom to know the difference. Amen. Keep coming back, it works if you work it!"

As these belligerents chanted, my heart splintered. On one side, I clutched Berry's hand, this giant lump of love, and on the other side, a total stranger, someone I would come to love as I learned I was exactly like them. Tears streamed down my bowed face. Deep voices cracked. Others grumbled with resentment, but all of us trying to hit the same note: Hope.

I swiped at my tears as the group dispersed back towards the smokers' area, or their apartments before breakfast, but the more I wiped, the more they kept coming. I looked into Berry's face, the morning sun spotlighting his beautiful smile. He looked like an angel.

"Welcome, Henriette," he said, opening his arms wide.

$\sim$

I GATHERED facts about my new family the way a squirrel stores for winter—eagerly, strategically—because in learning about them, I learned about myself. I had forgotten what it was like to talk with people other than medical professionals or Kevin, trapped inside our relentless cycle of accusation and denial. With them, I could breathe.

One afternoon, as we sat waiting outside the meds' room, the DJ princess confided when she'd added up how much she had spent on pills that year it had totaled over $30,000. She'd been thrilled when she found a drug dealer who sold her pills for $2.50 each instead of $4.00. I nodded, thinking that would have made me happy too, then felt a flush of jealous awe that she even had a drug dealer.

I found myself nodding all the time, like when I heard I wasn't the only one to obsess over unfinished drinks. One night after a dinner out with Melissa, she slipped away to the bathroom without finishing her $14 Grey Goose vodka and soda. Whirling from two goblets of red wine, in addition to the two I had gulped at home, I sat transfixed by her unfinished drink. She had barely taken two sips. Was she finished? Would she notice if I polished it off? If she did notice, would she buy I had thought it a shame to let it go to waste? From her red lips, the Columbia graduate confessed that she also flinched when half-finished drinks were taken away.

I never thought I would have laughed the way I did in rehab— deep, gasping-for-air hysterics. One day, after the gym, the hulking Texan boy observed my muscular arms and quipped, "You have the arms a junkie would kill for."

"I wouldn't know! You're the expert!" I shot back, and we snorted with laughter.

Looking up into this beautiful man's face, I wondered. How old was he? I didn't know his last name. I was straight. He was gay. I was white. He was of mixed race. I had been married for 16 years. He was a self-professed "playah" on the streets of WeHo. We had nothing in common but rehab. I had known him but a handful of days, yet I felt like I could tell him anything.

SOBER DAY 5. FRIDAY OCTOBER 21st, 2011.

ON MY WAY back to my room on lunch break, I ran into the pharmacist, whom I was closest to in age.

"You know, one time I chugged cough syrup," he said. None of it shocked me. Such truths filled me; freed me. Each revelation drew me closer to them, the thread of it binding our common fabric tighter.

Back in my room, I turned on my music for a few minutes before group. The in-house physician, Dr. H. had just informed me that mine was the hardest detox—alcohol and benzodiazepines. He wanted me in rehab for nine months. Sighing, I rubbed my forehead. At $17,000 a month, that was never going to happen.

The delicate strains of *Clare de Lune* shuffled onto my iPod. The gorgeous notes plunked down like divine tears from above. Closing my eyes, I drifted off.

God, I just want to go home.

~

A WRINKLED SLICE of lime lay in a pool of vodka water. *Already?* Pushing back my chair, I stumbled over to the refrigerator, trudging the way this Canadian child used to walk through mile-high piles of snow—laboriously, with joyful purpose. A whoosh of air hit my flushed cheeks as I yanked open the freezer door. Reaching down towards the bottom shelf, I started. Where was my vodka? I whipped around. *Fuck.* There it was, its empty neck sticking out from the recycling bin.

Stupid, stupid, stupid. What am I going to do? There was no way I could get into the car and drive to 7-11, not because it was 3 am and I had caught myself nodding off at my computer, but because the sound would wake my husband. Bracing myself with the fridge doors, I rocked back and forth on the balls of my feet, scanning its contents repeatedly, praying a bottle of wine would miraculously appear because I willed it to be so.

Is there any alcohol in the house? Maybe there was enough vodka in the empties to mix one more drink? Mouthwash? A shot of it had been fine to steady my nerves in the past, but I didn't really want to savor a glass of it. Bathroom. Alcohol. It was clear like vodka. It was just a higher proof. Rubbing Alcohol.

Grabbing the bottle from underneath the sink, I slipped it beneath my t-shirt, slinking past our bedroom door. I never wondered if my party-for-one was keeping Kevin awake. Or if he struggled to sleep, knowing I was marinating his precious gift in alcohol.

Hmmm. What can I mix this with? It's a shame we don't have any tomato juice. I could have made a Bloody Mary! Lemonade? A Lemondrop! Perfect!

My heart pattered as I watched the sunny liquid splash against the icy rock formation. Grabbing the rubbing alcohol, I poured once, then twice, completing my cocktail. *It's so pretty! What a shame I don't have one of those teeny umbrellas!* Then I raised the glass, toasting my ingenuity. The cool of the ice brushed my lips as I tilted my head back. Then I took a giant sip of my rubbing alcohol cocktail.

Fire coursed down my throat. I slammed the glass down on the counter and grabbed at my neck. I gagged, doubling over. Tears filled my eyes. It felt like boiling water from a whistling kettle had been poured down my throat. Like drinking flames.

Then I went in for another sip.

∿

DEBUSSY CONTINUED to swirl through the air. Something inside me was cracking, an entity that needed release. Hot tears dribbled down my cheeks and onto my chest for long minutes, soaking the sheets around me. I couldn't breathe. A force pushed me onto the floor. My hands found each other in a desperate grip. Burying my face into the side of the bed, I began to scream.

How had I forgotten this? But I had. With but a few sober days, my longest probable run since age 19, my mind had defogged enough to recall this insanity. What had I done? I had consumed rubbing alcohol on the kidney Kevin had gifted me four months earlier.

But on that July night, it had made total sense. The bottle said 70% alcohol. I knew of 80% proof rums, recalled that the legally reinstated Absinthe hovered around the 100 proof mark. Drinking rubbing alcohol would be fine. But alcohol proof is different from alcohol content. Proof is an expression of the strength of alcoholic content, defined as twice the percentage of Alcohol By Volume (ABV). So what I did not understand was the rubbing alcohol's 70% alcohol content was actually 140% alcohol proof.

More significantly, rubbing alcohol is not ethyl alcohol (beverage alcohol) but isopropyl alcohol, a totally different chemical than the alcohol of beer, wine, or liquor. The lethal dose of isopropyl alcohol in adults by mouth is about 8 ounces. I had poured 2 heavy shots into a glass and proceeded to drink.

On the floor I shifted, reaching for a deeper comfort than the endless stream of snot and tears. The Serenity Prayer drifted towards me like divine flotsam. I struggled, uncertain of the words, clinging to each syllable while every cell inside of me was breaking apart.

"God grant me the serenity / To accept the things I cannot change / The courage to change the things I can / And the wisdom to know the difference."

I was an alcoholic and an addict. I was in rehab. And I didn't know if I had lost Kevin forever.

Through the music and tears and prayer, I saw I had not just taken myself for a joyride down the winding roads of addiction, but that Kevin had been dragged along behind me for endless miles. Was it too late for us? His sagging blue eyes floated before me and my anguish rose again, a wailing siren without end. Every time the idea to get up entered my mind, something kept me on the floor.

I remained there for two hours unable to recall when I had ever felt so safe.

17. CAFFEINE

S ober Day 5. Friday October 21st, 2011.
   They can't take that away from me.

We laugh a lot in rehab, and I asked someone if that was wrong, "Absolutely not." It's because there is understanding.

We stood in the common area, arms dangling by our sides. Kevin's eyes flickered around the facility for the first time: Pajama-clad clients shuffled from their apartments to the smoking area. Thick plumes rising up from behind the meds' room like subversive smoke signals. Techs walked in and out of unlocked apartments, dropping off take-out dinners or notifying clients they had a phone call. On evening break (5 pm-7 pm), clients often congregated in this area to watch the community TV, work on their temporarily reclaimed laptops, or engage in monitored conversations on the facility phone. But tonight, we were alone.

Chewing on my nails, I wondered if I should hug him. I hadn't seen Kevin in a week. How long had it been since I had seen him with sober eyes? He looked so sweet and handsome in a plain t-shirt and jeans. He said nothing as he moved to sit down, but he was here. I had enough newfound clarity of mind not to complain.

He swigged at his Coke Zero. My heart thudded as I watched my husband take in every detail. Kevin is not a fan of the unfamiliar. He had probably Googled this place and every treatment center in the greater Los Angeles area trying to comprehend the new axis of our lives. Kevin had always hunted *and* gathered information, anything to help me, us. He had always been that kind of husband. Was he still?

The wail of a siren filled the empty space between us. *Please. Say something.* I knew I should start, but didn't want to say the wrong thing. An apology seemed like dropping a bucket of water on a forest fire. My stomach gurgled with anxiety. Sitting next to each other on a couch in a LA treatment center for drug and alcohol addiction ranked this day as the strangest of our 16-year marriage. Was it our last?

With a trembling hand I reached for his. He let me take it, but did not offer anything in return by way of a squeeze. I shifted closer towards him, breathing him in the way I had when we were first falling in love—from his soapy pine scent to his inherent kindness. I had missed him. I had forgotten Kevin was my husband, and not just a roommate I hid my drinking and using from.

I stroked the top of his left hand. He was not wearing his wedding ring. Neither was I. One day last summer, as we were driving through Burbank, our agitated conversation had escalated from irritated bickering into full-blown verbal warfare. I have no idea what we were arguing about. It could have been World Peace or the fact that it was Wednesday.

Inside the car, I spewed. He snapped, uttering the "d-word." Divorce! I saw white. My chest swelled inside a disorienting rage. With an angry swipe, I removed my wedding band and whipped it out the window. "There! Now we're divorced!" I had screamed, then sat fuming in the passenger seat as Kevin pulled over to search the grassy knoll of Zankou Chicken, combing its blades for a flash of gold.

I shivered as the incident came back to me. Kevin had been living every second of our narcotic nightmare with the crystalline clarity to which I was just awakening. Remorse burned my throat as I placed my husband's hand against my heart. I wanted to smother his face with retroactive kisses for the times I had raged and called him names. *Oh, God. What do I do?*

From behind the meds' room, a whoosh of laughter cut the silence between us. Without my axis of pills and alcohol, I spun lost inside my emotions. I shifted on the couch. Two cushions existing like two separate planets for as far away from him as I felt.

"I'm going to Winnipeg on Tuesday." Kevin said.

My stomach tightened. *Winnipeg. That figures.* "For how long?"

"I don't know. A week? 10 days?"

My skin grew hot. Jealous globules began to drift down my cheeks. Kevin would hate the tears, but I couldn't help it. I could just picture it. His family would spend all their time sitting around that kitchen table talking about me. I frowned at the thought of the endless Dainties and cups of tea consumed as they tore me apart, bit-by-judgmental-bit. That stupid table, where the only time I had ever felt comfortable was floating away on my mother-in-law's stolen Xanax.

It wasn't fair. I was his wife! I was in rehab! I wanted my husband here with me. First he had stayed away for a week, and now he was leaving the country. Kevin was taking a break for first time in our marriage, and it scared me.

"It bothers me. Your blog. That you are laughing here."

"What?" I dropped his hand and wiped tears from my chin. What was he talking about?

"In your last blog. You said you guys laugh." His eyes flared. "I'm not laughing."

It had become my thing. Among the techs and clients, I was known for posting a nightly blog. On evening break I would write a piece for *Hey, Buddy, Can You Spare a Kidney?* I loved it, lived for it: The tap-tap-tap on my keyboard transforming muddled thoughts into lyrical posts. The thrill of hitting "Send" before 6:59 pm when my laptop turned back into contraband. As I wrote, friends and family read, and collectively we puzzled over how a screen-testing actress devolves into a two-time overdosing patient in recovery.

I sighed, reclaiming his hand. What Kevin did not understand was that fueling our laughter was a pilot light of pain. Underneath this canopy of lights and trees existed people treading water inside such a vast reservoir of pain it threatened to tsunami us all if it ever became undammed. Klean was helping me dismantle it brick-by-brick. How could I explain that I was not laughing because I was happy? I laughed because I no longer felt alone.

Kevin looked away. His stern profile pierced my heart. He had heard the discordant rattle of my pills, and the sound of my breath petering away to flat-line. He had listened to these sounds with ears wide open, not clogged with a narcotic thickness. When was the last time Kevin had heard laughter?

When he looked back at me, I flinched. I wasn't stupid. I could see what Klean looked like from the outside. As if I got a fabulous break from life's responsibilities in the form of twice-weekly maid service, and Sober Fun Day at *Pinz* bowling alley on Ventura Blvd.

We talked about my daily schedule, including group therapy and the doctors who were treating me, yet it was impossible to communicate the heart of my first week. How could I explain that a simple shower had become like daily baptism into my new world? No longer an inconvenience, sheeting hot water felt like purification of a body no longer crumpled in agonizing withdrawal. With each drop of water, I would think, *I can do this without pills.*

I would stand over the kitchen sink and devour spoonful after spoonful of peanut butter drizzled in honey. I could not get enough. I had been disinterested in food for so long I had forgotten. Food was awesome. Orgasmic. With every bite, I would think, *I can do this without pills.*

I cannot say my mind stilled during that first week, but it pinged with thoughts other than *Should I get my prescription phoned in to CVS Burbank or Rite Aid Sunland?* Before group, I would grab my pen, paper and coffee with first-day-of-school excitement and think, *I can do this without pills.*

For Kevin the act of showering, eating and thinking were actions he had never lost. But for me, these fundamentals of human existence, taken for granted by most people on any given day, had become transcendent experiences.

Kevin rose to leave. Fresh tears brimmed in my eyes.

"You're leaving already?" I clung to his hand.

"I have a long drive home." When had Kevin ever complained about the drive to this area of town? "I'm glad you're doing well."

His arm dropped to his side as he walked away without acknowledging when he might return, without ever touching his wife.

My heart cracked. Yet more tears fell. I watched my husband disappear through Klean's gate and out into the real world. Self-piteous bile rose in my throat. I remember thinking he still had everything: his health, career and family, and I had lost it all. I could not see that in losing his wife to addiction, Kevin had lost just as much as me, and that night, unlike me, he was very much alone.

Kevin went to Winnipeg, but he never took a break from us. Years later, he admitted that several times during that first week, he made the hour-long trek to West Hollywood. He would circle the quiet residential streets, seeking a glimpse of the tribe that had claimed his wife. When he finally told me, I was unsurprised. I'd had a feeling. Not that he was circling the facility at an exact moment, but that somehow, someway he was still orbiting my world.

SOBER DAY 7. SUNDAY OCTOBER 23rd, 2011.
Just Grateful.

THERE WAS a man on Saturday who spoke and for me it was deeply profound. He has been sober 16 years, and he said, "Now when I have fun, everybody has fun," and I thought of all the times I was having fun, and it was nothing close to fun for Kevin at all. Closer to hell.

Grateful to my husband who is still willing to listen, even though he has every right not to.

18. PEN AND PAPER 2011

Sober Day 13. Saturday October 29ᵗʰ, 2011.
      Rebirthday.

I SHOWERED and blew dry my hair (on loan from contraband). My now long again, strawberry blond mop blown straight and parted down the middle, makeup free, naked as a newborn. I smeared free the mirror of steamy diversion and gazed cleanly into the eyes, if you didn't look too closely, of a woman who could have been the girl of yesteryear. 23 years ago, when a discharge nurse after Transplant #1 mentioned I could get Tylenol 1 with Codeine over the counter if I still had pain. When those cunning, crafty tentacles of addiction stirred awake and affixed themselves to a gaping, welcoming sanctuary...

As SOBER DAYS turned into sober weeks, I embraced my daily tasks, simple chores understood by a defogging mind. Klean's rules did not suffocate me. The structure felt like a hug of encouragement. Not walls I wanted to bounce off, but a safe place against which I could lean my head: Make your bed. Dress yourself in clean clothes. Participate in the communal breakfast. Agree to drug testing. Take your detox meds. *I can do this without pills.*

In my first private session with Klean's on-staff psychiatrist, Dr. C., I unleashed an unstoppable torrent, confessing self-hatred when I remembered stealing pain medication from Kevin.

"What's wrong with me?" I wailed. "Why would I do that?"

Dr. C. listened much more than he ever spoke, but as a seeming comfort he offered, "Alcoholism is listed in the American Medical Association."

In 1956, the organization declared alcoholism / addiction an illness. Then in 1966, proclaimed it a disease. In 1991, the AMA further endorsed the dual classification of alcoholism by the International Classification of Diseases under both psychiatric and medical sections. As defined by the AMA, alcoholism meets the three standard criteria for being declared a disease: 1) It has an identifiable set of symptoms. 2) It follows a predictable and malignant progression if not treated. 3) It responds to treatment.

That these words came from the mouth of a man of science changed everything for me. It legitimized addiction. Maybe addicts weren't ne'er-do-wells who lived under bridges, needles hanging from their arms, slamming heroin eight times a day because they were losers with no will power. Apparently, they were sick. I could get on board with this. I was a girl who understood disease.

SOBER DAY 17. Wednesday November 2nd, 2011.

"ADDICTS OFTEN EMERGE from childhoods of profound trauma and rigid, regimented upbringings that manifest in OCD/control issues."

When Dr. C. presented this theory in group one afternoon, I had to suppress the urge to jump up and down and cry, *That's me!* Profound trauma? I submit Daddy's alcoholic death when I was 10, chased by my CKD diagnosis at age 13, capped by a kidney transplant at 19. A rigid and regimented upbringing? How about Mum's checklist of chores I had to complete before I could go out and play. OCD issues? There were those lists I had been driven to keep from age 6, so similar to the ones I had seen spattered across my mother-in-law's kitchen backsplash on the night I stole my first Xanax.

As a girl, I would amend my standing list every night by proudly crossing off the items I had completed that day. But through my teens and as an adult, more lists materialized. Some nights, in addition to this standing list, I would go through my "master" list. This was a now book of lists and sub-lists cataloguing old lists from days gone by. Deep inside my nightly ritual, my body would quiver on the verge of tears, but I could not afford to focus on the neon digits blinking by. If I did, I might forget something that had to be added. Or removed. Or highlighted. Or cross-referenced. I could not stop. I had to complete these lists.

When I finally finished, it would have all been worth it. Having wrangled every thought, feat and desire, I could breathe. I felt in total control. Untouchable. Invincible. Until I wondered if I had forgotten something, and a searing darkness would shatter the brief peace I had just found.

As I made my way over to the meds' room for my scheduled time on the phone, Dr. C.'s hypothesis began to gel inside my 17-day old sober mind. His information was like oxygen for my crazy cells. I had never known why I made these lists, and often felt insane in my inability to stop.

I signed my name and the time on the sign-out sheet, grabbed the cordless phone and collapsed into the same couch where Kevin and I had sat nine days earlier. Something was tugging at me. At an earlier point in my life, list making had worked. Bringing me comfort, a sense of control, for at least one day. But with this ritual came a point where I crossed some line. Almost as if I were no longer writing the lists, like the lists were writing me. The process became so agonizing, providing me with such a brief flicker of relief that it hardly seemed worth the effort anymore. The ritual had backfired. And yet, I kept making them.

I was not in rehab for making lists. I was in rehab because of an overdose of 132 benzodiazepines. Yet, it had been exactly the same with pills. I had crossed some line. Once upon a time, just the thought of Her had brought me relief. Then, the delicious ritual of Her: Step 1: The Ordering of the Medication. Step 2: The Picking up of the Medication. Step 3: The Swallowing of the Medication. Until that June day in 2010 when I picked up 120 misprescribed Fiorinal, and realized I couldn't return Her to the pharmacists. In the ER, everyone believed I had tried to kill myself. I shivered. There was a truth crawling on my skin: I had not tried to kill myself. She had tried to kill me.

Was it really was a disease? And was Dr. C.'s theory the reason I had become an addict?

My heart pounded as I phoned Winnipeg. Kevin had never understood my compulsion to make lists so I had hidden the majority of my obsessive scribbling from him. But now I wanted to shout from the rooftops—and most particularly to him—that there might be a reason why I had done the things I had done. Why I had become an addict. Lists had been like my first drug. And then I had found Codeine.

"Addiction is a disease. It can stem from childhood trauma," I offered excitedly. My heart fluttered in the seconds his pause eroded into a loaded silence.

"That's no excuse," he shot out. My cheeks burned.

"Well, I thought it was interesting."

My hackles surged. What the hell did Kevin know about childhood trauma? He had been raised in the perfect nuclear family—father, mother, daughter and son. Unconditional love all the way around that kitchen table: Hockey, highland dancing, and hugs. My mouth went dry. For the first time in forever I did not know how to defend myself. With his click goodbye, I felt a wall go up between us.

I had expected this information to resonate in his bones the way it did in mine. How could he not care? Later that night, I would run Kevin's comment by a tech.

"No, it's not an excuse, but it is an explanation."

On the edge of my odd little bed, I trembled with emotion. Was I angry because Kevin was right? That addiction was a disease was not an excuse for the things I had done. This information had empowered me, but not my husband who needed answers to entirely different questions.

Why couldn't you stop after I gave you a kidney? And will you stop now?

Indeed, Dr. C.'s theory explained perhaps why I had become an addict, but it did not explain how I would stop.

That night, we slept in two different countries staked on two different sides of one terrifying disease. I stood planted on side "Explanation" while he remained on side "Excuse." How could I bring him over to my side of the wall? And did he even want to?

SOBER DAY 20. Saturday November 5th, 2011.
   Miss Understanding.

I FEEL the disconnect between myself and those who don't suffer with addiction. It echoes back on a string between two empty soup cans. I feel their love, but their inability to relate rattles (me) like a storefront garage door coming down and I'm left locked inside.

It's loud and dark and I am afraid.

19. TYLENOL 3 WITH CODEINE

S ober Day 21. Sunday November 6th, 2011.

THREE WEEKS INTO REHAB, I had attended about 15 AA meetings. Besides those first days when I slept nearly 24/7, I only missed meetings when I was sick. Clients were never forced to go to 12-Step meetings like AA (Alcoholics Anonymous) or NA (Narcotics Anonymous). Legally, California treatment centers cannot subscribe to any one form of therapy, but it was suggested we go and keep an open mind. I went every chance I got. After 7 pm, I no longer had access to my laptop, and evenings in rehab stretched long. But it was more than that. I began to love meetings, crave them, not unlike the way I still craved my pills.

The walk from Klean through West Hollywood to the regular 7:30 pm meeting was seven minutes long. Usually five or six of the eleven in-house clients would attend. I kept close to the front of the pack, masterfully avoiding their pervasive cloud of smoke. Our nightly stroll was taken during this neighborhood's witching hour: Restaurants thrummed with anticipatory bass lines. Designer-clad boys prowled up and down Santa Monica Boulevard. I'd watch them strut and wonder, *Will it ever be fun to get dressed up without a drink in my hand?*

This night, a waiting maître'd' nodded as I passed his restaurant's patio. Three weeks earlier he would have escorted me to a table where I would have ordered a glass of wine. Or two. Probably three. I made brief eye contact with him and then looked away at the sight of the empty wine glasses standing at the ready. My stomach rumbled. This physical ache was my witching hour. Getting high on an empty stomach was all I had lived for but a month ago. I swallowed tightly at the thought of washing down pills with a chilled vodka/soda. A cold sweat dotted the back of my neck. God, how I missed the euphoric melt entering me, slithering through my veins, soaking my soul.

I glanced back at the maître'd. What did he think when he saw this motley crew trudge by? Did he know we were on a field trip from rehab? Was he one of us, periodically scurrying to the back of the restaurant to swig from a hidden bottle of booze the way I used to stash wine behind our water heater? I sighed and ran my fingers through my thinning hair. Through sober eyes the world was a changed place, everything reminding me that pills and alcohol would always exist, but could no longer exist for me.

"Hi. Welcome."

A small group of well-dressed men nodded to us as we shuffled through the facility door. I nodded, averting my eyes as I scurried through yet another thick cloud of smoke.

When I had first stepped into this utilitarian space, I was unsurprised. The meeting room appeared exactly as depicted on the big screen: Casual to well-dressed people sat in rows facing a podium. In the corner by a sink was a bare bones coffee set-up: coffee maker, white Styrofoam cups, powdered creamer and dollar-store cookies. On painfully bare walls hung two banners: "The 12 Steps" and "The Twelve Traditions" from the Big Book of Alcoholics Anonymous (aka: The Big Book).

We were wrangled into seats by our chaperoning tech. My pack. Always together. Animated conversation swirled around me as potent as the smoke I had dodged on the way in. I sat very still, both hands holding a Styrofoam cup. The teabag bobbed in the steaming clear, seeping rusty plumes until the cup was fully saturated with life. In those final minutes before the meeting began I liked to close my eyes, and like the tea, allow myself to become steeped in the energy of the room. My body relaxed as if I had just swallowed a Xanax.

The meeting's secretary (that I later learned is a rotating commitment) read the AA preamble, and then volunteers read regular selections from the Big Book. With a warm smile he asked, "Are there any newcomers here with less than 30 days of sobriety? If so, please stand and identify yourself by first name only so that we may welcome you."

One-by-one the newcomers stood, willing to declare themselves members of this tribe. My heart pounded as I rose.

"Hi. I'm Henriette and I'm an alcoholic, addict."

"HI HENRIETTE!" With each name, the room exploded, bursting into applause when the final person sat. My head spun. To publicly declare myself an addict was: Terrifying. Confusing. Relieving. I exhaled deeply, allowing myself a small smile. But shaming? No, one thing this raucous greeting was not, was shaming.

At last, the night's speaker approached the podium. He began to talk about what his life had been like when he drank, what happened to bring him into the rooms of AA, and what his sober life was like. He would say something, and I would nod. He would say something else and someone else would nod. Sometimes we would all nod. Mumbled testimony filled the air around me. We were with him.

"At first, my drinking and using was fun. Then it was fun with problems. Then it was just problems," he shared.

My blood iced over. Washing down the odd Fiorinal with a beer was so controlled some twenty years ago. I pictured Vegas nights not so long ago when Kevin and I frolicked intoxicated in an enormous plush bed and he would whisper, *I like Drunk Hen.* On a more recent trip, Kevin waited downstairs in the casino, as I got ready for the evening's concert. Every time I raised my hand to apply more eye shadow, I'd raise my glass. Every time I popped the cap on my lipstick, I'd pop Her cap, too. By the time my face was plastered, my body and soul were as well. Shifting in the plastic chair, I teared up, unable to stand the memory of catching Kevin's devastated eyes across a crowded casino floor.

What happened? Why could I no longer stop after one or two drinks or pills? Drunk Hen had stumbled down the street, and become so lost she could no longer find her way home. Would Kevin come looking for me as he always had? Of our 21-day sober marriage, I knew one thing for certain: Kevin did not like Drunk Hen anymore.

The speaker's laughter landed like a spray of rain on my face. I was invigorated. Electrified. He had cheated, stolen, and lied. Yet he seemed relieved of the crippling burden of remorse. Kevin's face floated before mine, and the tears that threatened began to fall.

YOU ARE A FUCKING DRUG ADDICT!

As I wiped at my unapologetic stream of tears, the speaker continued.

"Every addict remembers their first high."

As he spoke, I pictured myself at 19 hunched over a coil notebook in bed. It was February 1988, two weeks after my first kidney transplant. That night, my skin was crawling. I scanned the left side of my abdomen that Mum's kidney now called home. The scar throbbed mildly, but it was healing well. I looked at the clock: 9 pm. Long past my nightly dose of Tylenol 3 with Codeine (Acetaminophen / Codeine / Caffeine). Interesting. I hadn't even noticed the time for my painkiller had come and gone.

Irritated, I tapped my pen. At the time, my boyfriend had been away for five months in Indonesia on a student exchange program. After my surgery, his mother didn't bring my flowers to the hospital as instructed because, as she later confided to me over the phone with a sigh, *I just don't like hospitals.* My chest had swelled with rage. *Well lucky you, you dumb ass.* Conveniently forgetting she had taken me to dialysis and rented movies for me to watch in their home so I didn't have to be alone while my mother was at work. An indefinable ache gnawed at my gut. My boyfriend needed to know about this.

Restless, I stared at the empty page, grappling for words. I reached for the prescription bottle, popped the cap, and swallowed one pill. I couldn't stand the fact that I couldn't talk to him right now.

When that single pill flooded my bloodstream, I near levitated off the bed. My head swirled with relief. Uninhibited, I sharpened my pen as sword and began to carve out my missive. With contemptuous flourishes across the page, I jabbed at his mother, outlining her failure. Then I sacrificed my pride with an unabashed literary surrender: I miss you. I need you. I want you. I love you. As I wrote, my soul soared. I felt connected to myself in a way I never had. Untouchable. Invincible. Authentically Henriette. Empowered by a source that annihilated all my fears. I laid down my sword that night convinced everything would be OK.

That night I learned pills were for all kinds of pain.

Maybe a month later, my boyfriend's response to my diatribe was a single telling sentence scrunched into the corner of the final page of his last letter. "Be careful who you crucify." *What?* I had only been telling the truth. What did he know about pain? I had had a *transplant*. 23 years later, my cheeks burned with embarrassment as hot as if I had just read his words.

A couple months later, we would break up, but I would find a new obsession. Post-transplant, my discharge nurse handed me a prescription for Tylenol 3 and shared information that would change the trajectory of my life.

"If you still have pain after this, you can get Tylenol 1 with Codeine over the counter at any pharmacy."

A month later, I found myself in the back of a Mom 'n Pop pharmacy asking if they carried Tylenol 1 with Codeine. The pharmacist was most obliging, so polite, so Canadian, delivering me not only the inquired-after drug, but introducing me to its generic version, saving me two-thirds the cost. This innocent purchase initiated me into my longtime relationship with Codeine. It became my daily dose of relief, no different than a morning cup of coffee to kick start my day. I would take Tylenol 1 with Codeine every morning for the next 23 years.

Every addict remembers their first high.

How many sober days had I had since I was 19? I sighed and gripped my cup. The warmth I was feeling was not from the heat seeping through Styrofoam. In this room, I felt good. Safe. The speaker had blown my mind. I did remember my first high, every delicious and empowering moment of it.

His voice suddenly dropped, and I made eye contact with the man next to me to see if he too was struggling to hear.

"I bet you if he was in a bar he wouldn't have any trouble speaking up," he said, wiggling his eyebrows.

I burst into loud laughter. Mortified, I clamped a hand over my mouth, muffling my snorts. I couldn't help it. What he said was perfection. An undeniable peace filled my heart. I had not felt these feelings in so long. Belonging. Serenity. Hope. Whatever these strangers had, I wanted.

SOBER DAY 21: Sunday November 6th, 2011.
Easy like Sunday morning.

THERE IS something remarkable that happens when that door shuts and the gavel pounds twice. Between 4 unadorned walls a roomful of eclectics sit, shifting and sipping. But when the meeting starts, an aura drifts down blanketing the crowd below. Understanding.

In my first 30 days, I still do the newcomer bop; standing quickly, eyes shifted downward as I quickly blurt, "Henriette, alcoholic, addict..."

"Hi, Henriette!"

"Done."

I am accepted.

Judgment doesn't squat here.

Demons spill forth after the first handshake. Laughter flows freely, like a sandbag removed from a dam.

20. SEROQUEL

S ober Day 33. Friday November 18th, 2011.

MY ROOMMATE KAREN and I were in the kitchen saying goodnight. She always turned in just before II pm, rising at 6 am to meditate alone before Morning Meditation. Suddenly, I grabbed the counter, my legs wobbling beneath me.

"Are you ok?" she asked.

"Yeah. I think it's just my blood sugar dropping."

She nodded, closing the bedroom door behind her. Inside our apartment, we orbited each other like two polite satellites. I did not dislike her, but outside these walls, I could not imagine we would be a part of each other's worlds.

Sweat beaded on the back of my neck. I hadn't eaten enough today. That was it. I stuffed half a pastry into my mouth and stumbled into the living room, planning to watch the news while my sleeping med kicked in. I hated this feeling—like you are falling through space.

I lay down on the couch and placed my shaking hands on my chest. I was not frightened. I knew what was happening. A blood sugar crash is when your blood glucose level drops below normal. In people who don't have diabetes like myself, poor diet, too much alcohol, intense exercise, and certain illnesses or medications can cause your blood sugar to drop causing hunger, anxiety, and sweating. I knew the pastry, as rapidly absorbing carb, would stabilize my blood sugar.

Suddenly, it felt like a fist punch to the back of my neck. I gasped, crumbling to the floor. Sweat streamed out of me. My heart was pounding so hard my entire body rocked. This feeling I did not recognize. Tightness gripped my neck. I tried to swallow, but my throat was closing up. Desperate to breathe, I sucked air through my nose. What was in my mouth? I had to get it out. I stumbled over to the bathroom, clutching my neck with both hands.

In the mirror my eyes were wild, my cheeks two circles of shocked red. My tongue protruded like some agitated creature smeared in dough. Was this an allergic reaction to the pastry? I had never had a food allergy in my life. My head whirled. I grabbed at the sink's cool edge, my legs buckling beneath me. On a final surge of adrenaline, I launched my body against the bedroom door and screamed.

"Karen! Help me! I can't breathe!"

Our door flew open. Without a word, Karen caught me as I collapsed. She is shorter than me, but hurtled us through the apartment and down the steps into the common area. I managed a strangled cry. The sound made when terror renders you mute.

"HELP! HELP! SHE CAN'T BREATHE!" Karen screamed.

I spotted Buddy, one of the techs, outside the meds room. He would later tell me my body resembled The Incredible Hulk—every vein engorged—as I collapsed onto the patio steps.

In the driveway outside Klean, oscillating lights swirled from atop two ambulances, slicing the dark night with their angry red beams. EMTs emerged from the shadows, wielding their flashlights into our faces. I raised my forearm against the flickering lights. The walls of my lungs felt like they had collapsed. Every breath burned. I planted my hands on my knees and wheezed like an old dog.

Inside the cluster of men, Buddy was gesticulating. Why had no one come to offer me a hand? Bring me a chair? Or even help me lean against the ambulance's tailgate? My chest seared with pain. I had to sit down. The driveway was packed with cars, and there was no patch of grass. Shuffling over to the street, I squatted in the gutter, dropping my head into my hands.

There was something in the air. It was not the moonless night that made it difficult for me to see the face of the EMT who finally did question me. It was the way his dead eyes stared as I struggled to answer with an uncooperative tongue. The way he recorded my information with a flaccid pen. The throng stood with their backs to me, offering nothing but the occasional glance. I began to shake as the cold cement seeped through my pajama bottoms. Why was I still on the ground? I looked up to see Karen moving towards me. She squatted on the curb and threw her arm around me, planting her feet in the gutter beside mine.

With a sudden shiver, I realized it was imperative they know I had a pre-existing condition. I told the closest EMT that I was a recent kidney transplant patient. God, why wouldn't my mouth work? My lips were as effective as two wriggling worms. I had a legitimate medical theory. Ten days earlier my immunosuppressives had been cranked higher. Maybe this was a reaction? He acknowledged my theory by walking away.

Eventually, I was packaged onto a gurney and inserted into the back of the ambulance. When the EMT looked the other way, I wormed an inch of breathing room between my body and the restrictive straps. Why were they so tight? I told them I couldn't breathe! Finally, he placed an oxygen mask over my nose and mouth. With one huge and grateful breath, the mask slipped down the side of my face. The EMT did not move to help me. My stomach flipped in confusion. I wriggled one arm out of the straps and placed the mask back over my mouth myself.

"Has your doctor ever told you there are certain medications you can't take?" The first EMT was standing by the open back doors holding a chart encased in a silver box.

"I'm allergic to Vancomycin, Amoxicillin and Clindamycin." His brow crinkled. I breathed in and out through my nose the way I had learned in yoga. This forced breath had always calmed me down in the past. His unfriendly eyes narrowed. I was not calming down.

"Has you doctor ever told you there are certain medications you can't take?" My heart quickened. Why was he repeating himself?

"Um...I can't take Advil or any other NSAIDs because of my transplant." His eyes flashed with impatience.

"That's not what I am asking. HAS. YOUR. DOCTOR. EVER. TOLD. YOU. THERE. ARE. CERTAIN. MEDICATIONS. YOU. CAN'T. TAKE?"

Hot tears formed behind my eyes. Why was he yelling? I couldn't breathe. I could hear just fine.

"I don't understand." He sighed, slamming the doors shut. With an ominous wail, the ambulance lurched forward the short ride to Cedars. Clutching the sides of the gurney, I realized in 30 years as a patient, I had never once taken a ride in an ambulance.

The back doors swung wide and my gurney clunked to the ground. I squinted, overwhelmed by the sudden assault of florescent light and directed shouts. The EMT removed my oxygen mask and escorted me to the ER waiting area where I crumpled into a chair. When I looked up, he was gone.

As I fought sleep from my prescribed sleep med, I stayed awake to a nagging tug in my gut. In the hospital I had always been treated like a queen: helped into wheelchairs, offered masks, and escorted to procedures. The tilted-headed wonder that is my two kidney transplants had afforded me the Gold Star treatment, a fast pass for every procedure and pain. Tonight, for the first time ever, I sat alone, waiting alongside everyone else.

A couple hours later, Kevin arrived just as I was being bought into a room.

"Hi," he offered, sagging into the chair beside the bed.

"I'm just waiting for the doctor." Kevin nodded, pulling out his phone.

I opened my mouth to say more, then stopped. I glanced around at the familiar cupboards filled with medical supplies. My reddened skin from a recent IV line was par for the course. My heart beat wildly. Something was off.

A physician whirled into the room, declaring the incident an allergic reaction to Seroquel. Seroquel was my current sleep med. Ten days earlier the transplant clinic—in addition to increasing my immunosuppressives—had switched me from Trazodone to Seroquel because the former presented unsafe interaction with my protocol. It had taken ten days to kick in, but the offending Seroquel was hereby discontinued. I was told to return to rehab and rest. Then he whirled away as if through a revolving door. Mystery solved.

Inside a stifling silence, we waited for the nurse to come around with my discharge papers. Kevin shifted in his chair. I shifted on the bed. Everything between us, too, was the same as it had even been. I wore the ubiquitous hospital gown as Kevin took swigs from his Coke Zero, but everything felt different. Many nights we had sat together in hospital silence, but it had never hurt my ears. Crossing my arms, I took a good long look at his profile. What was vibrating off him? Resentment? Disinterest? Kevin looked out into the bustling ER. He was here, but not. Everyone was acting like there was some place else they would rather be.

The doctor had barely taken in the medical marvel that is me. His eyebrows had not risen when I pointedly shared that Kevin had given me his kidney seven months earlier. Suddenly, a shiver of understanding traveled down my spine. The only nuggets this doctor had digested from my impressive medical history was that I had been admitted 36 nights earlier for a benzodiazepine overdose and was currently living in a drug and alcohol rehabilitation center. I thought back to my slumped body in the gutter outside Klean. The EMTs must have assumed I was loaded, and not having an allergic reaction.

My heart dropped. In the eyes of my steadfast community, my clout had vanished. Once again, I looked over at Kevin, head bent over his phone.

"What's wrong with you?" I snapped.

"I'm tired, Henriette. It's nearly three in the morning." Then. "Did you have to come in an ambulance?"

I felt my breath catch. I had been strapped to a gurney with an oxygen tank! It's not like I had stubbed my toe and scored a ride to the emergency room. What had he imagined I do? Hail a cab? Skip the 12 blocks to Cedars? Hitch?

"Walking wasn't really an option, *Kevin*." I heard the way I emphasized his name. Economical. Frigid. Two could play at that game.

"How much is an ambulance going to cost?"

My face burned hot. Was he fucking kidding me with this? In what world was the cost of an ambulance more important than my ability to breathe? I released a slow and deliberate exhale.

"I have no idea. I was too busy trying to breathe."

Kevin stared at me. "I'm allowed to ask."

There had been many times Kevin had bitched about our $800 combined monthly premiums, for-profit hospitals and overpaid doctors, but his frustration had always been spewed in a general direction—at the American Medical System or at ourselves for leaving Canada's beloved Universal Health Care. It had never felt like he was blaming me, like somehow being sick was my fault. Until now. His tone so scornful, it felt like I could wipe its residue off my gown. Kevin's red-rimmed eyes spoke to his exhaustion, but he held his laser-focused stare. I shivered. My husband was no longer looking at his wife, but at the medical burden I had become.

Tonight, no one had seen a woman sustaining an allergic reaction. They had seen an addict. The EMTs and ER physician had treated me efficiently and coldly, as if I were a subspecies of patient: Trauma Patient, followed by Very Sick Patient, Sick Patient, and at the end of the line, Addict Patient. They had discriminated.

My blood boiled. This was Cedars-Sinai Medical Center! Surely they understood I hadn't chosen to add this to my medical repertoire. An icy revelation flooded my veins. These medical professionals believed I had chosen to become an addict. But with everything I had already heard and read, and what I could feel in my soul, I knew I had not chosen this path. Born this way or due to circumstances beyond my control, addiction had taken me. Somewhere along my winding road through procedures and prescriptions, the pills had taken me. After only 33 sober days, I believed I had lost the power of choice because of an illness—a physical craving that can never be satisfied once triggered, coupled with a mental obsession to try, try again until death.

I pulled at the neck of my gown, my heart racing. I wanted to shed the hospital garb that had always felt like a second skin. To leave those who lead with shaming stares, and be around those who rendered understanding. Kevin stood. With a gut punch I realized he didn't want to be around me. I wanted to go home. To Klean.

That night, I'd been rushed to the ER because I had been unable to breathe. Curled in my tiny bed I watched Karen sleep, listening to her snore for several long minutes. I thought about how much easier it was for me to talk to her than my husband. Inside gunmetal gray walls, I realized my world now existed inside the sleeping hearts and minds around me.

Then I turned onto my back and exhaled.

∼

SOBER DAY 37. Monday November 22nd, 2011.
Zoo Station.

NUDE, *silver slats, peering through into dark,*
    sweating, convulsing, mind tearing up thought.
    you are far from my arms now,
    you are far from my heart.

~

SOBER DAY 45. Tuesday November 29th, 2011.
   I heart AA.

AA IS NOT A CULT.
   aa is not a gathering place for the tribe of the morally defective.

NOR IS *aa a hub for the l.a. jet set; clutching their recyclable starbucks canis-*
ters, sucking down hard on camel lights.

FOR ME, *aa is a place that should be mandatory for all. like death and taxes.*

IT IS NOT *a crutch. it offers you one until you no longer need it, when you*
can pass it down to another hobbling soul...

IT IS NOT ABOUT RELIGION. *it is at heart, a spiritual program. about under-*
standing yourself, your destructive ways of thinking and changing them, so
that you can be of service to another...and another...and another...

AND IT IS NOT *about judgment. there is no "failure". the person who has 47*
days (me) is as welcome as the person who has 47 years. for the 12 steps are
a program that can be plugged into anyone's life at any time...

...FOR THE FIRST *time in 47 days, i truly understand what this disease is. it is*
a disease of my thinking. i am learning how to change the way i think, and
then create new solutions. pills/alcohol were not my problem. they were my
solution.

. . .

...*TONIGHT, i stand in 100% belief of this:*

IF THE WHOLE *world went to aa meetings, the world would be that better place that exists in all our dreams.*

21. CELL CEPT 2012

S ober Day 58. Tuesday December 13th, 2011.

EVERYWHERE I LOOKED WAS BLUE. Cloudless blue. A lovely breeze brushed the back of my neck. The *bha-ha-ha*-ing of goats underscored the thrum of the freeway. Our canyon unfurled into the distant smog, where the towers of Los Angeles protruded as dazzling beacons to ambition. I was home.

I wiped my palms against the "L"-sized sweats I'd picked up on one of the Sunday Target runs to accommodate my rapidly expanding body. The world literally lay at my feet, and yet I could not move. How could I wash dishes next to my Secret Cupboard knowing I would never again find Her there? How could I go into my closet and see boots that upheld bottles of wine for me to nip at in the night? Coming home was like returning to the playground after being sent to the principal's office and discovering all my friends had gone home. Who would I play with now?

I had left rehab one hour ago and was already homesick.

A few days earlier, in my final session with Dr. C., I'd asked about continuing our sessions. "I think you are going to be just fine," he stated cryptically. Did he mean to say I no longer needed therapy? Or that he didn't want to see me? I had not asked. Then, Dr. H. who oversaw our detoxes and medications closed my file with a proud glint in his eye.

"I've waited fifteen years to see a file like that."

In theatre school, winning the part of Girl Most Likely To Stay Sober would have thrilled me, but in recovery, it left me unsettled. Their comments inferred I would stay sober. These were professionals giving their Grade-A medical stamp of approval. Squinting into the distance, I shivered. What was I missing?

The hairs on my skin vibrated as I felt Kevin join me at the edge of our world. How long had I been out here?

After the Seroquel incident, Kevin and I entered into a kind of ceasefire. His unchecked anger seemed to have been triggered more by the night's circumstances (long drive, another medical bill), than a permanent position of resentment towards his wife. Every Sunday, he came to the Family and Friends BBQ, and stayed for the in-house AA meeting. As we ate potato salad and hot dogs in the common area, we would talk. Love still flickered in his eyes, dim as it was.

"I love you, Henriette, but I can't go through that again."

"I know. I know." But did I?

During these weekly "dates," we took baby steps towards the wall that divided our understanding of addiction. Kevin stopped insisting, *Well, it's not a disease like your kidney failure,* that calling it a disease was just some big Excuse. I stopped trying to Explain it away. But who were we to each other now? Once defined as husband and wife, today, Addict and Normie.

"Are you coming inside?" He put his arm around me.

The afternoon sun flared off the faraway towers. I leaned into my husband. How could I explain to him that I felt consumed? Without the walls of Klean protecting me, the world was too big. There was too much air. I no longer knew how to breathe this air without pills.

I cannot do this without pills.

My heart pounded with equal beats love and fear. I recalled the many times we would go out—pre and post transplant—and I would bring nothing but my drivers' license and a lipstick to slide into my back pocket. I insisted it was because I wanted to be unencumbered by a purse, but really I wanted to be unencumbered by life. To drink and use unconditionally, always assuming Kevin would be the night's designated driver. Never once asking if he might want to partake in the fun.

He had force-fed me my immunosuppressives. Rearranged his work schedule to accompany me to every appointment. And then there was the way he left me at Klean—like a giant Marital Time Out. Kevin had always assumed the role of caregiver without me ever having to ask. The way a parent loves a child.

He gave me a squeeze. I snuggled deeper into the nook of his armpit and sighed. I liked our parental frequency. Pure. Uncomplicated. I wanted to stay here forever. I had gained 15 lbs in sixty days and would continue to as I discovered sugar as a substitute for my drug and alcohol cravings. My hair was falling out and would be chopped into a bob the next day. In my prodigious sweatpants I barely felt like a woman, never mind a wife.

"What can I do?" he asked, intimating wisdom only a parent has. The knowledge that everything will be all right because they are older and wiser and have lived through it. But Kevin wasn't my parent, nor did he possess the blueprint of How To Move Forward in a Sober Marriage. But I did.

At Klean, I had been schooled to treat the disease of addiction with AA meetings and a sponsor who would take me through the 12 Steps of Alcoholics Anonymous. Before I was discharged, the techs told me to line up a meeting. I had found a Big Book study in a place called The Burbank Group that was 12 minutes away. With a pang, I wondered what time it was.

"There's a 6 pm meeting in Burbank."

"I'll come with you." Then he took my hand and squeezed it. "C'mon."

Walking inside would be unadulterated immersion into a sober new world. There would be countless firsts: Driving a car. Having a bath. Washing our dishes. Despite the fear weakening my legs, willingness flooded through me. Kevin's gentleness was a welcome downshift from his standoffish presence at Klean. Perhaps Al-Anon meetings (a recovery program for the friends and family of alcoholics) and his community of men with shared experiences accounted for his willingness. Or maybe there was fairy dust magic in the simple fact I was home.

I squeezed back. With Kevin walking beside me, sobriety seemed possible. I didn't realize that I needed to let go of his hand in order to find my way home. Not alone, but without Kevin.

"OK," I said.

But this day we walked inside holding hands. Where for the first time in 22 years there would be no pill to welcome me home.

❧

FOR THE FIRST few weeks after I left Klean, Kevin would often join me at open AA meetings sitting alongside twitching addicts with single-digit days of sobriety. Newcomers took chips for 30, 60, 90 days, 6 and 9 months and 1 year of staying clean. They took cakes—like birthday cakes—for continuous years of sobriety, and thanked sponsors, sponsees, friends and God for helping them stay sober. We listened to Old-Timers in pressed suits or tailored dresses with 10, 20, 30 years of sobriety talk about how they'd had everything only to lose it all to alcohol. Then with AA found an even better life, a life beyond their wildest dreams. What the hell did that mean? *A life beyond my wildest dreams.* Did that mean I would finally become a big movie star?

If I had any doubt that Kevin still loved me and was willing to try again, it vanished every time I stood up in a meeting and identified, *Hi. I'm Henriette and I'm an alcoholic* and he didn't bolt. In fact, sometimes Kevin would be the one getting me into my seat. One night I threw a tantrum outside an AA clubhouse, terrified to go inside. *I don't know anyone! I don't know how to share! I want to go home!* But when I went home, I felt worse. My husband sat with me like a sober companion—a person of significant sober time hired to help a client maintain total abstinence and harm reduction. (A job frowned on by AA purists.) In early sobriety, that was the dynamic we found. Kevin was there to do a job, and I let him.

SOBER DAY 104. Thursday January 26th, 2012.

"WHAT ARE YOU HAVING?" Kevin asked.

Inside the darkened booth of the steak house I fidgeted, tugging my dress down over my knees. I had agonized over what to wear for his birthday, and chosen a shift dress to hide my now 20+ lb. weight gain. With a hair straightener, I'd yanked at my coarse bob of hair, trying to coax it into the luscious locks of yesteryear.

Over the menu, I scanned the tables, taking note of those indulging in wine. The patrons' laughter taunted. Glasses clinked melodic. By candlelight, the dark bottles gleamed like rare jewels I could no longer afford to enjoy. No longer anchored by alcohol to a situation like this, my body sat, but my soul suspended from the forbidden tastes and smells. The waiter set down Kevin's Coke Zero and my sparkling water. The birthday boy caught my eye and I forced a smile. Laughter did not fall easily from my mouth on Day 104.

"Are you ok?" Kevin asked.

"I'm fine." But I wasn't. "You can have a beer, you know."

"I know," he replied. But he didn't.

I had enough clarity of mind to understand my husband wasn't drinking because he thought it would bother me. Kevin could not enjoy himself if I was not enjoying myself. I had no idea how to enjoy myself at a steakhouse without a drink. We had not slipped into our old roles, because we had not yet surrendered them. Kevin should have been able to celebrate his birthday with a drink, and I should have been able to celebrate my husband, but we were still functioning the way we had in the last years of our marriage: Me, obsessing on the wine not going into my mouth, and Kevin obsessing over me. All that had been removed from our marriage was the symptom of alcohol, not the problem of addiction.

I raised my glass and toasted my husband. "Happy birthday, sweetheart." He smiled.

But we were trying.

~

ADDICTS new to recovery are often instructed by treatments centers or sponsors to hit 90 meetings in 90 days. But by January, I had already drifted away from what my sponsor, Liz, had suggested I do. I stopped going to a meeting every day. I stopped calling her every day. Often inside that iconic grouping of chairs I rolled my eyes, chest burning with resentment as someone complained about their deck needing repair or their hormonal teenager, even as Liz smiled lovingly and rubbed my back.

I did relate to some things, particularly the obsessive thinking. One woman confessed excitement upon learning she was pregnant because she knew in nine months she would get drugs. That I got. But unlike at Klean, I did not feel a part of this AA world with their high-powered jobs, nice handbags and half-salad lunches. Their quality problems. In January 2012, I was only nine months post-transplant. I took toxic medications. Had side effects. Might reject. I had real problems. I was different. I had had a *transplant*.

After my June rejection episode, the Prograf / Cyclosporine fiasco that ended in August, and my October benzodiazepine overdose, my doctors' immunosuppression strategy had evolved from cautious to overprotective. 10 days prior to the Seroquel incident, Cell Cept had been jacked up to I'd-never-before-seen-levels: 1000 mg twice a day. As a result, so had my side effects. My still detoxing body was blowing up with: edema, headache, G.I. issues and abdominal bloating. (By end of day my distended belly resembled a 7-month pregnancy.) While Kevin slept, I would cry in the bathroom *I can't believe I'm an addict,* desperate to escape a body that was now home to not one, but two diseases.

Obviously, I could not take anything mind-altering, transplant patients cannot take any NSAIDs, and Tylenol was a joke. (Tylenol is to addicts as Pez is to candy. What's the point?) I was stone cold sober. And so I complained. To Kevin. To the doctors. To my sponsor. On my blog. Complaining became my new drug, and once again, I couldn't get enough.

By February I was complaining so much to Liz that she took me down with a single shot of her tough love rifle. Liz had been suggested by one of the Klean techs, and we began talking on the phone while I was still there. She was a nurse of 30+ years whose husband died of liver cancer. She had enough experience to perhaps not trump me—because let's face it, who could? —But at least meet me medical-toe-to-medical-toe. She told me to stop complaining to Kevin and even to my doctors unless there was something new to report. I was to call three other alcoholics a day, email her a list of 10 things I was grateful for every day, find a transplant support group and volunteer at a dialysis center. And then she said she loved me.

As I hung up the phone, my skin sizzled with emotion. Part of me reveled in the sting of her gunshot wound. I got it. She was being cruel to be kind with these tasks. But another part of me raged. No one had ever spoken to me this way before. *Who the hell are you? You don't know! You don't know what I deal with!*

SOBER DAY 177. Friday April 6th, 2012.

ALMOST ONE YEAR to the day post-transplant, Kevin and I sat in one of the clinic's rooms waiting for the doctor.

A new kidney transplant gestates with frequent appointments and closely monitored blood work for one year before it is truly born. Doctors strive to find a balance when medicating, an invisible line that is different for each patient. Once again, overimmunosuppression causes intense side effects and leaves the recipient susceptible to viruses and infection. Underimmunosuppression creates a lapse in the protection of the kidney. The recipient's immune system can attack the donor kidney and cause rejection. It takes twelve months of tracking blood levels and titrating medications before doctors are comfortable "delivering" the kidney. My day was finally here.

Restless, Kevin got up to pump from the wall sanitizer station. As he rubbed his hands together, a backdraft of isopropyl alcohol wafted beneath my nose. My breath caught. With a shiver, the smell brought me back to my deepest descent, while titillating my nostrils with memories of conscientious nurses swashing their hands before they injected me with The Big Relief.

Kicking my legs against the side of the bed-chair, I sighed. I had come for follow up appointments once a month for the last six months since getting sober, but it still felt strange knowing the option to hit the restroom and crush a few Xanax between my teeth was gone.

I looked over at Kevin as he scrolled, grateful that nothing floated between us but annoyance at having to wait. He caught my eye and winked. I was excited. Even my wistful craving could not overshadow the significance of this visit. There was no reason to think today's blood results would not be the coronation of Kevin's indefatigable kidney. Over the last six months my results had been showing: 1) Healthy glomeruli (filters) meaning good blood flow, thus a bounty of urine. 2) Normal, almost low, blood pressure even without medication as had been necessary throughout my first transplant. 3) Perfect regulation of minerals in my bloodstream, and 4) Four medications a day, down from a dialysis-dependent 23: Myfortic (Cell Cept coated for abdominal upset), Prednisone, Lasix, and my old buddy, Cyclosporine.

Advancing footsteps echoed down the hall. Kevin and I locked eyes. One tumultuous year had passed since Kevin's kidney had become mine. We were ready to take The Kid home.

Dr. P. and her tousled ponytail entered and pulled up a rolling stool next to me. We picked up the conversation exactly where we had left off a month earlier.

"We can't lower your Cell Cept, Henriette."

"I know."

"You rejected on the lower dose."

"I know."

I looked at her hair, annoyed. How busy was this fancy doctor that she couldn't take a brush to it? Had Dr. P. ever lived with toxic medications in her bloodstream? I thought not. I was doing it sober! As she brought up my virtual chart, I remembered what I had learned at Klean. Medical students get about seven hours on addiction. And even though Dr. P. was a transplant specialist, studying something and daily grappling with two medical conditions is profoundly different.

Kevin had survived Her late-night hysteria and enabled pharmacy runs. Now he was asking questions. Inch-by-tentative inch, I was revealing the details of my sticky-fingered past: Medicine cabinets I had pilfered. The many times I had driven altered. Bottles of alcohol consumed. The pill parties in my mouth. Curious combinations. Heath Ledger combinations. Yet at the unveiled shock in his eyes, and at Liz's suggestion, I refrained from revealing it all. Kevin did not have the whole story. How could Dr. P?

She was rambling on about recent studies proving the long-term effectiveness of Cell Cept at the higher dose. If I were unwilling to stay there, or switch back to that hellion Prograf, I would have to take Imuran. Imuran is an older immunosuppressive that was prescribed to me from 1988-1995 until discontinued because of increased risk of lymphoma. It is a drug considered so dicey, so suspect, they never put transplant patients on it until the First Year mark has passed. As if. I swallowed. This was my window.

"Dr. P." My mouth went dry. "I respect your studies. But I took half the amount of Cell Cept for over 20 years with my first transplant. I know I rejected, but I cannot stress enough how much I abused drugs and alcohol last summer."

Dr. P. tilted her head to the side and pursed her lips. The cubicle went tomb silent.

"That's true."

As we left the hospital my heart floated on her vague promise.

Let's see what your creatinine is today. Kevin squeezed my hand, adding *That's promising.* I nodded, distracted, scanning the pharmacy shelves, noting the prescription pad bulges in passing lab coats. Places and things no longer mine, forever altered by sobriety.

When my creatinine came back at 1.0, so close to the 0.9, post-surgery baseline, Dr. P. would lower both Cell Cept and Cyclosporine. I was triumphant. She had concurred with my theory that drug and alcohol abuse played a part in my June 2011 rejection episode. The day was a win for both my quality of life and The Kid. So why did I feel like a loser?

I could not concede to my innermost self that getting Dr. P. to lower my immunosuppressives had not been what I wanted from my Cedars experience. I wanted pills. Deserved them. I was a patient. A chronically ill woman. I should have been able to take Fiorinal for my migraines, Klonopin for my tremors, Ambien for my insomnia, Xanax for my anxiety, and opiates—for it all. It was punishing and ridiculous that I could not have what Normies can take with impunity.

If I called Liz, I knew she would tell me to go to a meeting and share, and then call another alcoholic to get out of my self-obsessed thinking. I didn't. The Big Book said the main problem of the alcoholic is centered in his mind, rather than in his body. Pg. 62: "Selfish-ness—self-centeredness! That, we think, is the root of our troubles." *Easy for you to say! There were no transplants in 1935. You'd think about yourself, too, if you were trapped inside my body!*

In recovery, it is a stroke of bad luck to be chronically ill.

I cannot do this without pills.

22. VICODIN

S ober Day 178. Saturday April 7th, 2012.

"WHY DON'T you hang out here while I run Zoey?" Melissa suggested.

The flat and sandy property was broken up into several pens for horses. Lawn equipment littered the yard. Cats roamed. Garbage bags oozed. On a concrete slab next to the run-down bungalow stood a swinging couch. I eyed its cushion suspiciously.

Melissa kept her silver-haired stallion, Zoey at this boarding home in Temecula, and needed to run her in her friend's absence. I had jumped at the invitation to drive a couple hours out of LA, not because I particularly loved horses, but because I loved my friend more than the early Saturday morning meeting Liz was always pushing me to attend.

"Where's the bathroom?"

As I reached for the handle of a nose-marked sliding glass door, I glanced over my shoulder. Zoey's ears twitched with recognition as Melissa approached. I smiled to myself. Sweet. I stepped over the metal track, dodging the two old and smelly perpetrators of said nose marks, tails wagging at half-mast. I spotted the open bathroom door just a few steps down the hall and to the left, just as Melissa had described.

All the plastic accessories were that curious pink 80's aesthetic. As I pulled up my jeans, I wondered if this bathroom had been cleaned since that decade. Flushing with my elbow, I stepped over damp and threadbare towels. As I washed my hands, I scanned a counter crammed with suntan lotions, and hair care equipment for the extended limb of a sanitizer pump.

In a blinding flash of light, I saw it. My heart stopped. I blinked, and then blinked again. Was it real? A white mushroom cap poked through the cluster of containers. Blood whooshed through my ears. *Oh, my God. Oh, my God. Oh, my God.*

*Calm down. It could be anything. An antidepressant, an antibiotic...*I watched my hand reach for the prescription bottle. *I'm just going to look.* My fingers tingled as I brought it up towards my face. It was not full, but it was certainly not empty. I could hear Them rattling around inside Their plastic home. As I turned the label my eyes squinted, then widened with stark and reflexive joy: Hydrocodone or Vicodin.

My left hand flew up to cover my mouth. *Lock the door.* I rattled the doorknob gently. I wiped my hands on the front of my jeans, and then palmed the cap. The lid cracked open with the satisfying click that flooded my veins with unadulterated joy. Tilting the bottle onto its side, I counted as 1-2-3-4-5-6-7-8 tablets rolled into my palm. I stared at Them. They stared back. My mouth began to fill with saliva. There was one last thing to check—the date. I turned the bottle ever so slightly towards me: Date Filled: 09/2011.

I gasped. It was April 2012. This Vicodin had been prescribed seven months earlier for acute pain that had run its course before the pills had. Or maybe Vicodin's owner was a Normie—that curious breed of person who declares, *They make me feel funny* and elected to discontinue the prescription. (The kind of statement that elicits addict head-scratching the world over.) Whatever the reason, the date sealed the steal. I always felt better about stealing pills when the victim wouldn't miss them.

Slipping all 8 tablets into my front jean pocket, I returned the bottle to the exact spot I had found it. As if that would make any difference when Vicodin's owner discovered it empty. To me, it did. By returning it to its original bottle outline, I could more easily convince myself I had not committed any crime. Then I slipped away leaving the bathroom door cracked just the way I had found it.

Shielding my eye line with the same hand that had just stolen a stranger's opiates, I scanned the property for Melissa. She and Zoey were cantering beneath a blinding blue sky, totally oblivious, as if I had not just sustained an emotional earthquake and the ground beneath me still rattled with aftershocks.

The couch creaked softly as I pushed off with my legs. I reached down to fondle my jean pocket. The pills bulged slightly, but not enough for anyone to notice. Already, I felt the bliss of their relief, as if rays of sunshine were shooting from my chest.

I pulled out my phone and called Liz. Static filled my ears.

"Honey, I might lose you," her voice crackled.

Part of it was the poor connection we sustained as she drove through a canyon, but I couldn't hear much over the neuro-fireworks exploding in my brain. Why had I called my sponsor? Was I hoping she could cut through the noise? All I had to do was spit it out *I have 8 Vicodin in my pocket!* and it would all be over. I asked about the meeting I had missed, and what was she doing for the rest of the day? I was enjoying my Saturday, hanging out with my best friend and her horse. I fondled my pocket once again. Her voice clicked in and out, and then she was gone. I did not call her back.

∾

A FEW HOURS LATER, Melissa and I stopped to eat before getting on the road. The family restaurant hummed with that early Saturday evening vibe—clinking dishes and shrieking children. As I followed the hostess to our table, I wanted to shimmy and shout like a crazy person to the entire restaurant *I have drugs in my pocket!* Shoulders slung back, I cupped my hand over the pocket the way I often protected The Kid when I felt it was being threatened.

As we picked at salads and fries, I watched Melissa's mouth move, but my head kept defaulting to the bigger story. Breaking News: To take or not to take. Nibbling on my straw, I nodded at appropriate moments while my head narrated as in a movie: *Although my best friend, Melissa had no idea I had ordered an iceberg lettuce salad because its empty calories would not fill my stomach. Just in case.*

My restraint was impressive to me. By waiting, I felt utterly in control. Unlike the time I had picked Her up at CVS Burbank and popped 3 tablets in the parking lot, unable to wait until I got home. I nibbled at a fry. The Big Book said I had lost the power of choice. I had not! I was deciding. There was no way I would take them in a noisy restaurant. Their power to transport was something to be honored. I would decide at home.

A sudden shiver passed through me. *What are you doing? This is no movie.* The 8 unswallowed pills had infected my thinking. My skin was on fire, feverish with possibility. The disease of addiction inflamed by their mere presence. With an awkward lurch, I jumped up from the table.

"I've got to pee."

As I turned the corner to the restroom, my heart thumped in my ears. *You can do this. You can do this.* I could do this. I would do it. Right now. I would flush them down the toilet.

Inside a locked stall, I removed the pills from my pocket. I stared at the 8 large oblong tablets. All I had to do was tilt my palm a fraction of an inch to one side, and 1-2-3-4-5-6-7-8 they would all be gone, drowned in the public waters of a restaurant toilet. I fingered them with awe and wonder. Anticipation marinated my tongue. I could taste their bitter puddle inside my mouth.

It should have been obvious. If I took the pills I would be flushing $17,000 from my in-laws and $10,000 from my Toronto friend, E. for the cost of rehab. It would be tossing almost six months of sobriety, and the snipping the gossamer trust woven between Kevin and me.

But pills were me. My flesh and bone. Nerve and sinew. Blood, sweat and tears. Pills had swum in my bloodstream every day since age 13. And pain pills? They were like accessories to my basic style. They had enhanced my soul from Codeine at 19, to Fiorinal at 21, to Roxicodone at 42. Where was my panache without them? I fingered them again. They belonged here. I curled my palm into a fist and slipped the tablets back into my pocket. My hands shook as I fixed my hair in the mirror, my eyes dark, electric.

As I arrived back at the table, I watched Melissa leave her half of the bill. My heart softened. She was such a good friend. All I had to do was blurt out *I have 8 Vicodin in my pocket!* and it would all be over. But then she would know I had stolen pills from her friend. That was not a conversation I was willing to have. My brow furrowed. How should I play this?

When we walked into the house, my heart flinched at the sweet smile on Kevin's face.

"How was your day?" he asked.

My stomach flipped as we set down our bags. I had to tell him. My lips tried to form the words *I have 8 Vicodin in my pocket!* but then they would both know I had stolen. My cheeks flushed with shame. I could just hear him. *Why would you do that?*

My head spun. No. No way. I couldn't tell Kevin I had stolen again. I could still just flush them down the toilet. Melissa's friend would never miss her long-forgotten prescription. Melissa would never know. Kevin would never know. Nothing had to change. My fingers itched. I just needed a few more minutes to figure this out.

"I've got to pee."

There they were in the palm of my hand. Vicodin. Pain pills. Pills. *It's just 8 pills.* Then my heart slowed. Inside our bathroom, I was no longer confused. Now home, the choice was clear. I would take them.

In just a few hours it would be April 8th, the official one-year anniversary of our kidney transplant. Oh, the timing was perfect. I would take all of them tomorrow morning to celebrate! This plan a most synchronous nod to that moment post-discharge when I toasted my new kidney with Dilaudid, Percocet and an ice-cold Corona.

Finding Vicodin had been so serendipitous! 8 tablets would be the perfect book-end to The Kid's first year.

When would I take them? Before our celebratory brunch or after? If I took them before, I wouldn't be able to eat much. I would have to claim nausea from my immunosuppressives—believable, as this often happened—and pick at my meal, food being the enemy of narcotic absorption.

If I took the pills after brunch, I would have to wait until my food was digested, or be unable to ride the narcotic wave. And how would I get through the day? Above the table, I would nod and smile at my husband, but my thoughts would wander to the pills hidden in my purse clutched in my hands beneath the tablecloth.

The mound beckoned. *Imagine how good 8 Vicodin will feel.* Yes. The first option made the most sense. I would take all 8 tomorrow, upon awakening on the one-year anniversary of our transplant.

My hand hovered over the doorknob. Or, I could take a few tablets right now by splitting the pile into two piles—4 tonight and 4 tomorrow. My body shuddered. Yes. The perfect compromise. Two highs are always better than one.

An unfamiliar sound drifted through the door. Kevin was laughing. I could just picture him: crossed arms, rocking back and forth as he and Melissa shared some inside joke about F-stops and depth of focus (or was that the same thing?). He liked Melissa very much, considered her a sister, but his lilting tone arose from somewhere else. It was a lovely laugh. One I had not heard in a very long time. Not restrained to dam pain, but elastic to release joy.

As I pictured him, I could not recall the darkness in his eyes or the way his shoulders would slump. I did not remember his retreat to Winnipeg when I wondered if our marriage was over, or the heartbreak associated with it all. Inside the eye of this narcotic tornado, I could not anticipate any storm to come. When I went into treatment, I had taken over 130 pills. This was 8. There would be no dopesickness, no pitiful and incomprehensible overdose. Of this I was certain. It would just be a fun way to celebrate. That's all. No one had to know. Nothing had to change.

Separating 4 pills from the pile, I tossed the remaining 4 into my mouth, and swallowed with a swig of tap water.

As the three of us stood chatting in the dining room, Vicodin flooded my being. My limbs went rubber, my shoulders soft. Through glassy eyes everything looked better. Every ache and pain in my life found equilibrium. One-by-one, my marriage, side effects, and sobriety were tossed overboard, as pills once again anchored me. How had I lived without this feeling for nearly six months? It was worth every second of hell I had ever endured.

As I watched them chat, my heart burst with goodwill for these two beautiful creatures. I wanted to shout *Guys! I'm high! Everyone should know this freedom!* Inside this blissful haze, it was so clear: This is where I belong.

In bed that night, my head rattled with old rhetoric unleashed from a six-month gag. *Thank God I haven't run out yet. I can't wait to wake up and take the rest. Should I check the baggie again?* Did I turn to kiss Kevin goodnight, reminding him we were at the Ramada Inn a year ago tonight? Or did I just turn off the light and roll away, riding Vicodin's waning waves into the night. I do not remember, but were I to place a bet it would be on the pills.

∼

THE NEXT MORNING, I swallowed the last 4 tablets as I dressed for our special brunch. As I dabbed on lip-gloss, the second rush was just as lovely. I saw myself bloom like a spring flower, bursting forth from the hardened winter soil of abstinence. I dropped my specially purchased, yellow pleated dress over my head and entered the living room. Kevin's eyes sparkled.

"You look pretty."

I wish I could write that I threw myself into my husband's arms and thanked him for saving my life. And maybe I did, but all I am sure of was my strict focus on the high: As we drove to the restaurant, ordered our meals, and made conversation. *Is this as high as I will feel? Is this now the half-life?* And then, as sure as what-goes-up-must-come-down, I knew the ride was over. As the waiter cleared our plates, agitation nipped at my skin.

Leaning into the restroom mirror, I scowled at the sudden bags under my eyes. I reached for more eyeliner, more blush, desperate to brush and blend my way back into feeling as pretty as I had that morning. I had been lovely. Everything had been lovely. Now a sour pallor blemished my skin. The narcotic light in my eyes, extinguished. As I reached into my purse for my gloss, I saw the empty Ziplock bag. Tossing it into the garbage can with an angry flick, I wondered why I had brought it. Did I think Vicodin was on the menu and could order some? *Idiot.* With a final scan of my reflection, I saw the whole picture, not just fragments of a vanishing façade. There were no more pills. I had relapsed.

And then like the wave in reverse that it is, a tsunami of regret dragged me out to sea, far, far away from the sobering anchor of the last six months.

When I returned to our table, Kevin had gone. I whirled around, white-hot rage bubbling in my chest. *Typical. Just takes off whenever he feels like it.* Storming towards the door, rippling fumes of wine fueled my charge. The patrons' laughter taunted. Glasses clinked melodic. I felt insane. A blur of yellow and rage. I burst outside into the beautiful afternoon. There he was, loitering on the sidewalk. *He's just Kevin.*

One year to the day that my husband saved my life, I shared three little words with him. They were not *Thank you, sweetheart* or *I love you* or even *You saved me.* When I went to open my mouth, a single beam of sunlight pierced my eye. I shielded myself against its bright light and into my husband's face, screamed,

"You ruin everything!"

23. EXCEDRIN 2012

U nsober Day 24. Tuesday May 1st, 2012.

MY HEAD WAS THROBBING, my neck a cement pillar of pain. It was two in the afternoon, and the curtains were drawn. I was sitting in bed, my laptop resting open on my legs. A single word filled the entire screen. *Dilaudid.*

I had been surfing opiate sites for hours having Googled, *Where to buy drugs online.* In a friendly font like Chalkduster, *Dilaudid* popped next to a single image of Caucasian nurse smiling at me from deep within illegal cyber space. Immaculate in white, she stood waiting in front of a pharmacy counter. My shoulders softened in Pavlovian response to the crammed shelves behind her. She was lovely. It looked safe and legal. It was picture narcotic perfect.

Squirming, I opened and closed my mouth in a futile attempt to unlock my jaw. I was obsessed with the click of its release even if it never alleviated my pain. I stared at the screen. I could feel them rolling down my throat, taste them on my tongue. How could I order pills without Kevin finding out?

At the time, one of our favorite television programs was *Nurse Jackie* about a functioning prescription drug addict nurse. I had stared slack-jawed at her brilliance when her character's escalating appetite for drugs went past stealing from her patients, to stealing an MRI of a brutal back injury to score even more. In one scene, she opened mail from what was clearly her personal PO box, revealing several credit card statements with multiple pharmacy charges.

That's what I would do! Get my own credit card! Obviously, the bill could not be sent to the house, so, I, too, would open my own PO box. But how would I pay the statements? Send cash? No. Of course not. Too risky. But in order to pay by check, I would have to open my own bank account, and then apply for checks. How could I withdraw enough money from our joint account to open my own account without alerting Kevin? Could I pay one credit card statement with another credit card? How good was my credit without Kevin? Could I even get a credit card? Grrr. If only I wasn't so *married*. I scowled and shut my laptop.

I was not high. I was stone cold sober.

～

AFTER MY MAD exit from the restaurant, Kevin had confronted me. *What's wrong? Why are you acting this way?* Like a child, I had sputtered and stomped a lame rationalization for my behavior. *You left without telling me! I might have wanted to sit a while longer!* Resigned, but not suspicious, Kevin walked away from my bad behavior the way he always had—silently, with bewildered eyes. As I followed him to the car, I knew I would not cop to my relapse. *It's just 8 pills.* In fact, I had already left my relapse behind in the garbage can with the empty plastic bag. Buried so deep, that I still believed myself to be sober.

One week later, I would take a 6-month chip at my regular AA meeting. That day I would get a migraine that would last 29 days. Today was Day 20.

Whether it was one long migraine or 29 migraines is irrelevant.

Categorizing migraines does not diminish their ruthless pain, but this type of cycle is referred to as a cluster.

On Day One, I took my Imitrex as prescribed, but the migraine continued for several days, so I tried the only other drug at my disposal—Excedrin. Transplant patients are forbidden to take any NSAIDs (Non-Steroidal Anti-Inflammatory Drugs) like Advil or Motrin because they are so punishing to the kidneys. Excedrin is made up of Acetaminophen, Caffeine and Aspirin. Aspirin is an NSAID, but since it only makes up one third of Excedrin's chemical component, I gave it a pass. Unsuccessful in arresting the migraine cycle after a week of daily Excedrin use (taking up to 6 tablets a day when the recommended dose is 1-2 tablets), I went to see Dr. A., my neurologist. I would see him three times in three weeks, and speak with him multiple times on the phone after hours.

He began by detoxing me off Excedrin with Methergine (used for severe bleeding post-labor, but found to be effective in treating headaches). Excedrin, he warned, could be wonderfully effective, but if used more than twice a week caused rebound headaches more painful than the original. We then tried Maxalt, cousin to Imitrex, from the non-narcotic Triptan family. He then prescribed a preventative "cocktail" of medications: Topomax (for epilepsy), Inderal (a beta-blocker / blood pressure med) and Gabapentin (for nerve pain like shingles). He chased the cocktail with Xanaflex. When that failed to work he prescribed Flexeril, another muscle relaxer that left me so brutally bone-tired the next morning it was hardly worth the brief seconds of relief I was never convinced it provided. Finally, he shot up my neck with tiny anesthesia-filled needles that did nothing but stir a craving for the head-spinning, bone-melting rush Dilaudid had provided in hospital days gone by.

None of these remedies took away the pain that consumed every thought, and challenged every breath. One desperate night I picked up the phone, my hand shaking. As my heart ricocheted off the walls of my chest, I heard myself explaining an option heard in the rooms of AA.

"If my sponsor holds the bottle, I can have pain meds."

He could have shamed me. He could have highlighted my transparent attempt with a scoff or a sigh, but instead gently replied,

"Let's try something else."

I got off the phone and tried not to burst into tears, because all that would do was make my head ache more.

~

THROUGH THE WALL, Kevin was laughing in *that* way. A little too loud, a titch too forced. I rolled my eyes. Sure, he thought whatever the client had said was funny, but I knew it wasn't *that* funny. The front door slammed. This meant his photography session was officially over and he was escorting his client down the seventy steps from our cabin to the street. Our house had been transformed back into a home. I left the isolation of the bedroom, and locked the bathroom door behind me.

My skin shuddered upon contact with my watery salve. As I surfaced from a plunge underwater, I felt the savage grip on my neck release. The 6 Excedrin I had swallowed half an hour earlier—as I had yesterday and the day before and the day before that—were kicking in. Two hot tears rolled down my face. *It's worth it.* This brief reprieve from Migraine's reign was so profound it was easy to nudge Dr. A's warning about rebound headaches from my mind.

A few hours later, Kevin entered the kitchen as I stood making tea. As the water began to roll, my neck seized up. Excedrin had reduced the pain to a general throb, but Migraine was finding its momentum once again. *God, it always comes so soon.*

"What's wrong?"

"What do you think is wrong?" I sneered, as I ground my thumbs into my temples. The water began to rumble.

"Maybe you should see the doctor again."

"There's nothing else he can give me, *Kevin.*"

"Maybe you should get a second opinion."

"And go through all that again? That's brilliant." The kettle began to scream.

"Hang in there, sweetheart."

"What does that mean? What do you know? YOU DON'T KNOW!"

I yanked the kettle from the stove with an angry jerk. I could feel my face contort, red and puffy. He needed to shut up. I wanted to throw the boiling water into his face, into my face, anything to detract from this pain.

We were at war. Another war Kevin hadn't signed up for. He could never say the right thing. If he offered a loving nugget like, *It will get better* I would pulverize his sweet suggestion into pulp. If he didn't suggest anything, I pummeled him with *Why don't you say something?* He couldn't win and we were both losing.

The only time we found peace was when he would massage my shoulders. As I sat cross-legged on the floor in front of him, he would grind his elbow deep into my upper back, or dig his thumb into my unyielding jaw until tears rolled down my cheeks. This silent pounding of my body was the only time we enjoyed each other's company anymore. Inside this wordless truce our old roles still worked—my husband the fixer, and me, the fixee.

Kevin went into his office and I went back to bed. It had been my go-to place to escape pain. Except without drugs, there was no relief to be found. I wanted Her. Now. Handfuls. I raged at Kevin, because I could no longer have Her, punishing him as if he was denying me. As if it was his fault I was an addict.

AA couldn't help me because now I was a liar. Every time I opened my mouth in a meeting, talked to my sponsor, or did step work, I compounded the lie I had buried in a restaurant garbage can. With my whole heart, I believed I deserved that 6-month chip. I had worked so hard. I was 99.9% sober. *It's just 8 pills.* It is no coincidence that the day I stood up and announced to the world I was 6 months sober was the day the migraines began.

I curled into myself on the bed, my brain screaming. It was 5 o'clock somewhere, but I was nowhere. AA couldn't help me. Dr. A. couldn't. Kevin couldn't. There was no fixing this relentless cycle of migraines. It had to be broken. We had to be broken.

I wrote earlier that there is no relief to be found in categorizing migraines. That it does not diminish their ruthless pain. I categorize this period as "Marital Migraines" hoping every time I do, I prove myself wrong. That the searing pain of this memory might diminish even a little.

One day, Kevin began talking about renting a photography studio and staying there overnight. Then, in one of the rare times I went to an AA meeting, I shared that I thought my husband and I were separating. A woman I barely knew said she was leaving for England for two weeks. Did I want to housesit? And just like that, it happened.

Unsober Day 31. Tuesday May 8th, 2012.

Against the soundtrack of Kevin's rumblings through the bedroom wall, I packed up the last of my clothes. His laughter might have been for his clients, or maybe he was reminding himself it was possible at all.

It was a quiet departure. No screaming. No tears. The fight had left us behind. Just the soft putt-putt-putt of our station wagon as I round the bend, and our cabin in the hills disappeared from view.

A few days later, my cluster of migraines broke.

24. PEN AND PAPER 2012

Unsober Day 141. Friday August 26th, 2012.

I'm at Urgent Care. My back went out.

I was standing in the upstairs bar of the Red Rock restaurant on Sunset Boulevard when the text came through. My first thought was *Oh, my God.* My next thought was *I wonder what he's going to get.*

Hopping into my rental, I waved goodbye to my friend, Tara (of the perfect red lips), and away from the AA meeting I had just lead. Times vary, but most leads in Southern California are 10-15 minutes long. You share your story: what it was like, what happened and what it's like now. Holding a meeting in a bar was surprising, but meant to support AA's philosophy that we can go anywhere on Earth where there is alcohol and not be tempted. I got the point—that spiritual work is an inside job—but I don't know that I'd ever want to testify from the pharmacy aisles as the benzos and opiates rattled their familiar tune.

My spine elongated with pride as I wound my way back to my apartment in Glendale. Driving again was a curious thing after years as a drug-addled passenger. Seeing life from the driver's side took some adjusting. In the three months since separating from Kevin, I'd been slammed with three parking tickets and run out of gas several times.

Today my brain was laser-sharp. Buzzing from sharing with strangers that I had downed rubbing alcohol. Watching a sea of heads bob up and down gave me the same sense of relief that came from that first sip or pill.

I had told my truth, that I had over 10 months of sobriety (October 19th, 2011). The truth my soul had yet to recognize was that 8 Little Pills had changed the date to April 8th, 2012. I had four months of sobriety, not ten. But by August, those 8 pills had been pushed so far down inside of me they had never existed. They had not been stolen. I had never swallowed them. They had dissolved from my life.

Half an hour later, I spotted what I knew I would lose if I ever came clean. Pulling alongside a Glendale Urgent Care, I waved at my husband. His face lit up. My heart skipped a beat. *He's just Kevin.*

We had been separated for three months, but in some ways, it felt like I had never left. From the night I drove off into a two-week hous-esitting situation in Sherman Oaks, Kevin followed. That night, he came to rub my head through the final wanes of my Marital Migraines. As his elbow dug into my shoulder, I could feel his eyes darting about, evaluating my temporary home.

A couple weeks later, we met my future landlords: A pregnant couple eager to cash in on the now owners' market that had nearly destroyed us when it crashed. They owned three rental properties in Glendale, and we were looking at one of them. Dressed in his kilt, Kevin stood near me, although not quite beside me. Legs cemented beneath him, arms tucked into his armpits in that oh-so-McIntyre way. He had raced from a Scottish Festival in Costa Mesa to inspect the furnished studio apartment only 20-minutes from our house. Renting me an apartment was only affordable because we were no longer paying our mortgage, having hardballed with Bank of America to qualify for a loan modification.

We had discovered the apartment together as man and wife, the same way we had found our cabin: Scouring Craig's List, me sitting in a chair pulled up beside his desk, and Kevin's arm periodically reaching for my back or my knee. His uncontrollable tic. Tourette's of the heart.

The four of us stood on the square patch of asphalt outside my new front door. The couple's slick exuberance annoyed me. Kevin and I were like the cracked reflection of what these ex-model-forward-slash-actors might become if one of them lost their way. When I met people for the first time now, I wondered. What was in their medicine cabinet? Was their recycling container crammed with empty bottles? *You have no idea, newlyweds.* If I hadn't already told my new landlords that Kevin and I were separating, would they have been able to tell? There didn't appear to be much difference between us, except for a few years and a few thousand pills.

We would sign the lease on May 27th, 2012, our 17th wedding anniversary.

Most Wednesdays we would meet at my place, where I prepared bagged salad and ready-made turkey meatloaf for our surreal version of date night. We would then drive separately to The Windsor Club, a 12-Step clubhouse down the street where Kevin brought cookies to an Al-Anon meeting, and I attended a 90-minute AA speaker meeting. As official greeter, I extended my hand to the restless, irritable and discontented as they passed through the front door for the 1st or 1000th time.

"Hi. I'm Henriette! Welcome!"

"I haven't seen you smile like that in a long time." Kevin noted one evening.

He was right. I was happy. I had come to love AA.

"What happened?" I called out, walking the few short steps from my car. Kevin stood hunched in the Urgent Care doorway, a back brace and paperwork dangling from his hand. The prescription had to be in there.

He didn't need to answer me. Three months apart had only refined our shorthand. In 2009, Kevin practically spat up Norco when diagnosed with an agonizing case of shingles because he didn't like the way they made him feel. For a month beforehand, he suffered intense neck pain (in retrospect this was the shingles virus bearing down), instead of taking himself to the doctor to get the shot that would have averted it. That Kevin had driven himself to Urgent Care, instead of waiting for me to return from West Hollywood to collect him was testament to an uncharted level of pain.

We scanned the X-ray report together. "He said I have several herniated discs in my back. I have to get an MRI."

My stomach flipped, trying not to notice the paperwork underneath. Back pain always equaled pain meds. Nurse Jackie was prescribed OxyContin for her horrific, albeit falsified back pain. Even without an MRI, they had to have given him something.

I looked up from the report into my husband's sagging 39-year old face. In the penetrating afternoon light, coarse gray hairs sprouted through his untamed stubble. His eyes caught mine and for a moment I couldn't breathe, a memory cutting off all air. A year earlier: A driveway full of suitcases, his sister and the calling of the pipes.

YOU ARE A FUCKING DRUG ADDICT!!!

I shivered picturing Kevin's face dotted with my spit. His dead stare. His vanishing smile. *You can't have my pills!* Back then I had been unable to see my destruction. Today, sustained collateral damage came back to me in painful, epileptic flashes. In sobriety, these memories were slow to return but arrived with a sucker punch to the gut every time.

A single bird chirped. I offered my husband a small smile. The air between us now was maybe not romantic, but friendly. His reddened eyes drooped, as he too smiled.

"What do you need?" I asked.

The phrase tumbled awkwardly from my mouth, and those weren't even the words of our marriage therapist. *What are you needing?* sounded like I should putter after my husband with freshly baked scones and clotted cream. When verbal warfare ensued between us, our therapist suggested one spouse pop the other spouse's ballooning rage with this question. Despite its corny construction, it had worked on me. Turns out usually all I needed was a hug.

"Do you want me to come home and help you?" I prompted.

"No. I'm going to go home and rest." My cheeks burned. It wasn't so much that my independent man wanted no help. That wasn't exactly breaking news. It was that he didn't want me to come home with him.

"What did they give you?"

It was slight, indiscernible to anyone other than a spouse. It could have been for any reason: a fly landing on his upper cheek, or a salty bead of sweat rolling into his eye. Kevin had narrowed his eyes—bright blue shifting to black.

"I don't want to tell you." My heart cartwheeled. I knew it!

"We don't even live together," I laughed, and then bit my lip. *Stop talking.*

"Norco." Kevin paused. "I'm not even sure I'm going to fill it. Why do you want to know?"

"I don't want you to be in pain." That part was true.

~

SHUTTING the door of my apartment behind me, I was awash in trendy Tiffany blue paint and wall-to-wall carpeting. On my immediate left ran a wall attached to my landlords' house and a glass sliding door closet. The remainder of the studio opened up to my right: a queen bed, a box television on a dresser, and an oversized chair. At the back of the space, a kitchen stocked with utensils, a fridge, and a two-ringed flat stove. Photos of Kevin and Maggie stood next to my handwritten post-its and DBT (dialectical behavioral therapy) diary cards. I'd displayed them like art, hoping to inspire me.

Turning on the A/C unit at the foot of the bed, I threw myself down and burst into tears. Fact: I cried every day for the first six months of my sobriety. A theatre school friend had shared with me how she cried every day for half a year after getting sober. So I recalled the day I drowned her watermark in a fresh flood of tears.

And the next day. And the next. I knew there were reasons why we were living under two separate roofs, but every time I saw him, I forgot why.

Sighing, I sat up and reached for my phone. "Hi Liz. My lead went well. See you at the meeting tomorrow. I love you!"

It's safe to say I fell in love with Liz the first time we spoke. Back in rehab, one of the techs had been sponsored by her and thought we would be a good fit. After I finally worked up the nerve to call, I paced Klean's common area waiting for our phones to connect.

"Hello?" a woman's voice rang out.

"Uh, my name is Henriette. I'm, um, in rehab. It was suggested I call you.

"Well, Hi, Henriette. I'm Liz!" Her pleasing laugh tickled my ears. "I'm at a medical conference in Atlanta and it's raining. I'm holding an umbrella and climbing into a cab. Can I call you later?" I broke out into a full-body smile. Who did that? Who picked up the phone in a situation like that? Who was this Liz?

A few days after that conversation, I would ask Liz to sponsor me. She told me to read the stories in the back of the Big Book. The first 164 pages outlined The 12 Steps in detail as a suggested design for living. The last 411 pages are 41 stories (averaging 4-10 pages in length) dating from 1939 to present day. Every night in rehab, I held the Big Book in one hand and a yellow highlighter in the other, soaking up every word, trying to understand how these self-diagnosed alkys were like me.

Bringing the book to my chin, I stretched my legs long on the coffee table. I had just finished reading about a woman in the 1940's who hid bottles of alcohol all over her house. Yes, I had done that, but only to protect Kevin. *You're an alcoholic!...I'm just having a glass of wine...You drink every night!...We know tons of people who drink every night...I don't care!...*

Drinking more than Kevin was comfortable with didn't make me an alcoholic. How could I win an Oscar and not drink champagne?

"I don't know, Liz. I mean I know I have a problem with pills." Liz's tone shifted into detachment.

"Well, I don't know honey, maybe you need to go out and get loaded and find out." My breath caught. When was the last time anyone had spoken to me like that? Had anyone ever spoken to me like that? I scowled, annoyed, but also impressed. I kinda liked it. She was calling my bluff. Had I been bluffing?

"Think about this. When you enjoyed your drinking, could you control it?"

I opened my mouth to snap, "Yes!" My drinking abuse had spiraled so quickly, from wine to vodka to isopropyl rubbing alcohol, seemingly over one long night, while Kevin slept and I stumbled on towards dawn.

"And when you controlled your drinking, did you enjoy it?"

Sitting on my hands as a waiter walked by, because I wanted a third glass of wine, did not qualify as control. She had a point.

"Henriette, do you believe in God?"

My pulse quickened. My answer was instant and surprising. The sky filled my mind. Bright, colorless.

"Yes." I stumbled. "I mean, I was raised Catholic, but I don't...I'm not practicing.

"This is a spiritual journey, honey. Not religious. Here you find your own God."

∾

THREE DAYS after I was discharged from Klean, I met Liz at her house and together we drove to a women's meeting. She was tiny, classically stylish—pearls and a cardigan or tailored dresses and heels. I adored her. My 20-lb. weight gain and me frequently smothered her with eager hugs. Almost every Tuesday night, before another women's meeting, we met at her house to read through the Big Book page by page.

STEP 1: We admitted we were powerless over alcohol—that our lives had become unmanageable.

.   .   .

MY FIRST PIECE of homework was to write a list of 25 ways I was powerless over drugs and alcohol. What's that you say? A list? And on my two favorite subjects! Pills and me! I'm in!

"After overdosing on Fiorinal, I was 51/50'd and handcuffed to a gurney." Liz explained.

My heart stopped. What? I was never handcuffed. Kevin had talked the ER psychiatrist out of a 51/50. Then I realized that had been Liz's experience. A nurse administrator who loved Fiorinal? How perfect was she? But these details were but perks. Her selling point was her rigorous honesty and time. After each meeting my love for her expanded. She was like my platonic lover who understood me better than I understood myself. A strong and sober woman who had loved pills as much as I did.

Kevin's hunched body flashed through my mind. I shot him a quick text. *How is your back?*

On the small table I would never eat at, my AA workbook lay open. Its blood-red leather cover housed thick, creamy pages onto which I poured my wreckage.

TOP 25 WAYS **I am Powerless over Drugs and Alcohol**

(FROM MY 2012 LIST. The following appear throughout *In Pillness.*)

1. JUNE 2010. Taking 120 Fiorinal in 3 days. Hospitalized at Cedars-Sinai. Kevin talking the ER psychiatrist out of 51/50-ing me.

3. WINTER 2011. Drinking every day and abusing Xanax on dialysis.

.   .   .

4. APRIL 15, 2011. Having a beer the second I was discharged from the hospital, post-transplant.

5. 2011. Throwing my wedding ring out the car window during a huge fight with Kevin.

6. BUYING 4 bottles of wine, hiding 3 from Kevin and placing one on the counter.

7. HAVING one glass of wine going and another hidden on the water heater behind the laundry soap.

12. Since 1996, every time I went to Canada, the first thing I would do is go to a Shoppers Drug Mart and buy Tylenol 1 with Codeine.

13. Since 1996, every time I would come back from Canada, I would traffic several bottles of Tylenol 1, 200 caplets each.

14. Ever since 1988, pretty much every day I have taken Tylenol 1. In 1988, it was 2-3 a day, ending in 18 a day by 2011.

15. My last pick up. Bending over the counter at the Rite Aid pharmacy, pleading with Karen to release my prescription by cash, a day early, only to have her discover that I had somehow managed to get 135 tablets in the space of 90.

16. My last prescription. Making Kevin go and pick up my Xanax

when the pharmacy opened on Sunday, only to make him go back when he came home with the wrong prescription of "only" 12. This made him half an hour late for shooting a wedding in Orange County.

17. Stealing Xanax from my mother-in-law.

18. Could only have sex when I was drunk or high.

23. Convinced the social worker, and psychiatrist at Cedars-Sinai to amend a form that I would not use Fioricet after my transplant, so I could still drink and take other drugs.

25. Drank rubbing alcohol with lemonade when I ran out of vodka.

29. Blew countless auditions, not there 100% because I would be slurring my words having just taken a pill to even out.

31. Replaced all of Kevin's Tramadol with my Xanaflex.

"YOU'RE LUCKY YOU'RE ALIVE." Liz stared at me with big eyes. "With your one kidney."

"Yes." I could see that.

"You are a hope-to-die opiate addict."

I should have said her monition felt like a compliment. This other Henriette, Mrs. Hyde, was a total badass. Internally, I wore the list like a demented badge of honor. In the writing of it, I had pictured Kevin's face, all blotchy skin and bewildered eyes. Great globules had rolled down my face as I recalled begging him for my pills, my desperate cries bleeding his ears. *Please. Please. Please.* But other than the initial reading to Liz, I found little humility in my list. Total insanity. Yes. I could see that. Why couldn't I feel it?

STEP 2: Came to believe that a Power greater than ourselves could restore us to sanity.

I TRIPPED up on the 2nd Step as well.

"Do you really think you got sober on your own?" Liz asked, cocking her head to one side.

"But I am the one who stopped taking the pills." Her eyes widened. What was I missing? I knew I wasn't God, but what value did that have if I didn't know what God was? I was the one who stopped calling the doctor, going to the pharmacy, and stealing from strangers. My eyes blinked, returning to the page.

35. Took 8 Vicodin on April 8th, 2012.

I CLOSED THE BOOK. Kevin had texted back.

I'm OK. Going to sleep now.

It took everything in me not to text back: *Did you pick up the Norco?*

That night, I got on my knees the way I had ever since Liz and I completed the Third Step.

STEP 3: Made a decision to turn our will and our lives over to the care of God as we understood Him.

BY CANDLELIGHT, our hands clasped over the Big Book, Liz and I had recited the 3rd Step prayer together: "God, I offer myself to Thee—to build with me, and to do with me as Thou wilt. Relieve me of the bondage of self, that I may better do Thy will. Take away my difficulties, that victory over them may bear witness to those I would help of Thy Power, Thy Love and Thy Way of Life. May I do Thy will always!"

The capitalizations did not bother me, nor did the religious overtones. Indeed, none of it touched me at all. I recited the words while driving, while doing the dishes, or on the toilet at the gym. I humbled myself to this new position on the floor because Liz told me to. I saw no burning bush, nor was I filled with a revelatory white light. I would check off this AA box twice a day: Pray in the morning. *Check.* Pray in the evening. *Check.* Completing this homework with the same motives as high school—because I wanted an "A."

Not because I wanted to learn anything new.

25. NORCO

Unsober Day 142. Saturday August 25th, 2012.

MY EYES SWEPT the disaster that used to be my home: unwashed dishes, unfolded laundry, and *sniff, sniff*—was that *pee*? I sighed. Between the cacophony of Maggie's where-have-you-been squeals and my brain churning in-which-order-will-I-clean-what-first, it took a moment before I noticed my husband.

I knew the posture. Rigid. A body resisting itself, against pain that threatens to consume if you breathe the wrong way. Standing in full bag piping regalia, recently tuned bagpipes lying at the ready, Kevin McIntyre was anything but. The bags under his eyes communicated today's shorthand. He had been up all night, suffering through 2, 3, 4 AM musings over how he would play the bagpipes with a broken-ish back. This afternoon Kevin was booked, as he had been for several years now, to play the bagpipes at Peaches' birthday party. Peaches was not a code word. Peaches was 94.

He would drive in pain if he had no other options, but he wasn't moving. Something fluttered in my chest. *So he got the Norco.* He would rather die then take a mind-altering substance and take the wheel.

"Do you want me to drive you?" I sighed.

He nodded with robot-like efficiency. I'm not sure what was more surprising: Me forgoing quality time with my fur daughter, or Kevin accepting help. Either way it was a milestone moment in the Ivanans-McIntyre household.

"Fine, let me just pee," I said. Kevin sent me a half-smile.

My narcotic frequency had always been impeccably tuned to the square footage of our cabin. All I ever needed was one of my senses to activate it. *Rattle. Rattle. Rattle.* My heart stopped. There was no need to peek out of the bathroom. *Rattle.* I continued to wash my hands, feeling Kevin bend over his bagpipe case. *Rattle.* The quick zip of its top pocket.

For the first few minutes, we drove in silence. Pain is inversely proportional to chatter when waiting for a narcotic to kick in: the greater your agony the less you dare to speak. Kevin was staring out the window.

"Don't speed." he mumbled. I rolled my eyes.

Fascinated, I snuck quick looks at his profile. When would the narcotic penny drop? My wings now clipped by sobriety, this legal eagle maintained a reasonable 68 mph as we headed out to Simi Valley. No freeway shenanigans for this #sobergirl.

"Everyone's really nice, sweetheart. You'll have fun," he murmured in a velvet voice. My shoulders softened with gratitude. There it was. The shift in his personality from neurotic back seat driver to Chatty Cathy. Freedom. Kevin stroked my kneecap the way he had when we were dating as his buzzy musings filled the car: Peaches' decade long stint in bed. Her daughter Lana's sacrifices. Subway sandwiches and champagne cake.

I nodded along, aware of a curious burn in my chest. Although pleased he was out of pain, watching Kevin get high felt empty. My husband had disappeared, vanished inside his glassy eyes. Was this what Kevin had witnessed? Watching me slip away through the windshield and out into a world that was whipping by too fast for either of us to keep up? I pushed the pedal down a little further.

Champagne cake. I wonder if I can eat that?

File it under: Things You Just Don't Think About Until You Get Sober.

∽

THE DOOR FLEW OPEN. She was all wild, gray curls, a tropical-themed muumuu and unabashed affection for my husband. She was Lana and she was a natterer.

"Oh!" Lana clapped her hands. "Kevin! You're here! And Henriette! I've heard so much about you!"

I doubt that.

"What can I get you to drink?" She was the kind of natterer, that if I had been asked that question a year earlier, would have most assuredly responded, *A big fat vodka-soda with three limes, please.* I could feel Kevin's eyes on me.

"Water is fine."

"Oh! That's why you're so skinny!" I resisted the urge to roll my eyes. Lana clapped her hands again and walked away. I leaned in to Kevin and whispered, "I'm just going to call Liz about the cake."

Pacing the short driveway of this suburban Simi Valley home, Liz and I shared a giggle.

"Well, honey, all the alcohol should be burned off, but the taste could be triggering. If you're worried about it, just don't have any."

Shutting the front door behind me, I entered the stale front room. Curtains drawn. Dead air. My eyes traveled over the shadowy outline of Kevin's bagpipe case. *Could I?* My pulse quickened. Voices burst forth from the neighboring room. *Keep walking.*

Eight people gathered on furniture covered in blankets arranged in a cozy circle. Water bottles, juices and sodas commanded the water-stained TV tables in front of them. Those drinks weren't mixing anything. *No wonder there's a champagne cake.* Peaches lay in a hospital bed off to the side. With her white hair and crinkly, smiling eyes she resembled Mrs. Claus. Kevin's opiate-inspired chattering had also revealed Peaches had been unable to talk for several years. Apparently her daughter was picking up the slack.

In the adjoining kitchen, I accepted a bottle of water from Lana's outstretched hand. On the counter—not the famously touted Subway sandwiches—but sliced meats and cheeses, fruit platters and the infamous champagne cake with neon-pink cursive spelling out, *Happy birthday, Mama Peaches.* Lana was babbling about her recent leg operation and the torment that was her therapy.

"But I've just taken a pain med, so I'm sure I'll feel better soon." I took a giant sip of water. *Jesus, does everyone in the world have pain medication but me?*

With a sudden screech, Kevin's bagpipes cut through the chatter. A cheer went around the room. Everyone shifted in their seats, electrified by the instrument's thrilling call. I followed Mama Peaches' gaze through the glass patio door into the back yard, as Kevin performed in his glass box on a fuzzy green stage. Unable to walk or talk, yet her eyes shone with joy.

"He's so talented! You must be so proud!" Lana cried out, unwrapping the candles. I nodded, annoyed that anyone would talk while Kevin was playing. I was. His cheeks puffed up and down with the intense rhythm. It is clear that the bagpipes are a complicated instrument. He made it look so easy. He made everything look easy, even with his moral compass so tightly wound. I bet he wasn't wondering where Lana's pain meds were.

As Lana placed the "9" and then "4" on the cake, she breezily reminisced about the day Kevin had piped his way into her life. Visiting a friend's gravesite, she had heard Kevin playing a funeral, and approached him afterwards. Kevin slid the patio door behind him, cheeks stained red with exertion, and moved to sit next to me on one of the couches.

"Then you pulled out a business card with this beautiful woman on it. When you said she was your wife, I thought, geez, what a perfect couple." Lana lit the candles and began to sing.

Every clink and murmur disappeared. Every committed, yet off-key note to "Happy Birthday" was suddenly sucked into our marital black hole. We exchanged no ironic chuckles, no soft-shoe shuffle kicks to the floor. Wedged between us, the Truth was like a third person we needed to ignore. If we acknowledged It, what would It unleash? Would It slap Its knee and howl, *Oh my God, Lana. You have NO idea!*

My shoulders tensed as slices of cake were passed overhead. My polite decline was either unheard or ignored and a large piece—the flagship piece with the gigantic pink rose—landed on the TV table between us. My mouth watered. I sat on my hands, pinching the backs of my thighs. The grainy blossom appeared to me a beacon. With just one bite, would I be tempted? One bite. One pill. 8 pills. It was all burned off. That's what Liz had said. She had laughed. It couldn't be a big deal if she had laughed. *Maybe just the rose.*

It was a simple gesture—surgically precise and quick. A covert action worthy of the opening sequence of a 007 Bond movie. In the few seconds I had pondered the sobering pros and cons of icing, Kevin had halved my piece, maneuvered it onto his plate, wolfed a reasonable portion thereof before squishing the remainder back onto my plate to resemble an abandoned, albeit thoroughly enjoyed slice of cake. Perfectly executing Operation Lead Me Not Into Temptation. Kevin, who hates icing, even ate the rose.

I shifted my body towards him, signaling him to read mine. Now shoveling forkfuls of his own slice, he angled his face towards me, and crinkled his eyes like Peaches. McIntyre. Kevin McIntyre.

Our truth had always been in the silence: Late hospital nights when there was nothing left to say. Sitting opposite each other in the common area at Klean. Navigating the confusing semantics of a slice of champagne cake. In the silence, when we had no words for what was going on, our love bloomed. Like a gigantic rose.

～

"THANK YOU FOR DRIVING ME, SWEETHEART." Kevin leaned against the bathroom door, as I washed my hands. Now in his sweats, stripped of regalia and responsibility and ready for bed.

"Of course." Had I ever thanked Kevin for driving me to Cedars, I wondered, drying my hands. Of course I had. I wasn't a *monster*. I flipped off the light.

Rattle, rattle, rattle. Through the open bedroom doorway, Kevin was hunched over his bedside table, pushing back the thin "secret" drawer at the top. I kept walking.

Slinging my purse over my shoulder, I grabbed my keys and watched my hand reach for the front door. My fingers curled around the knob and began to pull. Kevin was already at his computer, the telltale tappity-tap-tap rising from his keyboard. My arm dropped. Turning around I walked straight through the house and up to his bedside table. The top drawer rolled out silently on its velvet lining. Cracking the lid, I rolled 4 Norco into the rock-solid palm of my hand. *Tappity-tap-tap. He hates Norco.* Curling my fingers into a fist, I walked back to the front door. *Tappity-tap-tap. They give him a migraine.* Depositing the pills into the zippered pocket of my purse, I swung the front door wide.

Easy as 1-2-3. Not a bead of sweat dropped. Not a single hair mussed. Mistress of the Swipe was back. Ivanans. Henriette Ivanans. Mission Operation Free Norco accomplished.

"Bye, sweetheart!" I called out, closing the door behind me.

Then I popped all 4 into my mouth and drove the curious miles home to Glendale.

～

PICK UP SHIRT FROM BED. Stare at it. Wonder why I picked it up. Drop shirt back onto bed. I knew I was doing nothing. Giving hours of my life to a waning narcotic wave that never seemed to come ashore. Had I always felt this nauseous on Norco? God, I was swollen. My fingers felt like cocktail sausages. My heart? I couldn't feel that at all.

The next morning, my jaw cracked as I yawned. I reached for my glass of water. Why were my limbs so heavy? *Oh, fuck. Oh, Jesus. Oh, no.* With the break of my dawn came the soul-piercing realization that I had once again stolen. Relapse.

Wait. It was only 4. 4 Norco and 8 Vicodin made 12 pills. What was 12 pills? Not even half your average-sized, 30-tablet prescription bottle. I rubbed at my forehead. My brain hurt, pinging with these early morning rationalizations. Dragging myself to the floor, I pushed my aching forehead into the side of the bed and began to pray.

"OK, God. This is between us. You have to help me keep this secret."

No tears fell. No white light shone. Nothing. I felt nothing. Restless, I got up from my knees and walked over to the table.

When you don't have a god, you go back to your old ones: Lists. Pills. And Lies.

35. April 8th: Took 8 Vicodin.

I PICKED up a pen and began to write.

36. August 25th: Took 4 of Kevin's Norco.

THERE. Absolved.

26. PERCOCET 2012

Unsober Day 148. Friday August 31st, 2012.

"THESE ARE FOR YOU!"

A huge bunch of plump and open roses were thrust into my face. They bounced with the grand gesture, their delicate suede-like petals wafting their bold perfume. My breath caught. I laughed out loud, joyous. I don't remember their color, but I do remember I had to bite down on my tongue to refrain from crying out, *But I just stole from you!*

Half an hour earlier on the phone, Kevin had confided to his doctor, and then me, that Norco wasn't touching his pain. He was on his way to Rite Aid to pick up a different prescription before leaving for a Scottish Festival in Pleasanton. *What is he getting?* This time, I didn't ask.

With shocking and evolved ease, I dropped every borderline-OCD, leaving-the-house-for-the-weekend ritual: List checking and double-checking. Perfectly spacing my white plastic hangers. I might have even left dishes in the sink. I hopped into my car and burned the miles to Shadow Hills. Arriving at the house before Kevin became paramount to everything else. I had to know.

I was lying in the center of the cabin rubbing Maggie's belly, my narcotic frequency vibrating on high, when Kevin charged in.

"I have to pee!" he announced, breathless.

Burying my head deeper into Maggie's belly, I called out *Hello!* This calculated act was meant to assure Kevin I could see nothing, when in fact I had seen everything. Dangling from his hand, I caught the quickest blur of white, and heard that ol' familiar tune. *Rattle. Rattle. Rattle.* He raced into his office holding the Rite Aid bag. It took all of two seconds, and two sounds: *Bump. Bang.* I smiled to myself. I almost felt sorry for him. It was so obvious: The top drawer of his desk.

Kevin raced out of his office and into the bathroom, slamming the door. Once I heard the click of the lock, I was up. Out with the drawer. Bump! *Percocet! 60! They gave him sixty 10 mg tablets!* Then in. Bang! Walking out of his office, I clutched 5 Percocet in my fist.

Kevin went back out to the car, returning with a bag of groceries and the roses.

"They were on sale!" he beamed. I laughed. "Is that why you bought them?"

"They looked so nice. Then I saw they were on sale and thought, even better." He was right. They were beautiful. I buried my nose into the bouquet and inhaled. Their unusual fullness reminded me of our wedding roses. My groom's eyes were sparkling. He looked so proud of himself.

He doesn't have many, but if you can call it a flaw, it is that Kevin is not romantic. For example, he—and by default, we—choose not to celebrate Valentine's Day because it's "fabricated." It's not an equal opportunity holiday! Where are his flowers? Knowing Kevin could care less about flowers, I suspect this position is a curated ploy to spare him any wifely nagging lest he forget. Kidney-donator, yes. Flower-buyer, no. Until today.

But I just stole from you.

I remember the self-congratulatory glint in his eyes. The I-managed-to-knock-it-romantically-and-economically-out-of-the-park pride. How my heart simultaneously exploded, then shattered. We were happy. We were healing. For a deluded second I thought *See. I can have it all.* Then I realized I couldn't wait to drop him off at Burbank's Bob Hope Airport so I could swallow my first Percocet, and forget about what I had just done.

~

A FEW HOURS LATER, Kevin called me from his hotel room.

"There's 7 missing." I clamped my hand over my mouth. *SHIT. Shitshitshit.*

"What do you mean?" I stalled, leaning against the edge of our bed, the backs of my knees gone weak. Why had he counted them?

"There's only 53." He was slurring a little.

Suddenly, a cloak of calm dropped over me. My Mistress of the Swipe cape. My skin went cool. Ice cold.

"Wow. They gave you 60." I lied. "When did you take the first one?"

"Well, I took one at the airport and got so stoned that I missed my flight." *This I could work with.*

"Oh, poor sweetheart," I cooed. "Are you ok?" My husband was an amateur. I was the undisputed champ. In the pharmaceutical ring, he was swinging blind, headed for a total knockout.

"I know what happened," clipping my consonants with assurance. "Rite Aid messed up your order."

"By 7?"

"No. You took one at the airport, then one or two tonight. Right?"

"Right?" his voice wobbled.

"You know what. You seem very out of it. Check again."

His pills plunked in the background, echoing first into an empty plastic container, then landing against a jam-packed mound of drugs. The shift in the container's vibrations sent my heart racing. I could picture the pile of them growing. I could feel their powdery discharge between my fingers. I thought about the 3 Percocet (and 2

Norco), in the zippered pocket of my wallet, and my flesh began to hum.

"53."

"Hmmm. OK. Did you break up your stash? Leave any at home?" Drug addict tips 101.

"No."

"So Rite Aid messed up. Remember the time they gave you 90 Ambien instead of 30?" It was on the tip of my tongue to bring up The Accidental Prescription of 2010, but better not to remind Kevin of my subsequent overdose and the night he had to talk an ER psychiatrist out of 51/50-ing me. There was a long pause.

"True." Another pause. "But, I'm sure I've only taken 2."

"Well, they're very strong, sweetheart. You're not used to them. Maybe you forgot." The line went silent.

"Maybe." He knew. With a sudden chill, I knew he knew.

"Make sure you don't tell anyone you have Percocet. People steal."

"Yes. They do."

Kevin did not call me out. Maybe he didn't know. Or maybe he just didn't care. Maybe 99.9% sober was enough for us both.

27. PERCOCET 2013

Unsober Day 295. Friday January 25th, 2013.

IT WAS ABSOLUTELY PERFECT: Thick and oblong. A single Percocet. It lay on the linen tablecloth in front of me. I looked up into Kevin's eyes. It was his birthday. The big 4-0. Why was I the one getting the gift?

Everything fell away. I could not feel the breeze the waiters made as they pirouetted around our table, arms laden with exotic cheeses and juicy meats. The five-star dining room went dark, no longer ablaze with light streaming in from the floor-to-ceiling windows. In a black and neon color-blocked dress and leather boots, I waited. My meticulously painted lips trembled ever so slightly. I grabbed at the bottom of the upholstered chair. Offering no lift of my eyebrow, no curl of my lip into an appreciative smile.

I was transfixed. Not by the sight of my clean-shaven, sharply dressed man sitting opposite me, but by a single Percocet. Perfectly centered between rows of gleaming cutlery. He was waiting. His offering, like an engagement ring, required a response. *Will you swallow me?* Yes! YES! YESSSSSS! I wanted to scream at the top of my lungs. Fuck roses. This was the most romantic thing my husband had ever done.

~

WHEN KEVIN RETURNED FROM PLEASANTON, we never spoke of those 5 missing Percocet again. By the end of September, I would move home. I would steal (and meticulously record) three times in August (25th, 27th, 30th), four times in September (7th, 10th, 15th, 20th) and twice in October (9th, 10th) before my "sober" birthday on October 19th, 2012.

Unlike other, more pragmatic parts of the country, Southern California AA's exchange birthday cards, do lunch and receive flowers from friends at regular meetings on their sober birthdays—very California Dreamin'. Right before the big day, I asked Kevin to keep my secret from Liz, AA and our friends.

"Please don't tell anyone about this. They wouldn't understand."

Over 365 days, I had stolen a total of 32 pills from my husband: One average-sized, 30-tablet prescription bottle. An innocuous amount that could easily disappear into the bottom of a purse.

"So you took a few pills."

My heart had leapt, every cell in my body whooping with the joyous, hands-in-the-air revelation that Kevin always seemed to have my back. Al-Anon told us this was enabling, but my heart told me it made us a team. Kevin would confide that when I took my cake and gushed about my profound gratitude for AA and The Steps, he "felt bad for me." Regardless, my husband would continue to stand tall in my corner, even as that became increasingly difficult.

Kevin's back often went into spasm causing him agonizing pain. Yet, he would take the most mind-blowingly miniscule amounts of opiate, spurning its effects, taking just enough to reduce his pain to an ache. Obliteration was never on Kevin's radar. But I still was.

After my "sober" birthday, I stopped keeping track of what I stole from him. Maybe I no longer needed paper redemption after being blessed with his codependence. I didn't steal from my husband often, supplementing my habit by pilfering every medicine cabinet I encountered along my way.

Around Thanksgiving, he caught me, and unpredictably, saw red: He accused. I denied. He showed me proof of lift. I ran. He followed. I denied again. He insisted. I plead guilty, cried, and promised. And promised.

And every time I did, I meant it. I was sick and tired of the unsatisfying cycle. My pattern had become to swipe one pill every few days. It was almost—almost—not worth it. All one pill was giving me was a painful case of narcotic blue balls. I could never get off, because I could barely get any. I was becoming progressively aware of the subtle headache, the swollen skin, and the euphoric fog that never seemed to roll in and over me, but rather evaporate before it even touched my shore.

On the 23rd of December, Kevin discovered I had swiped two Percocet. In a blaze of Shakespearean anger, he dismantled our Christmas tree—stripping it from sparkling serenity to Charlie Brown bare—scattered pine needles and all. Then he drove to Orange County to spend the holiday with friends. It took me a moment to figure out what had pushed him over the edge. Rarely had I seen my husband display such specific and ferocious rage. As he stormed out the wreathless front door, he sputtered how my betrayal was lying during the role of designated driver, as we purchased last minute gifts for the Christmas celebration he would now attend solo. Yes, I had swallowed two pills. But Kevin didn't know that I had taken two swigs of rubbing alcohol as well, desperate to amplify my buzz for as long as possible.

Sobbing, I packed up our shiny trinkets from Christmases past. I rubbed at my eyes, smearing gold sparkles in with my tears. Why couldn't I stop? Alone on Christmas Day, I went to a Burbank Group meeting and sat with four strange men, crying my eyes out. Outside the hall, calmer, I searched the sky for a star, some kind of a sign. It felt good to be here, but I wanted to be with Kevin. I couldn't do this anymore. I had to stop. Yes. 2013 would be the year I got sober.

And it would be. For all of 20 days.

~

IN JUNE OF 2009, a shocking pain would shoot from my uterus down through my vaginal area, and into my anus. Around 5 am, after a sleepless night of accelerated pain that shot up into my right shoulder, we raced to Cedars' ER terrified something was happening to The Kid. It was nothing thousands of other women haven't experienced: A ruptured ovarian cyst. Like them, I would get a shot of morphine, then a shot of Dilaudid, and be sent home with a prescription for Percocet with my name on it.

On Sunday January 20th, 2013, I was struck with the same symptoms. Kevin was struck with the same tightness of face that plagued him whenever we were in an ER. Post-Dilaudid shot, I assured him I would be fine by group texting a number of friends —including Liz—who privately suggested I give her whatever bottle of pain medication I was prescribed. She would dole out my pills on an as-needed basis. However, once I had the all-too familiar triplicate in my eager hand, it made much more sense to give Kevin the bottle. Liz was, after all, 20 minutes away in the Burbank Hills. Once we were home, I was unsurprised that my husband did not want to get between Percocet and me. By default, I would hold the bottle.

I tried really hard. I needed those pills, but every day I would take one (or two) more than prescribed. Five days later, on Kevin's birthday weekend, the bottle was empty, three days before my follow-up appointment. No matter how long I stared at the "No" in "No Refills" it did not morph into a 1. Working my pharmaceutically inspired manipulations on Dr. D. could not happen until Tuesday. It was Friday.

I brought the empty prescription bottle to the hotel, fantasizing that the pills might replenish themselves in the dankness of my purse where many a bottle had taken root. Maybe the hotel had Percocet bushes you could pick from like blueberries. Or Vicodin vines— narcotics hanging like grapes to tilt back my head and nibble from. No, the Four Seasons had a lovely orchid garden tucked away in a greenhouse, but did not offer any such fantastical foliage. But my husband was offering the fruit of one of his bushes.

Kevin presented a smooth face, as if all his emotions had been ironed away. He glanced down at the pill, his eyes opaque. Was he sad that I was in pain or depressed that I, too, needed drugs? Or both. How serendipitous that he was on the very drug I had just run out of! His blue eyes shimmered with a kaleidoscope of worry, love, and shame.

"But what about you?"

"I have some." Then, "I feel bad for you. I know you're in pain."

My heart soared. Thank you! I was in pain! I was prescribed this medicine—first by a doctor, and now, my husband. If I took it as prescribed, I would still be sober. Why would I call Liz? What would prayer, a phone call, or a meeting do? My arms encircled my gut. How could AA help me with physical pain?

I looked down at the Kevin-approved pill. Could feel his eyes burning through the layers of my painted face and into my soul. I stayed focused on his offering. It was his birthday. I wanted him to have a good time. I wanted him to be happy.

There's a saying in Narcotics Anonymous: "One pill is too many and a thousand is never enough." Never.

With a slightly trembling hand, I pinched the Percocet between two fingers like the precious gem that it was. Raising my water glass, I popped it into my mouth and swallowed. And just like that, Liz and AA dissolved from my life.

◦◦◦

ON TUESDAY, Dr. D. offered me a one-time refill of Percocet, mumbling something about how half of one of these would knock him on his behind.

"They barely touch my pain," I murmured, with a calculated shrug.

After detailed ultrasounds by my gynecologist and then a special-ist, there was no explanation for my continuing pain, and the ruptured ovarian cyst was declared a misdiagnosis. So I switched specialties.

My U.S.A. Top Ten Rated gastroenterologist, Dr. E., would perform an endoscopy and diagnose me with "stomach abrasions"— one step down from a full-blown ulcer. Its image looked like a cracked out rodent had taken up modern art: red slash marks on my pink stomach as canvas. Dr. E. would prescribe Prilosec and Align. I even saw an infectious disease doc, but no one found anything that could explain my pain.

Dr. D. and Dr. E. would engage in a responsible conversation about pain relief. Because I was in recovery, Tramadol would be their drug of choice. I nodded along. My sobriety was very important to me. This synthetic opiate was the right choice.

It was their fault. They walked right into it. It was my junkie responsibility to run with the drug that confuses physicians, all the way to the pharmacy. I would tell Dr. E. that Dr. D. would prescribe the Tramadol because of my transplant, and explained to Dr. D. that Dr. E. would prescribe it because the pain was gastroenterological.

This deceptive ritual is known as "doctor shopping." It was so easy. I almost felt sorry for them. With this well-lubricated mechanism in place, I almost always had drugs. With the overlap of prescriptions, I could more easily binge without fear of running out and hearing the dreaded phrase that haunted this pharmaceutical whore: *Too soon to refill.* Tramadol's label read, *Take 1-2 every 4 hours.* I rolled out 3. That was February. By March it was 8. April it was 12. May it was 20.

By spring, I would often run out and fall into pharmaceutical "blank spots." Long days when I had to endure hand-shaking, pant-shitting periods of anxiety between prescriptions. On these days, Liz's words echoed in my ears.

You are a hope-to-die opiate addict.

On those desperate days, I would swipe from my husband. Maybe because it was so rare, that betrayal was sucked into our dysfunctional Bermuda Triangle of Kevin, Pills and me. He must have known, but never came after me. Maybe he was tired of every conversation revolving around my pain and lack of diagnosis. Kevin had bigger, more concerning pain to contend with: his own.

Over nine long months, from his August '12 visit to Urgent Care, throughout our separation, the Fall of our Christmas Tree and deep into the "ovarian-cyst-that-wasn't" winter, Kevin sustained great pain. He had been accessed at The Spine Center at Cedars-Sinai, and then the Spine Surgery Center at Keck Medicine of USC. Along with herniated discs, his official diagnosis was a "transitional vertebrae." This condition occurs in 6% of people. Kevin's was part genetic defect and part cumulative effect of years as a spine-abusing photographer and bagpiper. Cedars suggested a spinal fusion of his L5 and S1. USC said Don't. Kevin didn't know. He continued to take Percocet. I continued to swipe. And we both carried on.

During these pharmaceutical blank spots, I would randomly dissolve into screaming sobs. When unsuppressed by bliss, my CNS became upregulated, highjacked by fear. I would lose myself inside unparalleled emotional meltdowns. Up in my husband's face with a knife, not knowing how it had found its way into my hand. Hysterical, I would escape outside, panting like a feral creature against the side of the house, in bondage to myself, clueless as to how to break free.

After an episode like this, Kevin would suggest, "Why don't you go to a meeting?" My brain rationalized that while I was being prescribed pills, I couldn't attend AA. How could I go to a meeting altered, even if I still believed myself to be sober? And I couldn't stop taking Tramadol because I was in pain.

"No. I don't feel comfortable while medicated." He bought it, nodding, as if he understood. Kevin knew I was on Tramadol, but had no idea that two doctors were prescribing it. My husband the Normie, the almost-non-swallower-of-drugs that made him feel "funny" understood nothing.

UNSOBER DAY 414. Friday May 24th, 2013.

. . .

"FUCK YOUUUUUU!"

Spit flew from my mouth, flying across the dashboard. Kevin did not move as I pummeled his head, left arm and thigh with my fists. The car weaved between two lanes as I screamed into the windshield. My right foot descended.

"Sweetheart. Do you want me to drive?" His eyes were blank.

"NO! YOU CAN'T DRIVE! YOU'RE ON DRUGS!"

"Henriette, are you on anything?"

"Don't say it like that! Don't say my name like you give a shit. You don't care! YOU DON'T CARE!"

"Are you on anything?" he repeated.

"NO! YOU FUCKING ASSHOLE! I DON"T HAVE ANYTHING!"

Like lava it poured out of me, red-hot rage, shredding my throat. I sputtered and choked, unable to catch my breath. The thud of marital flesh-on-flesh filled the car, overwhelming the ignition's roar. Maneuvering the wheel with one hand, I felt the wheels beneath me skid me as the odometer continued to rise. I whipped my head to the left, locking eyes with a wide-eyed woman driving alone. *What the fuck are you looking at?* I glared, holding down the horn. Then I gave her the finger.

My heart pounded a heavy-metal beat, as I watched Kevin sink deeper into himself, withdrawing like a snail. No matter how hard I punched, I could not crack his shell. He would not punch back. I began to pound at my own skull.

"You're going to have an accident," he pleaded.

"WHO FUCKING CARES!"

"Do you want to go to a meeting?"

Bile rose in my throat. Tearing off the freeway, I whipped through the tree-lined streets of residential Burbank, wild and un-Wazed. The car screeched to a halt. Door open, directionless, I charged up into the Burbank Hills.

"Leave me alone! I HATE YOUUUUUUU!"

My fists pummeled the air as I ran. I wanted to rip my skin from my bones, to feel the blood pour out of me, to squish my flesh and sinew until pulp. Panting, I plunked down on a half-wall that bordered the front yard of a multi-million dollar home.

Wrapping my bony arms around myself, I rocked, relishing the punishing scrape of the brick beneath my dress. The sun was setting. Evening shadows crawling out to darken the manicured lawns. Up the street neighbors were walking their dogs, cars pulling into driveways. I punched at my head, unabashed. *Yes.*

Would Kevin come for me as he always had? I pictured his blotchy face accepting every blow, every slur. I wailed into the suburban air, moans wracking my body. What was wrong with me? Why couldn't I stop? I had never had more than those first six months of sobriety. Rocking back and forth, the repeated thud of marital flesh-on-flesh rang loud. I clasped my hands over my ears. Dual rivers of snot and tears poured down my face. I loved him. I loved him. He didn't deserve this. He deserved better. Why could I not be better?

Wiping the endless stream of goop onto my dress, I looked around. Oh, my god. I was on the street where Liz lived. I blinked, unbelieving. My heart dropped picturing her big eyes, her legs tucked beneath her as we chatted. Oh, how I missed her. What would she think if I just showed up on her doorstep, wild-eyed and withdrawing?

As the sun disappeared, the shift in temperature feathered against my skin. Welcomed cool against my remorseful flesh. I looked up into the sky. In the gloaming, they began to rise in voice. How I loved mockingbirds' romantic testimony. Sharp, full notes encouraging celebration of the day that has passed, and the beauty of descending night. Each chirp like the pluck of a harp, note by note, drying my tears.

Shaking, I inhaled awkwardly. A sharp and peppery breeze filled my lungs. Then mellow vanilla and rose. The farewell-for-nows of plant life closing up for the night. Caught between shadow and light, I sat. It was out there: In the birds. In the flowers. In the air. Hope. It was time to go.

My heart racing, I climbed into the driver's seat, armed with one last ultimatum.

"Don't talk to me until I get home." Then. "I don't hate you. I hate myself."

Kevin stared through the windshield. "I know."

∾

WHEN WE GOT HOME, I went straight into our bedroom and closed the door. Pulling out my phone, I clicked on *1 Unheard Message.* Liz had left me a voice mail in April. It was May.

"Honey, I just sitting here thinking about you. I know you go through a lot with your health. I want you to know that I love you. I will be here for you, if you call."

Sitting on the floor, back against the wall, my heart cracked wide. Unending tears dripped onto my bare legs, as I replayed Liz's promise over and over again. I wiped the phone against my skirt, and then my face with the back of my hand. This had to end.

Pills were no longer for all kinds of pain. They were my pain.

Holding my breath, my finger hovered over her number. And then, with the conviction of placing a prescription, I watched it curl and press "Call."

28. EXCEDRIN 2013

S ober Day 119. Thursday November 14th, 2013.

"HOW'S YOUR HEADACHE?"

"Actually, it's a lot better." I closed the front door behind me.

"I'll bet." My head whipped around. Scowling, Kevin stood across the living room with a prescription bottle in his hand. *Shit. Shitshitshit.* And just like that, the mellow, one-alcoholic-talking-to-another buzz that flowed through my veins all the way home from my 10 pm Burbank Group meeting, vanished.

"What's wrong?"

"Henriette. I know you took one of my Percocet." His eyes narrowed, turning arctic blue.

My heart stopped. I hadn't. "I didn't."

"There's half an Excedrin in here with my Percocet."

Oh, Kevin! I wanted to run over to my husband, and twirl him around in my arms like a parent comforting a hurt child. To bust a gut at his adorable Normie ignorance. *Kevin,* I would explain, hands on his shoulders, looking deep into his eyes: *I am no amateur. I never made a mistake like that. When I stole from you, I never mixed the drug I was replacing with the medication I was stealing.*

"Look again," I offered, swallowing. He locked the bathroom door behind him.

Plunk-plunk-plunk. His pills echoed as he dropped them one-by-one into the container. I could picture him squatting on the stone-tiled floor, a renegade bead of sweat traveling down from his hairline. Cleaning my fingernails with my teeth, I waited. There was no point in moving. My entire future depended upon this sum total. What did a guilty verdict look like when you were innocent? Brandishing lies to defend countless untruths had come easy. How would I brandish the truth?

The door clicked open. A sliver of light pierced my eye, then the shadowy outline of Kevin's body. His eyes locked with mine.

"There's half a Percocet missing."

"I didn't take it."

"I want to drug test you."

~

AFTER I CALLED Liz in May, I would slip one last time and steal pain medication from a friend in July. On the evening of July 19th, 2013, I surrendered unconditionally.

"I can't find God. I can't find God." I wailed to Liz. Once again, she took me down with a single shot of her tough love rifle.

"Honey? Are you using?" I chortled through my tears. Man, she was good.

"Yes. I was. But I'm done. I'm done."

I was.

We started doing The Steps again. She told me to go to a meeting every day. By November 25th, I had gone to 130 meetings in 130 days, but Liz had one suggestion I could not take. She wanted Kevin to get rid of his Percocet—to somehow get it out of the house. But that wouldn't be fair. In two weeks, he was undergoing a spinal fusion at Cedars-Sinai Medical Center.

"You'll never stay sober with pain meds in the house." Liz predicted.

~

KEVIN AND I PASSED SIZZLER, and the strip mall as we made our way up to the Vons pharmacy that was open until midnight. Rite Aid's sign flickered midway bright, beckoning even after hours as I recalled that two-hour, round-trip odyssey through a urine-stenched underpass, spit gobs and triple-digit heat. I could see myself straggling though the sliding doors, gratitude flooding my veins as the Freon breeze hit my burning skin, and then ecstasy that 120 Accidental Fiorinal would bring me home.

I would have crawled there. I had been willing to go to any length. That day, my soul believed She was the only thing that could save me. I glanced over at Kevin. He stared forward, clenching the steering wheel with two hands. What would save me now? Pulling out my phone, I texted Tara.

Kevin is drug testing me. What do I do?

Husband and wife drove in silence. There was nothing to say until there was.

"I'll wait here." I said, as Kevin headed inside Vons to purchase a drug test from the pharmacy that had gifted me the perfect pink pill: Roxicodone. I checked my phone. Nothing.

Suddenly, my stomach flipped. What if my test came back a false positive? It happened in 5-10% of drug tests. Decongestants sometimes registered as a false positive for amphetamines. Kevin had tested positive for opiates, during our own not-so-funny version of the *Seinfeld* Poppy Seed bagel episode.

Stepping out of the car, I took a few strides into the parking lot, taking in the night. Most of Los Angeles experiences a pasty gray sky barely freckled with light. But in the foothills, we see stars. Tonight, they were winking, wondering like me, how this would end. Against the soft putt-putt-putt of a backing car I inhaled, filling my lungs with the curiously calming blend of exhaust and neighboring jasmine.

Pulling out my phone, I called Liz. Her cell was off. I tried the home line, and her husband answered. George was polite and kind, just like Kevin if he was sixty-five and a dentist.

"Hi George. It's Henriette. Uh, Liz said I could phone her in an emergency."

"Oh," he stumbled. "She's sleeping. Let me get her." My heart pounded. There was a clunky metal sound.

"Hel-lo?" Her voice crackled, drugged with sleep.

"Liz. Kevin is drug testing me. I don't know what to do."

"Wh-a?" she slurred.

"Kevin is drug testing me," I enunciated.

"Was sleeping..." It was on the tip of my tongue to snap *No kidding,* but something inside me just let go.

"It's OK. I'll call you tomorrow." Kevin had joined me by the car.

"They don't have any," he said.

"Let's go to CVS. It's 24 hours." I said. Kevin hesitated, his hand on the driver's handle. That pharmacy was at least half an hour away, even in minutes-before-midnight, lack of traffic.

"It's OK," he offered.

"No. You need to know."

Driving the familiar miles from Shadow Hills into Burbank, I realized I had never driven to Her pharmacy like this: Neither on the toe-tapping verge of full-blown dopesickness, nor in manic, music-blasting anticipation. Tonight, my body was slouched with resignation, not defiantly turned away from my husband, deliberately fascinated by the mind-numbingly familiar roads. She wouldn't be waiting for me at the end of this surreal tour of my pharmacies. A drug test would.

My pulse slowed. Kevin's posture had relaxed. He felt my gaze and sent me a half-smile. I did not smile back.

As we pulled into the parking lot, I checked my phone one last time. Nothing. I got it. I was on my own. Kevin rubbed my kneecap.

"Do you want anything?" His eyes were soft. I shook my head.

"I'm fine."

Do you want anything? when entering a store was our code for "snacks." Chips, candy et al. Danish salted black licorice was my first choice, but impossible to find with the exception of the annual Scandinavian Festival in Thousand Oaks. Australian black licorice was a decent second commonly found throughout Los Angeles. America's Good 'n Plenty was a distant, but perfectly-acceptable-substitute-when-sugar-desperate third. The decision had to be made with intention. Once purchased there was no sharing. No bartering. Possession was 9/10ths of the law. We took our treats very, very seriously, but in this moment, I couldn't imagine swallowing a thing.

Another set of sliding glass doors closed behind my husband as he hunted for the drug test that would either cement the foundation of trust we had built over the last 130 days, or level it to the ground. Exiting the car, I inhaled late night's aromatic offerings: greasy fast food, a whiff of body odor, and diesel from the gas station on the corner.

Burbank was noiseless at a quarter after midnight. Once again, I took in the sky. It was not colorless, bright, the way I had described it to Liz when she asked *Honey, do you believe in God?* It unfolded in complicated shades of gray—the city's pollution blocking heaven's light from shining down. I couldn't see the stars from here, but I knew they were there. My eyes fluttered closed. I was powerless over what happened next, but I got the sense that if I just let go, everything would be all right.

I spotted her across the parking lot. Sexy wrap dress, blond highlights, 39 years old. She had just screen-tested for Ron Howard. She was pumping a bottle of chardonnay in one hand and a white paper bag in the other, charging towards her station wagon. The ignition sparked. I watched her rip open the bag, and together we gulped, 3 Fiorinal rolling down our throat with a swig of warm water from a bottle off the floor of the car.

A tear rolled down my cheek. I did not want anything that woman had. Bringing my hand to my abdomen, I cupped the slight bulge on the right side: My husband's life-saving gift: Kevin's kidney. Our kidney. Tonight, The Kid would create the few drops of urine necessary to prove to that she/I was no longer a liar. 8 pills had sent us on an 18-month odyssey culminating in this night. Kevin had been counting pills for 14 months. I wiped away the tear as my husband walked across the parking lot toward me. This had to end tonight.

"Did they have one?" Kevin reached into a bag and began to pull out a box. "I don't need to see it!"

I looked down at his hand. He was holding a box of Good n' Plenty.

Half an hour later, I sat perched on the edge of our couch, the Good n' Plenty lying on the coffee table, and Maggie at my feet, her tail wagging its metronome beat of unconditional love. *Click.* My heart jumped as the bathroom door cracked open. A shocking light shot out, so bright I raised my arm to shield my face. When it dropped, Kevin and I locked eyes. He was smiling.

I picked up my box of licorice, and stretched out my arm towards the light and smiled.

29. THE KEY

S ober Day 144. Monday December 9th, 2013

IT GLITTERED against the graying hairs of his chest, hanging on a thin piece of rope right above his heart. The key opened a lock box we had purchased to store Kevin's post-surgical medications including stool softeners, muscle relaxers, Valium and Percocet. It lay under our bed as we slept.

We both knew this distraction was like a pharmaceutical slight of hand—kind of like deleting your lover's phone number in front of your spouse. If you really want to contact them, you can always Google. Nothing could've stopped me if I really wanted his drugs. Even if that didn't include gently snipping the fine line around his neck as he slept, but rather tossing the box over our hill, and watching it smash open upon the craggy rocks. Although when I played this tape through, I did wonder if the plastic containers would survive the fall, or would the pills scatter, forever lost amongst the sand and succulents. Turns out, Kevin had Googled the exact same thing, discovering a desperate husband had busted open his wife's safe with a jack hammer in their back yard.

Gently sliding my arm away from his shoulders, I deposited my husband on the side of our bed. He slid back in increments, first inching his butt back towards a tower of pillows, and then leaning into the stack.

"Can you move this one?" I jumped to remove a flaccid pillow from the pile. "That's good," he said. Stretching his legs long, he flinched.

"Are you sure?" I asked. Kevin looked like he had aged a decade in four days. His skin no longer its vital pink-ish tone, rather a pasty gray. Beneath his pajamas, his abdomen sported a surgical Band-Aid covering his second laparoscopic surgery in two years. His hands shook as he adjusted his hand-knitted skullcap. The man who would rather go strolling in a Winter Wonderland than tiptoe through the flirtatious ebb and flow of a sandy beach was shivering. After tucking a blanket around his shoulders, I assessed the makeshift hospital room: drinks, flowers, and Maggie's tail gently bobbing on the bed.

"What else can I get you?"

"Maybe some grapes?" My heart squeezed.

Maybe some grapes.

∾

FIVE DAYS EARLIER, on Thursday December 5th, I went to my 140th meeting in 140 days. The next day, Kevin (who had been threatening not to go through with surgery right up until the stroke of midnight when he had to discontinue eating and drinking), underwent a spinal fusion of his S1 and L5 vertebrae at Cedars-Sinai Medical Center.

Inside Hospitaland, I assumed my wifely bedside vigil. Deaf to the grating beeps of his IV drip and heart monitor. Standing protective inches away from his bed, aware that even an accidental graze of the railing might shoot agonizing neuro-needles up his legs, back, or into his catheter. I did not inspect his IV bag, knowing that might aggravate the needle jutting from the top of his hand. Nor did I stroke his swollen legs wrapped in blood-clot preventing cuffs lest they unexpectedly inflate.

How many days and nights had we spent at Cedars? Countless. Endless. Through Ecoli poisoning, chronic transplant rejection, dialysis, and overdoses. Yet even with our transplant, Kevin had never been The Patient. He was the tea-bringer, kidney-donator, and joke-teller. My advocate, savior and friend. His eyes flickered open for a second. Maybe two. Just enough time for me to find him. I brought his hand to my lips. 32 years of being a patient had not prepared me to see my husband in pain.

He lay flat on his back, arms folded over his chest like a corpse. My arms turned heavy, barely able to stroke his cheek. The symbolism was not lost on me. Kevin had carried the load of our marriage for so many years. My Prince Charming had finally been knocked off his horse, and broken his back. Had I broken him?

During those three days, I would break away only to find refuge in the Cedars' Chapel. Amongst the inter-faith pews, I would cry on my knees. *Please, God. Help me. Help him. Take care of him.* Every night, I stayed with my husband until the hospital's final chime drifted away, pained to leave him behind in a place that, unlike me, he had never wanted to be.

~

THE KITCHEN COUNTER was cluttered with grocery bags filled with Kevin's favorite foods. They lay there mocking me. *Unpack us.* The kitchen was dark, and too quiet without Maggie clickity-clacking beneath me. She had elected to remain on the bed, curled up next to Kevin. Something fluttered in my chest. I looked down at my hands. They were shaking. I flipped on the light as darkness began to consume me.

Kevin had withstood this crippling powerlessness for years. This total inability to prevent the person you love most from suffering. He had set his timer to make sure I was still breathing through the blackest of Her nights. I had barely been able to round trip Ralph's, terrified he might pee unattended and fall. Oh, how I wanted to jump up and down on the hands of Time, propelling it forward so that my husband might be healed.

What could I do? I looked at the groceries again. I was a shell. A fraud. An Unwife. It began to rise in my chest, an awakened animal. An unrealized pain with teeth, heart, and a voice. My head spun. Falling against the counter, I screamed. Countless, endless seconds.

God. Help me.

I grabbed the edge of the counter, my legs buckling beneath me. I threw my head back and howled, tasting tears, bile, and blood. And then, flushed and spent, the emptying of my soul was complete. Moments later, my phone rang. It was the last thing I felt like doing, but I answered.

"Hello?" my voice shook.

It was Remy. We barely knew each other then. I don't think we would be considered friends today. She was sleek and stylish, thirty-something lady-who-lunches perfection. In her early 20's she was imprisoned for drug trafficking. We had exchanged phone numbers inside the rooms of AA, and a couple of calls.

"Are you ok?"

Out it came, all my self-loathing and shame. My surrender unleashed.

"IhavetounpackthegroceriesandmakehimasnackHesinsomuch-painIdontknowwhattodo…"

Remy paused. "It sounds like you need to go to a meeting."

"IcantleavehimIhavetolookafterhim…" I cried.

"You have to. It's your medicine."

Silent tears fell. Noiseless sobs cutting off all breath. But these were tears of connection. One-alcoholic-talking-with-another relief. She got it.

"Do you want his pills?"

Wiping away snot, I inhaled choppily. I pictured the lock box full of drugs beneath our bed, and the gold key gleaming against his torso.

"No. I don't. I really don't." I laughed. What I wanted was to be set free.

"Thank you," I whispered, choking out my gratitude to an almost stranger who had just shown me unconditional love. Loving me until I could love myself.

I lay down a tray and began to load it: ripped pieces of French bread, slices of cheese, and a smattering of tortilla chips and salsa. Lifting the grapes from the bag, I quickly rinsed them, and then set them next to a glass of soda, joyously exploding with bubbles. Patting away the remnants of my tears, I lifted the tray and walked toward the bedroom. Carrying the weight of this load comfortably, a small smile flitted across my lips, like the flutter of wings set free.

Tonight, I would carry the load. I would carry us.

Outside the bedroom door I paused, picturing my husband resting, his best basset gal by his side, and his wife finally on her way. I peeked my head through the crack.

"Hi, sweetheart."

And with a nudge of my hip, I pushed the door wide.

30. CELL-CEPT 2007/2019

Sometime in early 2007, I read an article about a woman with a kidney transplant who discontinued her medications herself. Just stopped. I can't find the article, nor can I quote her verbatim, but it went something like, *I didn't like the way they made me feel.* Unbelievably, her transplant thrived for years without medication. No Cell-Cept, no Prednisone, no Cyclosporine and certainly no Prograf. How her body had accepted its donor kidney for years without immunosuppression was a medical mystery.

I remember her pose for the camera. Folded arms resting across her chest in victorious calm. She was an anomaly. A one-in-a-million transplant patient. As I stared into her self-possessed eyes, my chest burned with jealousy. I wanted to be like her. Different. Unique.

Why can't that be me?

I approached my beloved LA nephrologist, Dr. D. with a radical idea. "Can we reduce my medications?"

"Why would you want to do that?" he asked.

Inwardly, I rolled my eyes. Only a person who has not suffered the long-term side effects of toxic medications would ask such a dumbass question. In 2007, I was 38 and generally felt great. Exercise, eating well, and relative youth was still working for me, even with my daily dollop of Codeine.

But during my first 10 years in Los Angeles, my creatinine had literally bounced all over the medical map. A normal range for the Untransplanted is 0.4-1.2. On May 7th, 1997 I charted an average 1.7. May 8th, 2000 was a concerning 2.2. June 27th, 2001 logged an astounding 1.4, and January 28th, 2002 landed at an upsetting 2.3. I knew this unsettling roller coaster ride was not conducive to titrating my medications downwards, but I had a plan.

I frequently got sick, and my colds/chest colds/flus dragged on forever. Even under the California sun, a flu bug would freeze me out of life for weeks. Given my interminable medical odyssey, well, quite frankly, that just didn't seem fair. Articulating this injustice to Dr. D. would be my gateway to a drug-free life. Unable to fight off the common cold, I was clearly overimmunosuppressed, and he would agree to reduce my meds. Then, I would respond so well to less medication, we would titrate down-down-down until I was forever drug-free!

"I get colds a lot." I did not tell Dr. D. I had read an article about a medical miracle.

"Some people are just more susceptible to colds," he shrugged, "Let's just keep things the way they are."

Diagnosed with chronic rejection a year later in February 2008, I visited Toronto in September 2009 before the symptoms of renal failure got real. I was suffering with increased headache, nausea, lethargy, and edema. My new American health insurance plan made it unnecessary for me to travel north to purchase my medications, but I wanted to touch base with Dr. C., my Canadian nephrologist who had seen me through my first kidney transplant in 1988. Kevin once remarked that listening to Dr. C. was as interesting as watching paint dry—cliché, yes, exaggeration, no. Dr. C. served dry, no frills medicine. His straightforward take on my diagnosis was what I craved.

When Dr. C. walked in, my skin warmed. He looked the same as always, just older. His dark hair gleamed with salt 'n pepper streaks. His familiar pinstriped suit peeked out from beneath his lab coat, the pop of his curiously slick tie so contrary to his intensely cerebral personality. Today, it was a shiny purple. Fidgeting on the tissue-paper-covered examination bed, I noted a spark when our eyes connected. I knew he had my back.

As he pulled up my virtual chart, a flash of a memory struck me. It was here in the hospital, in a different room. What year? 2001? 2002? That earlier time period when my creatinine had been bopping all over the place, along with my BUN (Blood Urea Nitrogen.) Urea is formed in the liver as the end product of protein metabolism, and then transported by blood to the kidneys for excretion. Kidney disease or a rejecting transplant can lead to the kidney(s)' inability to excrete urea, hence an elevated BUN. Numerous drugs can affect BUN by competing with it for elimination by the kidneys.

"Are you using drugs?" He looked me right in the eye.

My heart stopped. I lost the ability to breathe, my chest punctured by this surprising selection of words as bullets. This was long before opiates and benzodiazepines. Long before She took me down. But the day had been—as every day had been since I discovered It at age 19—a day of Codeine abuse.

"Your liver enzymes are elevated."

I maintained eye contact with him a la the Customs officer scenario, sternly instructing my cheeks from staining a deep red. Codeine flashed through my mind. It couldn't be that! It was over the counter! And yet, I knew. I was taking way too much every day. It wasn't like I'd lay out 12 Codeine tablets on the counter every morning next to my immunosuppressives before swallowing. Codeine and I did our mixing of bodily fluids on the down low.

But that the abuse seemed to be catching up with me was not enough to get me to confess. I couldn't tell him. I wouldn't tell him. How could I spin this?

"No. Only what you've given me. Fiorinal. For my migraines." *Make it seem like it's his fault. Not my fault. Hisfaulthisfaulthisfault.* Then, "I've never even tried a cigarette." Doctors were always impressed by this information. He didn't blink, insistent.

"It looks like you are abusing drugs."

I would not give up my daily cup of narcotic coffee. "I don't know why." But I did.

It is my fault.

Seven years after that memory, I sat in the same hospital, still abusing Codeine. Dr. C. had turned away from the computer to express efficient, yet kind regret over my rejection diagnosis. Nerves fluttered in my tummy. It was time.

"So what happened? Why did my kidney reject?" I asked.

"It's always hard to know exactly why."

"Yes," I prompted, "but why twenty years and then all of a sudden?"

"Essentially, there was a lapse in the protection of the kidney."

My blood iced over. My limbs wilted. I grabbed hold of the examination bed as my head spun wildly. *Ohmygodohmygodohmygod.* I avoided eye contact with Dr. C. fearing if I did, I might vomit.

That was all he had to say. It was his choice of words, and the blunt delivery. Something buried deep in my bones came roaring to the surface, rattling my body with the ferocious and inescapable truth.

It is my fault.

When Dr. D. told me to scrap the idea of reducing my meds, I couldn't let it go. *Why can't I be special like her?* By 2007, I had been taking medication daily for 23 years. I just didn't want to anymore. It was possible. She was proof. Doctors didn't know everything, even a nephrologist with 30 years of experience. I knew my body better than any physician ever would.

So, in April 2007, I stopped taking my prescribed dose of Cell-Cept. I continued to take Cell-Cept in the morning, but discontinued it at night. Half my dose would be more than enough. I told no one. I would be a medical miracle if it killed me.

One day, a few months into my decision, I opened the lid of our coffee table trunk, and Kevin noticed multiple boxes of Cell-Cept. My secret kept me bound to filling the same prescription, but consuming only half.

"Why do you have so much extra Cell-Cept?"

"I don't know," I said, shrugging my shoulders. Then I closed the lid and walked away.

For a while it seemed to work, which makes sense. Cell Cept is an extremely toxic medication, and if you refrain from metabolizing toxicity, your body will love the break. My creatinine came down, way down—to 1.4—and I believed I was on my way to achieving miracle status.

Over that short year, my body got strong. Too strong. It found its uncompromised legs again and realized Mum's kidney was a foreign invader, much like a flu bug, and went to war. My antibodies rallied, and attacked the kidney. By the time the damage showed up consistently in my erratic creatinine results, I was already in chronic rejection.

By February 2008, my transplant was 20 years old and considered a "senior." I had been taking Codeine every single day for 20 years. But by not taking my immunosuppressives as prescribed, I created a lapse in the protection of my kidney.

It was my fault.

~

No ONE HAS HEARD the Cell-Cept story. Not my first sponsor. Or my second. Or Kevin. Just six beta-readers. It is my last secret. Why? Maybe because it took me 30 chapters to understand how I could talk myself into risking the death of my transplant.

In 2007, I could not accept the truth: That I was a sick person who needed to take medication every day. In 2019, I need to take even more medication. First, for addiction: The 12 Steps, meetings, phone calls, prayer, meditation and sponsoring women. Then for my transplant: exercise, eating well, blood draws, education and taking my immunosuppressives. All of them.

It's not an official abbreviation, but essentially Cell-Cept stands for Cellular Acceptance. What if I had accepted Dr. D.'s decision? That 99.999% of transplant patients need immunosuppressives to safeguard their precious gift? Would I have rejected? Or become one of those rare patients with a 30-year old transplant? Would I have fallen out of love with my husband and sacrificed my soul for Her? Would I have become an addict? Or was I born one?

The definition of acceptance is: the willingness to tolerate a difficult or unpleasant situation. If I did cause my rejection, today I can say I carry no shame. I could not accept my intolerable until I learned how. Step by step. But regret? That my husband was the collateral damage sustained during the tornado of my addiction? Oh, yes.

There are moments I watch Kevin when he is unaware. The endearing smile that spreads across his face, elastic to release joy, no longer restricted to dam pain. Daily, I relive the moments that denied him the simple freedom of a smile. The overwhelming burden that falls upon my heart cripples my breathing for minutes at a time. And I fall to my knees; to the safest place I have ever known.

There are moments when She returns, swirling casually though my mind...*You are in pain. You never smoked pot. It will be fine*...I thought She lived in my heart. What I have learned is that She lives in my mind, ready to dictate the terms and conditions of my life . For today, I do not have to listen.

Prednisone was a bitter pill for this 14-year old innocent to swallow—in every possible way. But life with two diseases is no longer my intolerable. It has become my greatest gift.

With the exception of my June '11 rejection episode, my creatinine has vacillated between 0.9-1.3. Taking into consideration lab error, my creatinine has not changed since The Kid was birthed on April 8th, 2011.

I will not stop taking my Cell Cept.

I swallow it every day.

EPILOGUE

S ober Day 1564. October 29th, 2017.

IT WASN'T A TOTAL SURPRISE. For the last couple of years I had been hinting, wondering if it would ever come to pass. A week before my 49th birthday, Kevin sent me a text.

"If one was to get a...sweater...for one's birthday, what color would one like? Gold or silver?" My heart flipped. An irrepressible smile spread across my face.

"You have good taste in sweaters," was my reply, my eyes crinkling with joy.

On my birthday morning, a box stood on our dining room table along with a bottle of Pellegrino, coffee and salmon eggs Benedict. Inside that box, was a Little Blue Box. I clapped my hands together like a little girl. Kevin shot me a look that only a husband and wife who have known and loved each other for 26 years can decipher: a droll knowing, mixed with undeniable love. My heart rapped against my chest. I couldn't help it. I may be the anti-princess when it comes to summer jobs as a subway janitor, but when it comes to my Prince Charming I am a total Cinderella.

Six years after I tossed it out the car window and onto the grassy knoll of Burbank's Zankou Chicken, I stared at my wedding band. It was different from the one we had selected in 1995. Still 18K gold, this one was thicker and rounder, similar to Kevin's. I had teased my 21-year old fiancée about his choice of band—The Comfort Fit—because it had been $200 more than mine. My band had been much finer, corresponding with my elegant solitaire diamond engagement ring. I gazed at the singular band.

"It looks so small. I wonder if it will fit."

Together, we watched my finger take to the ring. Uninscribed. Unadorned. The band is twice the width of my engagement ring. At first glance, the rings are a total mismatch, but on my hand, fit together perfectly.

"It's perfect." My eyes filled with tears. "I can't believe I did that."

"I was horrible, too." Our eyes met.

"It's a horrible disease."

I got up to embrace my husband. Although Kevin had purchased the ring, his commitment had never been in question, and mine was now redeemed. One day at a time. The band was a gleaming seal, not the final step, but one more step together, marking our long day's journey into wife.

THE 12 STEPS OF ALCOHOLICS ANONYMOUS

Remember that we deal with alcohol—cunning, baffling, powerful! Without help it is too much for us. But there is One who has all power—that One is God. May you find Him now! Half measures availed us nothing. We stood at the turning point. We asked His protection and care with complete abandon. Here are the steps we took, which are suggested as a program of recovery:

One: We admitted we were powerless over alcohol—that our lives had become unmanageable.

Two: Came to believe that a Power greater than ourselves could restore us to sanity.

Three: Made a decision to turn our will and our lives over to the care of God as we understood Him.

Four: Made a searching and fearless moral inventory of ourselves.

Five: Admitted to God, to ourselves, and to another human being the exact nature of our wrongs.

Six: Were entirely ready to have God remove all these defects of character.

Seven: Humbly asked Him to remove our shortcomings.

Eight: Made a list of all persons we had harmed, and became willing to make amend to them all.

Nine: Made direct amends to such people wherever possible, except when to do so would injure them or others.

Ten: Continued to take personal inventory and when we were wrong promptly admitted it.

Eleven: Sought through prayer and meditation to improve our conscious contact with God as we understood Him, praying only for knowledge of His will for us and the power to carry that out.

Twelve: Having had a spiritual awakening as the result of these steps, we tried to carry this message to alcoholics, and to practice these principles in all our affairs.

Pg. 59 *Chapter 5: Into Action* from the Big Book of Alcoholics Anonymous.

ACKNOWLEDGMENTS

Without these people there would be no book. So there.

To the inimitable Jennie Nash who literally taught me how to write a scene, and changed my life.

To Anna and Julie, the editors who guided me through the overgrown adverbial jungle I'd planted, and scythed away to the heart of the story.

To Lisa Cron who saved me years of therapy and turned my writing on its mind-blown head in a single bound.

To UCLA's finest: Linda Venis, Samy Dunn, and Alison Singh Gee and the Offshoots: Natalie, Margaret, Meredith, Anne, and Lisa. Also, Kate, Rachelle, Scott and Angel.

To Amy Ferris, for blowing my heart up one day.

To Laura Hillenbrand.

To Roberta and Alex who, through impossible loss, expanded their hearts to cultivate struggling writers like myself, in honor of their beloved Allegra.

To my seven UberBeta readers: Miriam, Angela, Marlene, Susan, and Carrie, who read every single overwrought word, but especially Tim, who offered me the truth through sophomoric banter, brilliant insights and borderline inappropriate friendship. And to my sister-in-love, Kim. Your capacity to forgive humbles me.

To my other readers, from a single piece to several chapters: Melissa (my Luvah) Laura (Bouj), Jane(ski), Lisa (who gifted me Hennybird *tm), Tara (soul sistah), Amy M., Mona, Gesa, Alison, Rachel, Jentry, Karen, Sarah, Shannon L., Debbie, Torre, Alexis, Lori (my hero) Kelly (DO NOT GIVE UP!), Elyssa (Black Magic, baby!), Karin (who gifted me the title) and Laurie of L. (who read four chapters the night before brain surgery).

To Amy ("I'm 50!"), Diana (love you!), Antoinette (twinning!), Jean, Penny, Erica & Sarah, Malka and Kim E. (you funny lady) who humbled me by reading *In Pillness* in its entirety, unbribed.

To the Salonistas of Ronna's Garden: Lisa, Fred, Jonathan, Courtney, Don & Lisa, Ronna, and especially Margot (#loveyoumore).

To the spiritual muscle of Klean esp. Bradford and Berry.

To my social media supporters whose cyber generosity lubricated my insecurity with their words.

Toronto, Los Angeles, Winnipeg (esp. Auntie Bonnie), Vancouver, Israel and Denmark.

To Stacie (Sr. architect) and her MiniHe, Kent (Jr. Architect) who created a space for me to go forth and create.

To Wil and Amanda who made me a god mom again when I was 4 months sober.

To C, L, K, S, T & J who never let go of my hand, even though I'm sure they wanted to.

To Mum and Nick, V & M. #ivanans

To Lizzie and Danielle, and the Not Saints group. Without help it is too much for me.

To the Living Womb Women, and my fellows, especially Michelle A., Heather B., Steve M., Lauren A., and Dawn of the West.

To my chronic pain and illness Peeps.

To the women who allowed me into their innermost selves: T., B., M., C., C., and S., but esp. Justine, Shannon, Missy and Dawniebear. It is my profound joy to love you.

To Judaism and the bagpipes.

To Wahlter White McIntyre, the sweetest, most sensual senior basset hound there ever was.

To my sweetheart, Kevin, donator of my latest and greatest kidney, Mus Musculus, and one hot mensch of a husband. In sickness and in health, eh? This book? It's me squeezing back.

And to Big G. Thank you for your hand. I finally accept.

⁓

Some names in *In Pillness and in Health* were changed out of respect for Tradition 12.

PRAISE FOR IN PILLNESS AND IN HEALTH

"...This is more than just a memoir about addiction. The author's writing style, as well as what she has to say takes this difficult topic to a whole new level.

Quick-paced and raw, it is a fresh and brilliant mix of unflinching candor as well as keen observations. Reminiscent of Hunter S. Thompson, it sweeps us along with its rebellious riffing, unique and lyrical prose and wit, and comments on the dark absurdities of her reality.

It answers so many questions — from how did things get to this point, to how addiction "works" in taking over one's identity and life — to the final question that haunted me throughout: How did this person become the author capable of writing this stunning and sober account?

A must-read for us all..."

- Miriam Harris (Retired educator in the private and public education systems. Volunteer distress line responder and trainer. Avid reader.)

"...What an amazing read! I like to compare stories like this to a "high, inside" baseball pitch: High for the excellent quality of writing, and inside for first person POV by one who knows what they're writing about. To continue the conceit, the story comes at you at over ninety miles an hour and practically knocks you on your ass.

It's the artful telling of this harrowing tale that sets it apart. I wish I were an agent so I could talk to the powers that be and tell them about her wonderful turns of phrases, humor in the most dire situations, and raw honesty. I wouldn't stop talking until they agreed to publish *In Pillness and in Health*, because it deserves a wide audience..."

- Jean Badoud-Ridell (Author and director of the writing workshop, *Fictionweavers.*)

"...From the get-go, this raw and powerful memoir of a woman's turbulent descent into the abyss takes us along on a rollercoaster ride of pain, addiction and redemption. Told with meticulous detail and masterful scene-building, this gripping saga draws us in to a world of suffering and sickness, deception and manipulation juxtaposed alongside a marriage brimming with love and our heroine's courage and death defying resilience.

Chapter after chapter the author bares her soul and bravely shares her story with unabashed honesty. And just as she, at times, displays little compassion for her own life, she relentlessly shows no mercy for the reader. Chapter after chapter, I agonized, wondering if and how she would ever survive.

In Pillness and in Health is an evocative window into the soul of a truly remarkable woman whose struggle will leave every reader and anyone touched by addiction deeply moved and inspired. Her journey to sobriety, freedom and peace is a testament to her grit and infinite capacity to love and to persevere..."

- Marlene Garcia (Author and copy editor.)

"...Ivanans' memoir about her challenging drug addiction is, "an intentionally bitter pill to swallow." Her clever chapter headings create a fascinating armature for the narrative woven by her natural, powerful voice. Her eloquent grappling with the problems of addiction promises to raise the bar on its themes —dealing with the unknown, the monkey wrenches fate tosses into our lives, and the triumph of the human spirit — to a universal level..."

- Roberta Olson (Author of *Audubon's Aviary, Making it Modern* and *Fire in the Sky*)

"...She's a great writer. I love that she doesn't get all tangled up in trying to be fancy. She's eloquent with her words and uses writing as a vehicle for telling a good story, restraining from excessive word-smithery. I deeply appreciate it when I don't have to wade through a thick pool of bullshit to get into a story.

This is what stood out for me the most. Her voice. It's very readable.

The story itself: Holy shit, man. Reading about this was tough. She captures the mania of that addict state so well. The way it over-comes and leaves you powerless. It was like peering into the curtains of a very disturbed situation — both fascinating and deeply uncomfortable to behold.

This is what good writing is. It's honest. It's raw. It's infuriating and heartbreaking all at once. It's also inspiring..."

- Torre DeRoche (Author of *Love with a Chance of Drowning* and *The Worrier's Guide to the End of the World.*)

"...Compelling, inspiring, insane and hopeful. Have you ever wondered about the inner workings of an addict's mind? Ivanans' writing is intense, energetic, and mind reeling. Her memoir took me on a roller coaster of emotions I struggled to contain. *In Pillness and in Health* intertwines an addiction to pills and alcohol, and chronic illness, while navigating a marriage we wonder can survive.

This memoir had me cheering both for and against the author. I cried out in pain at the honest and transparent life of hell living as an addict. And it had me heartbroken and empathetic picturing the writer as a broken child and young woman, then wife rising to sobriety and serenity.

The writing is raw. The story is fascinating and so unique you imagine it must be fiction. But it is not. I am in awe of this woman as both an author and a person.

Do not miss out on this amazing read...”

-Kim McIntyre-Leighton (C.E.O. at *WASO* Winnipeg)

“...Henriette Ivanans' memoir is a vivid, no holds barred, searing account of the Hell that is addiction. The willingness she possesses as a writer — taking us on her journey, not gratuitously, but with a passionate urgency — is beautiful. Her openness and vulnerability places this memoir in a league of its own.

Greater still, is her inspired portrait of one addict's redemption: Redemption from the bonds of addiction into freedom.

She lets us in and what a gift it is...”

- Amy Atwell (Hospice Director and adoring Mom)

“...Henriette Ivanans has succeeded in writing an incomparably insightful page-turner about her love affair with drugs and alcohol. In vivid language, Ivanans describes how what started as a flirtation with prescription pills turned into an all-consuming romance that eventually turned on her.

With searing honesty, she recounts her insatiable drug cravings and the depths she would go to, to satisfy them. Through it all, Ivanans' indomitable spirit shines through. And when she finally finds the courage to break away from the relationship that tried to destroy her, she glows...”

- Diana Benjamin (Screenwriter, *Helen and Ted*)

“... *In Pillness and in Health* is a big, beautiful mess of humanity, in all its many contradictions. It's the relentlessly meticulous post-mortem of a soul unraveled, one nerve strand at a time. It's the hilariously glib Vaudeville of marital catastrophe, tap-dancing in the spotlight of a crumbling bedroom. It will make you angry and it will break your heart. Worst of all, it will make you care — deeply care — about a woman incapable of caring for herself.

The same manic compulsion that drove her to destroy herself with pills is the same manic compulsion that drives her to destroy herself on the page. She is acid and unsparing. It's like watching a woman jump off a skyscraper: you can't look away, even as she explodes on the pavement in front of you.

So why put yourself through it? Why read something so harrowing? Because in that long, terrible fall, my god how she soars..."

-Tim Rasmussen (Writer in Los Angeles. He lives with his wife Stacie, son Kent, Sweeney Dog the Demon Pupper of Flea Street, and hairless cat, Elaine Stritch.)

"...*In Pillness and in Health* is a harrowing, riveting, and courageous journey. The way Ivanans structured the memoir by the various agents of her addictions served her visceral writing style so well. Every chapter heading created a "What fresh hell is this?" moment. It's incredible that she lived to tell the tale, and that she did so with such skill, humility, and grace..."

- Linda Venis (Former Director of the *UCLA Writers' Extension Program* and author of *Inside the Room* and *Cut to the Chase*)

"...I hadn't realized how much I didn't understand what a person who struggles with addiction goes through until I read *In Pillness and In Health*. Ivanans' honest and emotional account of her struggles is heartbreaking, but important. Everyone can get something from this story of fear, strength, deception, gratitude, heartbreak, pain, and ultimately, love..."

- Angela Heine (Platinum card-holding animal lover and Mom)

ABOUT THE AUTHOR

In Pillness and in Health is Ms. Ivanans' first book. She won the Allegra Johnson Award in Memoir Writing (UCLA Writers' Extension) (2015). Her essay, *Alcohol May Intensify Effect* was published in Issue 19 of *Barrelhouse* magazine (2019).

She is currently working on her next book *How 5 Hounds Healed a Hen*, about the unconditional loving nature of dogs.

Ms. Ivanans is a two-time kidney-transplanted, sober woman and relieved ex-actress. She lives with her husband, Kevin and senior basset hound, Wahlter White McIntyre. You can find her at www. henrietteivanans.com

Made in the USA
San Bernardino, CA
18 September 2019